To Michelle

STOLEN
TEENS
(1939–1945)

step aboard with

Jayardy

The first seven years, bring up as a child:
The next to learning – for waxing too wild.

The next, keep under Sir Hobbard De Hoy:
The next, a man. No longer a boy.

Five Hundred Points Of Good Husbandry

Thomas Tusser, 1515-1580

STOLEN TEENS

(1939–1945)

by
CH/X 113124

CJWT SOLUTIONS
St Helens

First published in Great Britain 2007
© CH/X 113124, 2007

The moral right of the author has been asserted.

A CIP catalogue record for this book
is available from the British Library.

The author has taken great care in writing this book.
The publisher cannot be held responsible
for any inaccuracies in the text.

ISBN 978-0-9555393-0-5

Published by
CJWT Solutions
Sutton, St Helens WA9 4TX
www.cjwtsolutions.co.uk

Printed and bound in Great Britain

FOREWORD

Apart from the loss of his appendix in Newton Abbot and of another appendage in Hong Kong, Jim was fortunate to survive the 1939-45 war unscathed. That of which he was also deprived, and with more regret, was his teenage life.

Hardly into his teens as war clouds gathered in 1938 in Austria and later in Sudetenland in Czechoslovakia, he was 14 when war was declared. At 15 and together with his father - an air-raid warden - he was grappling with incendiary bombs and dousing fires caused by them. When 16 he joined the Home Guard. On duty every fifth night, at the age of 17 he was hospitalised in consequence of a strange incident while safeguarding a building of strategic importance, in so far as it supplied the City of London with 37 million gallons of water each day. In the Royal Marines two days after his 18th birthday, at 19 he was coxswain of a small landing craft on the 100 miles crossing of the English Channel on the eve of D Day. It was not until well after his second birthday spent in Hong Kong in the 3rd Commando Brigade that he returned to England, by then classified as adult.

Like all of that generation confronted with the dilemma of war, he merely reacted to events according to which option offered the best solution. Bravery the response was not: at most it was a conquest of trepidation. But the book is not confined to the tragedy of war.

Should elements of humour be detected, they serve only to mirror the indomitable spirit with which adversity was faced. Humour was as essential as air-raid shelters and as uplifting as the all-clear.

I. Jayardy

DEDICATION

This book is dedicated
to the memory of
Captain A.H.N. Gooding, R.M.
and to all who served under him
in 606 L.C.M. Flotilla

PART ONE

PER MARE

HENRY V

If we are marked to die, we are enow
To do our country loss; and if to live,
The fewer men, the greater share of honour.

He which hath no stomach to this fight,
Let him depart; his passport shall be made,
And crowns for convoy put into his purse:
We would not die in that man's company
That fears his fellowship to die with us.

This day is called the feast of Crispian:
He that outlives this day and comes safe home,
Will stand a tip-toe when this day is named,
And rouse him at the name of Crispian.

Old men forget: yet all shall be forgot
But he'll remember with advantages
What feats he did that day.

And Crispin Crispian shall ne'er go by,
From this day to the ending of the world,
But we in it shall be remembered;
We few, we happy few, we band of brothers;
For he today that sheds his blood with me
Shall be my brother; be he ne'er so vile
This day shall gentle his condition:
And gentlemen in England, now a-bed
Shall think themselves accursed they were not here,
And hold their manhoods cheap whiles any speaks
That fought with us upon Saint Crispin's Day.

St. Crispin's Day – 25th October
Date of the Battle of Agincourt (1415)

Wm. Shakespeare, 1564-1616

1

ALL ASHORE, WHO ARE GOING ASHORE

When this 'bloody' war is over
Oh how happy we will be
Just to get our civvy jobs back,
No more dodging mines by we.

No more deaths from shells or bullets,
Far more peaceful hours of sleep:
No more need from storms to shelter –
Gone all peril on the deep.

Jim began to ponder … though not anxiously, repeatedly. Had he bitten off more than he could chew?

Whereas his decision was considered by family, friends and workmates to be foolhardy if not stark crazy, being adventurous in attitude and to ensure that he would be able to serve in the branch of the armed forces of his choice Jim had volunteered for service in the Royal Marines in 1942, when only 17 years of age.

It was not until the beginning of the following year that he was summoned to report to the same naval recruitment centre, at Deansbrook Road, Hendon, where he had previously undergone his rigorous medical examination some months earlier and from where, two days after his 18th birthday, he re-emerged as government property.

Enlisted as CH/X 113124, he was cautioned by a colour sergeant that he was, forthwith, On His Majesty's Service and as such was liable for duty 24 hours daily and for 365 days each year. Conjecturing insubordinate might be the first entry on his record of service in the corps he refrained from asking whether, each leap year, February 29th was designated a day of leisure.

Provided with and required to sign on three separate forms for three shillings subsistence allowance, Jim was none too sure the NCO was not enjoying a rather profitable war, but again thought better than to enquire. Also presented with a one-way rail warrant to Woodbury Road Station, Jim was then given detailed instructions on how to proceed to the destination and, he thought, an ominously emphasised wish for the best of luck.

The rail journey was by far the longest he had ever undertaken, but in the company of several others making the pilgrimage to Woodbury Road the distance rapidly dwindled. Like himself, most of the others had only a vague notion of what to expect on eventual arrival, but one fellow- traveller spoke animatedly and incessantly of an uncle who had served in the Royal Marines prior to and throughout the first world war. When mention was made of the medals awarded to the relative a degree of reverence was conferred upon the nephew, which awe was gradually tempered as it became abundantly clear that the decorations were merely campaign medals. Inevitably the nephew became known as 'gongs'.

When at last the train pulled into the station on the branch line between Exeter and Exmouth, Jim and the others with whom he had travelled gazed at the stern looking sergeant resplendent in red sash who stood on the platform on the other side of the railway track. Obeying the sergeant's command, to alight on to the track from the carriage doors which were counter to the platform at which the train had halted, the recruits manhandled the suitcases each had brought containing items they would require until equipped with service issue, and in which suitcase would be returned to their home the clothes in which they had arrived. At another ear-splitting bellow enough to awaken the dead anywhere between Exeter and Exmouth, the aspiring marines were ordered to climb on to the platform on which their tormentor stood and beyond whom was parked a camouflaged lorry with the insignia of the Royal Navy, assumed by the rookies to be for their convenience by transporting them and their belongings to their destination.

Their surmise was not entirely mistaken. Their luggage was obligingly conveyed, but although there was more than enough room in the back of the vehicle for themselves they were instructed to form up behind the lorry and, with the sergeant comfortably ensconced in the back as protective chaperon, they were sped on foot, at the double, up hill and down dale. Just when it seemed the ascent of another gradient would be beyond their achievement, at a dip in the road the vehicle turned off the public highway, and after careful scrutiny by armed sentries patrolling the camp perimeter the straggling columns passed through the entrance to Exton Depot and toward their destiny. A banner read 'WELCOME, TO THE CORPS D'ELITE'.

Reunited with their possessions, unceremoniously flung out of the back of the truck behind which they had trailed, the new intake were formed into squads and under the authority of NCOs they marched to the large wooden huts which would accommodate them during the coming weeks.

Although by the time they had settled in the light of day had long since completely disappeared, and despite the imposed blackout, for those inclined to investigate their new environment the moon shed sufficient light. The wide roadway stretching from the gates through which they had previously staggered was bordered on one side by the guard room and adjoining armoury, the large orderly room, the adjutant's office, the quartermaster's stores, the padre's office together with a chapel, and a vast gymnasium. Further along was the transport section, a none too tidy conglomeration of workshops, stores, garages, Nissen huts and parking bays. Towards the end of the site and appearing to be most ominously situated, for a relatively small encampment a disproportionately large sick-bay was conveniently placed for any slipshod performances on the nearby, fiendishly constructed assault course. Opposite, as though to encourage recovery amongst the bedridden and the otherwise incapacitated, the NAAFI canteen, the garrison cinema and the dormitory of the WRNS collectively or separately aroused more enjoyable expectation, though not in that order of preference.

To the rear of these buildings was the parade ground, upon which surface square-bashing boots were destined to daily pound, and where arms would accustom themselves to the monotonous transference of rifles from one position to another. Here, too, squads would come to clearly understand that once mastery of a drill order had been achieved any lapse in its subsequent execution would invoke the displeasure of the drill instructor, whose ire would only be appeased by the sight of trainees running round and round the parade ground with rifles held at arms length above the head until limbs could no longer bear the strain.

The several huts in which rookies at various stages of training were (to be generous) cosseted, stretched almost to the bank of the River Exe and were very widely spaced, presumably as a precaution against air attack. In what would come to be regarded as home, the huts were not exactly en-suite although the separate facilities for ablutions and for the pressing needs of nature were within a day's march, or a night's dash.

The living quarters could not be spoken of as likely to merit accolades for sumptuous décor, nor would the description of 'lavishly appointed' have been altogether appropriate. Equipped with nine bunk beds on each side of the hut, the space in the middle was adorned with two trestle-type tables, one to each side of a cast-iron stove which graced the centre. Further creature comforts provided for the inmates took the form of four roughly hewn, rickety wooden benches for wearied, aching limbs, and blankets to forestall hypothermia, should a few hours of sleep be possible in between lights out and reveille.

As steps were retraced to their hut that evening, and continuing long after lights out had been sounded, three dozen randomly appointed individuals proceeded to forge bonds which would endure when the war permitted those who had survived to return to the county or to the country distinguishable by the dialect or accent in which they spoke. In addition to those from each of the home countries there were a few from different continental countries which had been occupied by the Germans, one from distant Brazil, a Canadian and another who insisted upon being referred to as an Afrikaner, not a South African. Jokingly he was nicknamed Lady Smith. Among other squads, their squad became known as the foreign legion.

It was Lady Smith who had spent the evening in the NAAFI canteen who returned to the hut to hold centre stage. When patter turned to the fairer sex, what Smithy revealed was unbelievable; reluctantly so, but surely too good to be true. Insistently claiming he was not mistaken in what he had heard, he revealed that at Exton every marine was allotted a female companion . Knowing no better, not even Gongs who could invariably recall a snatch of his uncle's reminiscences relative to any aspect of naval custom, the squadies conceded. After all, the allocation was rather like other creature comforts for the troops, in aid of which appeals were often made by such venerable institutions as the Salvation Army.

The squad were awakened the following morning at an

exceptionally early hour by the blast of reveille rendered by the camp bugler and by the simultaneous yell of 'Wakey, wakey; hands off cocks, on with socks', from the duty sergeant who had burst into the hut. Bleary eyes and drowsy minds ultimately brought the situation into focus and, reinvigorated by the sub-zero January air on the long traipse to wash and shave, with ravenous appetites they eagerly made for the mess.

Whatever it was the cooks deposited on outstretched plates, the substance was resolutely forced down reluctant throats with the same disdain for the same duty sergeant's rhetorical quip 'Are there any complaints?' as there had been for his earlier repartee.

After the early morning parade the day entailed attestation (decorous), documentation (tedious), inoculation (barbarous), depilation (preposterous), ecclesiastical ministration (god'elpus), and examinations/medical (obnoxious), optical (scrupulous) and dental (hilarious). The last mentioned check involved a recruit who had an upper denture from which two false teeth were missing. Classified by the dentist/lieutenant RN as dentally deficient, the misnomer initially entered on the man's medical record is not difficult to visualise.

Another source of amusement was due to the unusual surname of one of the new intake, whose name was Bastard. Embarrassing as unquestionably this name would seem on particular occasions, it was aggravated by the lack of vision of his parents who further encumbered their son with the Christian name of Walter. Displaying the dignity of gentilitial lineage in which the prohibitive seventh commandment would un-doubtedly have been sacrosanct, Wally Bastard took all ribaldry with commendable fortitude and would proclaim he was probably the only legitimate bastard in the whole camp.

Humour was also derived in consequence of Wally's surname at frequent roll calls on that first day. When conducting muster, on their first encounter with his name and until each officer or NCO could concoct an acceptable pronunciation there was always a distinct pause in their alphabetical progress: 'Adams', 'Allen', 'Baker', 'Barnard' ... had opinion polls been held during Wally's career in the corps, of the contrived pronunciations top of the surveys would probably have been the phonetically devised hyphenation 'BURR-STIRRED'.

There was one episode which did tend to wipe smiles from faces on that day. It occurred during the issue of kit, after measurements had been taken for uniforms and other items of wear: a puzzling exercise, really, insomuch that only two sizes of any commodity were available – too large or too small. Once completed, incidental items of equipment were handed out, the quartermaster sergeant specifying each item to be supplied while his underlings carried out his orders. 'Badge/cap-brass, mug/drinking-enamel' ... the staccato went on and on, 'Housewife/canvas – contents, needles thread, and wool/darning.'

For Lady Smith, the penny dropped. Looking cheated and musing on the topic overheard in the NAAFI, he realised it wasn't a marine's feminine companion someone had made off with but his housewife compendium, a standard item of the marine's kit and it was this accoutrement for which another was provided. What a bloody stupid name to give to a collection of needles and thread, it was vainly but repeatedly protested in the hut that evening in defence of his misunderstanding; but his annoyance met only with the taunt that perhaps Lady Smith would be prepared to deputize and to oblige.

With preliminary checks of suitability for service in the corps completed, training commenced. Much of each of the early days consisted of foot drill and arms drill. Having served in the Home Guard prior to enlistment in the Royal Marines, execution of the commands was familiar, if thought by the drill instructor not exactly up to the required precision. When not square-bashing, and ludicrously proclaimed as recreation, physical training was imposed.

If the objective of the physical training instructors was to reduce healthy, even athletic specimens of manhood to decrepit wrecks then their efforts were beyond reproach. Indicative of their perverted concern for the innocents at their mercy, prior to the 'off' on long cross country jaunts and with the thoughtful provision of a caveat, they dictated 'You will run until you drop: then you will crawl'. Alluding to the immense pain that was inflicted, had Winston Churchill not lost the script of the speech which he had intended making, instead of the ad lib 'up with which the nation had to put', he would have declared 'Never ...... in the fields ...... on human conscripts ...... was so much bestowed ...... by so few ...... upon so many'.

When, in the fields of Devon, PTIs were not in pursuit of pounds of flesh with the vigour of Venetian merchants, they sought retribution in the more secluded confines of the gymnasium where fearsome apparatus hinted at the possibility of make-weight.

In the rare interludes when humanity did prevail, lectures were delivered on the history of the Royal Marines. Formed in 1664 as the Duke of York and Albany's Maritime Regiment of Foot, it was subsequently re-named the Maritime Regiment of Foot of Prince George of Denmark following his betrothal to Queen Anne, which monarch gave birth to no fewer than 17 children. Arguably giving birth to the saying 'Tell that to the marines', King Charles the second commented that, drunk or sober, Prince George was inert! In 1748 the regiment ceased to be part of the establishment of the British army and came under the control of the Lords Commissioners of the Admiralty.

During their glorious past the corps of Royal Marines served with remarkable distinction at sea and on land in every quarter of the globe, as symbolised by their badge portraying the globe wreathed with laurel, and as embodied in their motto – Per Mare, Per Terram. Aboard the larger ships of war they manned X and Y gun turrets under command of RM gunnery officers, while bandsman serving afloat filled the role of stretcher bearers during battle. On land, as infantrymen, they were supported by the heavy guns of the Royal Marine Artillery, but in 1923 the RMA was decommissioned: although marine gunners were said to man the huge cross channel batteries which were located on the cliffs above Kingsdown, near Deal and opposite Cap Griz-Nez, during the second world war.

Said by one of the Sea Lords that if the real hour of danger should come to England the Royal Marines would prove to be the nation's sheet-anchor, there have been no fewer than ten Victoria Crosses among thousands of rare and priceless awards bestowed since their formation.

Among the squad there was less noble admiration but distinctly more coarse titillation at the disclosure that, undetected as women, Hannah Snell and Hannah Whitney had served in the ranks. A couple in the squad looked keenly and questioningly at others, and there was not a little regret among all of them that preliminary medical examinations were now more thorough.

Together with the 'encouragement' to lustily sing the words to the regimental march of the corps prior to the commencement of the evening's film by those able to steal time to visit the camp cinema, the lectures promoted a feeling of something more than merely belonging to a specific militia; more of being in brotherhood. Facetious as the trainees had been to the endless commands and unaware they were being conditioned to respond to authority unhesitatingly and precisely, the goadings and blasphemy with which they were reviled by the instructors were now recognised as necessary stimuli in pursuit of the coveted green beret of the commandos, while sufferance of the physical torture inflicted by the PTIs merely added to the aspiration.

Conscious he had instilled strict obedience in the recruits, from time to time their instructor relaxed discipline a little. Whereas at one time none would have dared to answer back to whatever was insinuated, if his demeanour indicated he was in a good mood he would tolerate good-natured or witty response.

Regarding less than flattering graffiti daubed on the walled entrance to the mess, and in pursuit of the culprit responsible for the insinuation the cooks were 'useless xxxxs', the squad was interrogated and threatened with all manner of reprisals. In unmistakably plain English, the least fluent of the overseas contingent asked who had inferred the 'useless xxxxs' were cooks. Whether, being of the lowly rank of corporal and therefore fed the same gut-liner as other ranks he was in accord with the Brazilian's jibe, or perhaps believing the South American did not fully understand the slanderous nature of his words, the NCO was as tickled as the rest of the squad and pursued the matter no further.

So much better disposed towards their erstwhile tormentors that even the physical training brutes were forgiven their atrocities, the rookies began to view time as the chief foe.

However, contrary to the mind-boggling impression given to them on their enlistment at Deansbrook Road, that at best they could only expect time in which to idle or revel each February 29th, it was not entirely so. After completion of each days training the fledgling warriors were free to please themselves. Well almost.

To pass scrutiny on parade each following morning squadies were faced with the necessity of burnishing all brass accoutrements from cap badge to ankle gaiter buckles, and all webbing equipment needed to be treated with blanco, but once boots had been so highly polished that faces would reflect in the toe caps which in previous hours had been scuffed climbing brick walls or surmounting other obstacles, then all that remained for the morning's inspection to be a formality was the removal of every suspicion of any microscopic trace of rust from rifle barrels.

Similarly, to safeguard against default at unannounced kit inspections, bringing in their wake the theoretical loss of liberty in confinement to barracks, it was vital to keep uniforms immaculately pressed, holed socks and woollen gloves darned and missing buttons replaced on shirts, trousers and overcoats.

Unanswered mail from family and friends could be left to accumulate, but from the enemy of mankind intervals were borrowed, and acknowledged they were. For the moment, at least, anxious relatives would be comforted and, though too shameful to be openly admitted, the prospect of further food parcels from them would be enhanced.

On completion of such tasks and provided the whole squad were not on guard or fire duties nor on fatigues, or, individually, one was neither mess orderly nor hut orderly, then each marine was free to do as he wished. Should the wish be to venture beyond the boundary of the establishment it was essential to ensure appearances were bound to pass inspection on the compulsory parades, attendance at the earlier of which was virtually impossible other than for unfettered camp staff, and the later 'liberty boat' was too far into the evening to make it worthwhile going 'ashore'.

It was remarkable how subtly naval jargon had crept into the vocabulary of the landlubbers. It was not affectation nor were the words and phrases specifically chosen as alternatives to avoid repetition. In fact, orally the terms were used unconsciously; it was only when they were written that the tendency was realised, but the influence was absolute. The ground had ceased to exist, as had floors. Each was now the deck. None went to bed, but spoke of climbing into their hammock. When any needed to answer the calls of nature it was no longer to the lavatory or if in camp to the latrines they went, but to the heads. One was not permitted to enter premises, but to come aboard; and clothes no longer needed washing, but dhobeying. Regardless of how nonsensical it sounded to speak of going ashore when stationed at a camp countless miles inland, ashore one went: not out. Even in this make believe fraternity only the most seriously impaired visionary could liken presence on an inspection parade, hopeful to pass scrutiny and be granted leave of absence, with the spectre of a ship's launch conveying members of its crew to and fro between ship and shore; but catching the liberty boat was the vernacular for attending the parade.

As time passed, all weaknesses in the character of each individual were eradicated and with robust self-discipline beginning to bloom the initial training came to an end with an impressive passing out parade and, in the evening, an equally impressive feat of drinking, causing a couple of the inebriates to pass out for the second time on that day. A few others, insisting it was a time honoured tradition, were intent on tossing the squad's corporal instructor into the river Exe but he, perhaps bitterly aware of previous immersions in the murky waters of the estuary, left the gathering after only a couple of rounds had been served.

Having escaped from the rigours of training unscathed and having survived the frantic drinking session on the previous evening, the next morning and to the martial strains of 'A life on the ocean wave' played by the depot band, the squad marched out of camp.

*****

In case any of the local righteous citizens of Devon astir in the vicinity of the gates to the camp should consider the exodus a sacrilegious mockery of the gospel according to St. Mark, and should become 'sore afraid, and should cry out in the belief that the apparitions they witnessed walking upon the surface of the waves were spirits', on this far less miraculous occasion it was better by far that the squad should march out of camp rather than 'go ashore'.

2

THE PARTING OF
THE BEST OF FRIENDS

Like passing ships in still of night
On voyage bent, soon out of sight,
The legion strode to duty's call

Along the way, alas for Jim
A 'special op' awaited him,
And end to friendship with them all

From the relative grandeur of Exton its graduates were banished to the desolation of Dalditch.

The location was so unmentionable that it did not merit specification on even the most detailed ordnance survey maps. The wretched landscape gave the firm impression of a spot to which the Almighty decided not to return for the purpose of completion after his weekend break, following six days of frenetic global labour.

Lacking any recognisable boundary, the new arrivals only realised they had entered the base when, dotted across an endless gorse covered common, half hidden but completely rusted Nissen huts came into view. Initially and erroneously they were assumed to be storage huts.

If the scene which first met disbelieving eyes tended to depress, it was as nothing compared to the utter horror which confronted them on crossing the threshold of the hut to which the squad were directed. Tunnel-shaped, it was of corrugated iron construction and had a cement base. It would have been far from true to say the hovel was uninhabitable. It was teeming with all sorts of life, though the insects soon recognised their awful mistake and swiftly returned to the comparative comfort of the wind-swept common. Hob-nailed boots aided and abetted by burrowing creatures with the penetrative power of pneumatic drills had, over the years, reduced the cemented deck to layers of powdery rubble. Those in the squad who were perceptive and quick enough to commandeer a bed which had a short leg supporting each corner, literally nestled in the dust. Those who reposed on beds which were lacking legs virtually peered up at it.

All hope that some measure of compensation might be found in the cuisine was shattered even before any of the foreign legion reached the entrance to the mess. Prompting their discouragement were an appreciable number of earlier diners who were leaving the building, and who were seen dumping considerable portions of unfancied food into a collection of conveniently placed swill-bins. The Afrikaner, now objecting to being referred to as Lady Smith and who had spent his formative years in India remarked upon the fact that the anglicised noun 'Dal' was derived from the Hindi term 'Dhal'- a common foodstuff in India. Deliberating upon the derivation of Dalditch, his conclusion was it must have resulted from the bloody common foodstuff that was ditched there.

The meal provided being everything short of edible, several in the squad flocked to the NAAFI canteen in order to pacify complaining stomachs. Seated within earshot of other, obviously more senior marines who had returned from active service and who were waiting draft to other units, fragments of conversation could be overheard discussing the possible authenticity of the rumoured Commando Order, concerning the treatment of captured commandos, allegedly issued on the instruction of Adolf Hitler. The sources of the rumour were obscure and many, but none among the group debating the matter seemed to have first hand knowledge of its origin. The more often the declared penalty of death for any commando taken prisoner was aired the more incredulous became the reason for the edict; but whereas the old sweats had no demands upon their time other than to scan daily orders first thing every morning for notice of draft, a variety of calls beckoned the comparative rookies which compelled them to vacate the canteen with the discussion still in full flow.

However, that evening the eavesdroppers pursued the topic vehemently, attracting the interest and gradual intervention of others in the hut. Some suggested the order may have been a reprisal for the mission towards the end of 1942 when, in what after the war was immortalised in the film *The Cockle-Shell Heroes*, a raid was carried out on fast, blockade-running ships anchored on the River Gironde at Bordeaux, but this school of thought was ruled out when it was pointed out the raid took place after the order had been issued. Another conjecture, somewhat vague in detail, was that it may have been in retaliation for an attack on one of the Channel Islands but as none, other than the person voicing the opinion, had heard of an attack on any of the islands it, too, was discounted. Yet a further reason given for the threatened death sentence was the daring raid on Field Marshall Rommel's HQ during the campaign in North Africa, the intention of which was to capture or, in the process, kill the Desert Fox, as Rommel was known.

As the evening progressed and as more and more joined in the argument, the few known facts of various missions became embroidered with all manner of highly contentious anecdotes, which in turn were further embellished. A generally scorned belief of one individual's claim, that German propaganda had broadcast an accusation of the enlistment of criminals in the commandos, did find a form of support from a small number. One of them pointed out there had been persistent whispers that several convicts, adept in the practice of safe-breaking, were released on parole on condition they accompanied the raiders and ransacked the safes at Rommel's headquarters. Surpassing this in imagination was an account of a passenger, seated next to a commando on a bus in the south of England, who was reputed to have asked for how long he was 'in' before release from jail. Another suggested the rumour must have been whispered very loudly to have been heard both in Germany and in the South of England.

Rejecting every single word as rubbish, and as ill-founded as the concept that all commandos were six-footers with shoulders as broad as barn doors, the majority conceded that the only known facts were that neither Rommel nor secrets were captured and, audacious and heroic as the mission was, it ended in failure and in the death of the C.O., Lieutenant Colonel Keyes, who was posthumously awarded the Victoria Cross for his bravery in the attack.

As the argy-bargy dragged on, one after another of the group turned in for the night. Further speculation was abandoned with Wally's remark that the reported existence of the order may have been designed to ensure that ranks fully understood capitulation would mean extermination.

If, during the night, uncomfortable, rickety beds were

conducive to dreams, such would have been of the end of the world; equally, wakening glimpse was not of the beginning of paradise. As those who were light sleepers knew only too well, it had rained on and off during the night: mostly on. Those who may not have been disturbed by its patter on the tin roof were made aware of it by the pool of water inside the hut. When, soon after breakfast, orders posted on the notice board for the remainder of the week were painstakingly examined, the suspicion formed on arrival the previous day was confirmed. From the very first moment the squad clapped eyes on Dalditch they strongly felt their existence would be entirely different. It was correctly surmised the kid gloves were about to be removed and the halcyon days spent at Exton would be pined after. In retrospect it was found that despite the relaxation in the level of spit and polish and perfection in drill and in personal appearance, beyond Exton's fence the grass was not greener.

The main items on the agenda displayed on the orders board were weapon training, bayonet combat and field-craft, with only two short periods set aside for physical training. A whole day was to be spent on an unspecified firing range. As to when it would take place, the appointed day was quite specific. Unmistakably, unexpectedly and uncharitably on Saturday. With the exception of church parade at 1100 hours, Sunday seemed to be free but in the interim none were so unwise as to bet that that small concession would not be rescinded for one reason or another, justifiable or not.

Recollection of the first encounter with the recruitment colour sergeant in Hendon was still vivid, with the intercalary date of February 29th still nearly a year off and its significance still an unknown quantity. How imprudent it would be to look upon every Sunday as a day of rest.

While untidiness, as such, was not a concession, boots laboriously smoothed by use of the back of a discarded tooth brush and then polished to perfection were forthwith heavily smeared in greasy dubbin, a sure sign they were destined to squelch through thick mud. Denim, fatigues attire pegged to clothes lines in other areas of the camp gave clear hints it would not be boots alone which would be plastered in such mire.

In training, a variety of weapons were gradually introduced. Viewed according to the number and diversity of staged stoppages during its simulated firing, which faults had to be identified and repeatedly corrected, the Bren gun, a light weight machine-gun, did not inspire unwavering confidence in the trainees. There and then Jim decided that, if as a member of a Bren gun team he should happen to be appointed, he would opt to serve in the heavy weapons troop of the commando unit to which he was posted. The machine guns in such units were far more formidable.

Brief acquaintance was also made with, and demonstrations were given on, the effectiveness of sub-machine guns, notably the Sten and the Thompson, the latter more widely referred to as the 'tommy gun', especially by film star gangsters. It had the disadvantage of a relatively low range of fire, but the guns displayed had the decided advantage of not being lumbered with the barrel-type magazine favoured by film producers. Mortar crews explained their respective routines and the situation in which these weapons were best employed. The teams laid down a devastating barrage and, as their finale and under which they withdrew, enveloped their audience in a blinding smoke-screen. From other instructors there were severe strictures on the handling and priming of hand grenades, according to the method by which they were to be dispatched. The wrongly timed fuse, four seconds or seven dependent upon whether to be thrown by hand or fired from a cup attached to a rifle barrel, could result in tragic consequences.

But, perhaps, the entertainment which made the biggest impact both literally and figuratively was the pièce de résistance served up by the demolition officer. Hoisted with his own petard as being a man of little faith, nevertheless in the eyes of the entire squad his method of moving mountains was just as effective.

Fieldcraft wasn't without interest or diversity, either. Wearing the three chevrons which entitled him to be addressed as sergeant, a rough and ready looking individual held periodical sessions in cookery. When the term was first posted on the daily orders board there was scope for amazement. It was visualised that either the squad were to don aprons, not entirely in keeping with the public image of commandos or, worse, there was a mis-spelling. 'Rookery', a term introduced by Gongs, no doubt recalling his uncle's yarns, was an Australasian and less explicit term for sodomy.

As it turned out, aprons were not called for nor was….. The instruction was in the culinary art but few of the ingredients or recipes would have been found in books on cookery. It was a prescription for living off the land and upon the edible creatures which inhabited it. Frequently, and not entirely by coincidence the squad thought, the session was a late morning exercise when appetites were keen and susceptible to the delicacies offered by the NCO. Of what they partook was only revealed after its digestion and to the mortification of the diners, few of whom would have been suited to deputise for Oliver Twist.

Another facet of fieldcraft on which much time was spent was camouflage. Once the art was fully explained and demonstrated it was quite remarkable how effective it could be.

Even in terrain which provided little scope for concealment, with the aid of scraps of adjacent foliage with which to break up tell tale outlines, and unless those in hiding made deliberate and exaggerated movement in order to attract attention to where they were positioned, detection was far from an easy task – in some circumstances from only a few yards. In its most skilful employment, far removed from comic portrayals of a whole line of saplings advancing across barren tracts of land, the art of camouflage was the subterfuge of the well trained sniper.

Jim was very uneasy in his mind regarding the role of snipers. It was one thing to open fire upon an advancing throng when under attack, or to do so when mounting an attack where it was a matter of slay or be slain, but it was an altogether different kettle of fish to lie in wait and calmly pick off a specific, unsuspecting foe posing no direct threat. Granted the fact that situations occupied by snipers prevented them taking prisoners, and presuming successive Geneva Conventions did not forbid their role, nevertheless to him it was completely unconscionable. He dwelt on the approaching day to be spent on the firing range, the purpose of which was to qualify as marksman, from which pool snipers were chosen. While he had no intention to deliberately fail the test, he knew full well that if snipers were not a voluntary body and should he be ordered to operate as one, he would find himself in considerable difficulty.

During the period leading up to the day to be spent on the firing range Jim wore a permanent frown. Whatever task required his effort, the concern was continually at the back of his mind. Though it required the observation of a close mate, he definitely smoked more cigarettes than he normally craved, but on the actual day fixed for the shoot he found the target practice to be quite relaxing. With careful aim and with rounds of ammunition to spare, marksman-ship was achieved. Rather as though its accomplishment had been his preoccupation, he adopted the attitude that he would deal with the consequence if, as and when it arose.

With others who had qualified he made his way to the butts, where they became markers for the next firing party. On hoisted targets below which the markers sheltered, with the aid of a large disc attached to the end of a long pole the results of each shot were indicated by placing the disc over the bull's-eye, the inner or the outer ring. Shots which had missed the target area altogether were indicated by waving the disc from side to side.

Though by those responsible the stunt was seen as nothing more than a prank, an accident occurred when someone on the firing range, with rounds to spare, foolishly aimed a shot at a hoisted marking disc, which rebounded and seriously wounded a person operating as a marker.

For those that did qualify as marksman, the magnanimous sum of three pence was added to the basic daily rate of pay.

By the time the last rifleman had finished firing, Jim's melancholy of previous days had lifted. The mere fact of a change of surroundings and an entirely new routine probably aided his change of mood. He doubted whether it was entirely down to the increase in pay. On the return journey to camp, when the lorry overtook a bus displaying the destination of Budleigh Salterton, he wondered how its citizens managed to squeeze the name into some of the very limited spaces on various forms, but he found it just rolled off the tongue. He reflected upon a snapshot seen among the family memorabilia, of either a jaundiced, distant relative or a sepia tinged photograph of the individual while on holiday in historic Anglesey, posing on the platform of a village railway station, looking distinctly bemused. As opposed to Llanfairpwllgwyngyllgogerychwyrndrobwyllllantysiliogogogoch, the scene of the photograph, Budleigh Salterton was not in the same league of tongue twisters, but idle curiosity prompted a visit to see what it did have to offer. There had been no intimation throughout the week regarding last minute plans for

Sunday afternoon, so he planned to make his way there.

At Dalditch, as in other matters connected with 'bull', church parade was low key. There was inspection prior to the march to church but it was more to ensure trainees were tidy rather than faultless in appearance; a recognition that, like cleanliness, tidiness was subordinate to godliness. Lacking musicians, as most other things at Dalditch, there was no band to march behind or to play hymns during the service; but whether this caused more upset to the Almighty, or to his terrestrial, uniformed, disciple conducting the unmelodious singing is a matter of sheer speculation.

In the afternoon, trusting in his sense of direction which had served him pretty well in the past, Jim set off across the common for B.S. on what he hoped would be a shorter route than by road. After about an hour the journey of discovery was accomplished.

What might one say of Budleigh Salterton? That it was sleepy, for sure: another certainty was it captured his heart – completely. The main road, practically the only road, led to a pebble beach on which were a few, apparently, stranded boats, the tackle in which suggested lobster was the prey of the indolent fisherman: certainly the public would never be induced to take a trip around Lyme Bay in such boats. On each side of what proclaimed itself High Street, stout, heavy looking doors of a variety of shops looked capable of resisting entry of would-be customers; but, being the Sabbath, proprietors were free to recuperate from the strain of dealing with the need of the odd client who had managed to gain entry during the week.

Without actually constituting roads, at intervals, on the seaward side, tracks from the cliff top descended towards the High Street. It was not the case that these path-ways ran down to the main road. Speed was not of the essence in Budleigh, where municipally provided wooden benches constantly beckoned and cajoled leg weary holiday makers and elderly, gregarious members of the local community, numbers of whom ambled from one seat to the next where they paused for conversation with those sauntering in the opposite direction.

From the other side of the High Street a bus service operated. Presumably this was for the convenience of visitors as it was altogether inconceivable that any of the inhabitants of Budleigh

Salterton would ever wish to depart. Although for the present Jim knew that, reluctantly, he must, it was there he decided he would settle down after the war together with his intended.

*****

In the absence of an equipped gymnasium at Dalditch, physical training was in the open. Gone was the tendency towards Swedish gymnastic exercises. The fitness and stamina created by these movements were put into practice in grappling with hindrances which might be encountered in action. Heights were scaled between Budleigh and Sidmouth, but at first not without moments of immobility for a small number of persons due to fear. To those afflicted with debilitating tenseness, instructors were quick to give assurance that all who climbed were subject to spasmodic bouts of anxiety and vouched the predicament would ease as climbing technique progressed. If, in the ascent, the concern was psychological, in the descent it was decidedly physical. Although the art of abseiling was not actually or even nearly perfected, it was managed, but not without rope burn to the lower controlling hand and weals in the crotch where, acting as a brake by an upward jerk of the rope grasped in the lower hand, the manner of descent was arrested. Many swore no gelding was ever dealt such unmitigated agony.

Methods of crossing rivers and ravines were also taught and more or less mastered, but again not without mishap. Descent of what was fancifully referred to as the death slide caused a host of different injuries, mostly and fortunately in the nature of recovery incidents as opposed to discharge events. Though the risk to life and limb was appreciably less, the most abhorrent element in training was the mental resignation and bodily submission when acting as a human footbridge to help other recruits surmount barbed wire obstructions.

Tests of endurance and ingenuity were given unlimited scope when, in small groups, they were transported quite considerable distances to Exmoor or even further, to Dartmoor. During hours of darkness they were abandoned without means or sustenance and were required to return to camp by an appointed time. Inevitably, ravenous hunger was appeased to the detriment of adjacent farms on the return route, while thirst was quenched with purloined bottles of milk from doorsteps of late risers.

As at Exton the demands on time caused the weeks to pass quickly and, on completion of training, those favourably assessed found themselves in the holding unit at Dalditch awaiting transfer for the ultimate test at the commando base at Achnacarry, to the north of Fort William and in the shadow of Ben Nevis.

Then, on the day before the draft to Scotland, Jim developed appendicitis: the attack was quite sudden, on a Sunday morning. He had not bothered to get up for breakfast, not as the result of feeling ill but from disinclination. To rise at the necessary and relatively early hour on the Sabbath, for gruesome grub he would not consume with any satisfaction, seemed pointless. When, ultimately, he did rise he became conscious of a severe pain in the centre of the abdomen which faded after a while, but only to recur after another few minutes. Although no food had been consumed since the previous evening he began to retch, and gradually the pain moved lower and to the right, becoming continuous. While shaving after he ultimately got up, he thought his appearance was ghastly and his temperature feverish, while later, back in the hut he collapsed in great pain.

Attended by sick-bay staff summoned by his hut mates and examined by the doctor, the camp ambulance whisked him off to a naval hospital at Newton Abbot. To alleviate his condition a sedative was administered and he was bedded down. Although drowsy, he was aware he had been placed in a bed, with legs which kept it off the floor instead of nestled in dust; of the luxury of sheets in which he was pampered and the comfort of a mattress beneath his body. It was as though he had passed away and, contrary to the expectation of all and sundry, had been allowed through the Pearly Gates by the duty janitor who had either failed to recognise him or who truly was a saint of the most forgiving kind.

On the day following arrival at hospital and preparatory to the removal of the offending organ, his nether regions were shaved by a member of Queen Alexandra's Royal Naval Nursing Service, which young lady wielded an offensive looking implement which defied all resemblance to a safety razor. Jim fervently prayed she was not conceived and reared by a member of the women's liberation movement who remained of the opinion that the majority of men continued to enjoy the dominant position in most affairs, so to speak; and that his appendix would be unaccompanied on its journey to the incinerator.

Thankfully the unwanted hair was removed without grievous mishap as was the appendix. Although in childhood he had twice been admitted to hospital, never having had an operation but aware of fondly recalled details of heroic recovery by those that had, when he regained consciousness he was agreeably surprised at his sang-froid. From the onset of the coma, around the count of six following instruction to commence counting following injection of the general anaesthetic, to resumption of his sensibilities there were no problems whatsoever. Prophetic warnings of intense nausea did not materialise; there was neither trace of debility nor any soreness. Certainly there was no sight of an anxious group gathered at the bedside. In fact, refreshed by respite from all care, Jim felt akin to an intoxicated reveller on the eve of a long weekend in which to contemplate further indulgence.

Until the removal of sutures, the only after-effect was due to the fact that joviality became a sorry business, best avoided, as belly-laughter pulled stitches in the wound. Clearing the throat, or worse still the need to cough, was resisted until unavoidable and then with dread.

After two weeks, with stitches removed, attentive nursing, the novelty of food fit to be eaten and with only the minimal exertion of lying to attention on the daily round of the medical officer and his entourage, recovery was rapid. Allowed out of bed at the beginning of the third week, and after a few more days wobbling around the ward on unsteady legs, permission was granted to go ashore for a few hours. With another convalescent from his ward, Jim spent the afternoon in Newton Abbot. His companion had enlisted for regular service in the corps for the compulsory, initial term of eleven years, long before the outbreak of war. In terms which seemed to epitomize the old sweat's outlook, he was seduced into signing-on for a further ten years with the lure of a pension on completion. He considered the arrangement comparable to prostitution. The provision of personal services for payment, but he bemoaned the fact those in the oldest profession insisted upon payment on demand rather than after providing service for 21 years.

Like so many other mariners, almost without exception, the

long-term serviceman seemed to have but one topic of conversation, of boastful conquests world wide with girls in every port from Valparaiso to Vladivostok, deeming that deprived of conjugal rights it permitted debauchery whenever and wherever opportunity existed. The tendency of the self-styled Lothario was to presume that adultery was the duty of every adult.

The only aspect of conversation which permitted any response arose in consequence of the hideous regulation hospital blue in which both were attired, the colour perhaps more accurately described as recoil blue rather than royal blue. In turn this led to the disclosure that a new, second, dress uniform issued at the beginning of the year to the regular was surplus to his requirement. Badly in need of funds for an undisclosed purpose, the spare uniform, vouched by the seller to be a lady-killer, was purchased for the sum of one pound on return to the hospital.

During the third week, with the implication of unwanted junk mail sent back to whence it came, Jim was discharged 'RTU'. On his 'return to unit', while on the journey to Dalditch and sitting alongside the driver of the ambulance instead of in the back, on a stretcher as on the outward route, Jim was made aware he would be placed on light duties for three months, the first two weeks of which would be on sick-leave, at home.

Although home was at the address of his parents and to where the military police would call if he failed to return to camp after expiry of the 14 days, it was the thought of spending two whole weeks with his girl friend of over two years and with whom correspondence, in both directions, had been almost a daily occurrence since he joined the marines … momentarily he was speechless. Although he would have to leave camp in standard-issue battledress as his newly acquired dress uniform had not been official kit issue, he would take it with him. Out of camp he could wear it with impunity.

Arriving at Dalditch and informed he would be posted to a new squad as that of which he was previously a member had been drafted to Scotland, for what remained of the day he was detailed for duty in the cook-house. For most of the time which he spent there he was completely ignored and remained idle. None of those engaged in preparing food were inclined to consider what contribution he could make, while others who had the appearance of being surplus to requirements displayed little enthusiasm for a break.

Recalling allegations of cooks lacing tea with some form of bromide, which rumour first surfaced at Exton, surreptitiously Jim kept a watchful eye for such machinations. On the sex drive of his companion in Newton Abbot, Jim felt the implied inhibition had not succeeded too well.

Instead of returning to his new quarters to collect knife, fork and spoon for the midday meal, some thirty minutes beforehand he was beckoned to collect from one of the cooks quite the most appetising meal he had had since he first arrived at Exton. As he ate he wrestled with the previously aired views of the Brazilian regarding the expertise of cooks in the corps. That they could produce food fit for human consumption was no longer the issue. The boot was rather on the other foot: whether, in the consideration of the cooks, those for whom they provided meals could be considered humane.

After the main body of troops had eaten and had left, Jim was pressed into tidying the debris left in their wake. With the assistance of one of the unemployed extras the trestles at which food was consumed were scrubbed, to the extent of giving the appearance of having never been used since manufacture. Similarly with the benches which were then placed on the tables, then aligned to the utmost degree. Ashtrays were empted, scoured and piled one on top of another, as erect as sentries upon the approach of officers. Salt and pepper pots were marshalled at the point from which meals were collected, again in faultless alignment. The uniformity was immaculate.

With no other demands upon his services, Jim made his way to the orderly room to collect his free railway warrant to London, consumed with the thrill that tomorrow Eileen would be in his arms again, the contemplation of which did not augur well for much sleep that night.

While awaiting the issue of his ticket to tenderness, it struck him that the ill-named orderly room was a complete shambles. Overflowing waste paper baskets had spewed their crumpled contents all over the floor. Piles of cigarette stubs and small mountains of ash surrounding battered ash trays suggested that a contest was in progress to establish who was the leading chain-smoker. Boots which had trudged copious amounts of mud into the orderly room had been kicked off and were strewn where they had landed, while typewriters in various stages of repair by courtesy of those machines being cannibalised had resulted in daubs of grease everywhere. Hanging from the ceiling at an unplanned angle, the stationary electric fan provided ideal anchorage for webs of unseen spiders.

Such disarray portrayed the 'orderly' room. Conversely, the 'mess' which he had just left was the epitome of tidiness and perfection.

The eagerly desired rail warrant was issued after what seemed to be an interminable length of time, then checked by the orderly officer to ensure the details were correct. Dated for the next day, the homeward portion was for travel between Exmouth and Waterloo stations, via Exeter Central: the return, a whole 14 days later from and to the same termini. As he walked back to the hut with the treasured possession he visualised the journey rumble by rumble along the whole of the permanent way between the two stations, well aware of the precious minutes which would be lost as the engine paused at the numerous stops en route, but the irritation was not long lasting and was as nothing compared to what was revealed on the return of his new hut mates after completion of their training for the day.

He was made painfully aware that Exeter was served by two lines to and from London, on either of which service personnel could elect to travel. The one on which he was scheduled to make the journey was the Southern Railway route. The other, from Exeter (St. David's) to Paddington was the Great Western Railway line. Instead of the countless number of stations at which trains would halt on the Southern line, each stop increasing the danger to Jim of apoplexy, from St. David's express trains only stopped at Taunton, Newbury and Reading before arrival at Paddington. The time taken to complete this journey was only three and three quarters of an hour, as opposed to over five and a half hours on the route which had been chosen for himself – an unpardonable waste of precious cuddling time.

However, the cloud which at first overhung any future patronage of Southern Railways did have the proverbial silver lining .For the return journey to Exeter a train left Waterloo at 0120 hours each weekday. Whereas all leave expired at midnight, for those able to evade the military police patrolling in the neighbourhood of Waterloo Station at that ungodly hour, the trains arrival at Exeter Central enabled those travelling on it to be present for roll call on the first parade of the following morning, thereby extending the period of leave beyond the day on which it officially expired.

As the day ceaselessly dragged on, he went though the motion of eating whatever it was that was served as the evening meal, neither fancying it nor fully aware of its taste. In consequence of his laboured dispatch of the meal, his delayed departure from the mess resulted in further contact with the person together with whom he had tidied the place after the midday meal, and from whom he learned that early each morning a truck left camp to pick up those returning from leave on the over-night train. It was intimated the appointed driver might, for the paltry value of a packet of cigarettes, be persuaded to provide a lift, but it would be necessary to be ready at an early hour.

Believing he would probably not sleep that night there was little fear he would not be ready. To ensure the truck driver's craving for nicotine was satisfied, Jim went straight to the canteen and purchased a couple of packets of the weed. All that then remained was to pack the items of kit he would take on leave, most importantly his recently acquired blue dress uniform.

3

PUPPY LOVE

Together, one day, a house they'd find:
There, in peace, their lives to bind.

Each life increased – by sharing it.
Duties halved, between them split.

If so blessed, their tots they'll cherish
And pray, in war, they'd not perish.

Urgently called to the front door of the house by her mother following Jim's unexpected arrival, Eileen's look spoke volumes. At first, words did not come from either her or himself. Besides being unnecessary, conversation would have been indistinct: in the throat of each of them a restrictive lump had developed.

They kissed. Not sensually nor over-frequently. When lips did meet they did not demand, they brushed. When lips parted, it enabled them to look into the eyes of each other, which conveyed to both of them what they wished to learn – that, parted from one another, hearts had indeed grown fonder.

When first they met over two years earlier it was to search for her cat which had gone astray. It was seen, significantly only by herself, in the back garden of his parent's house. This was situated in Culford Grove, which formed the base of a triangle with Ardleigh Road (where Eileen lived) and Culford Road. This disposition meant that at both ends of Culford Grove, back gardens shared a common wall with the corner house in each of the other roads, as was the case with the gardens of her parents and his.

For many weeks before the disappearance of the cat, from an upper window of his parent's house Jim had admired the newly arrived young lady, whose family had moved into the neighbourhood. Whether from her garden she had noticed his gaze was uncertain, but the girl upon whom his eyes dwelt was adorable. Her long, flowing hair covered sun-tanned shoulders. With a flick of her head she would transfer her auburn locks from the back of her shoulder to the front, there to nestle on her well developed bosom. Slim in the waist, rounded hips accentuated her long shapely legs. He looked-spellbound: but he dared not hope.

In closer proximity in the search for her family's missing pet he was struck by her hazel coloured eyes, mischievously bewitching and yet causing him to look away in case his look betrayed his wanton thoughts. So averted, he recommitted his eyes to the search but devoted his brain to the pursuit of other goals. Occupied as was his mind, most of the conversation was made by her. Trusting that his responses were the appropriate ones, he also hoped he was not conveying the impression he was more than just a little wet behind the ears.

Regaining his thoughts, it dawned upon him that in a relatively small garden the attempt by two people to find a relatively large animal was taking much longer than might be considered reasonable. Though it was unfortunate that during the search, as one set of digits manfully parted overgrown shrubbery while the other ten groped in the clearing, hands did not come into contact, Jims' understandable disappointment was compensated when generous stretches of stocking-enhanced thigh occasionally became visible; and when Jim's feeble attempts at humour surprisingly coaxed warm smiles, it induced the belief that the obscured sun partly emerged, giving promise of better things to come.

Inspired by the notion from above of heaven on earth, Jim casually made mention of what was a contemplated trip to the botanical gardens at not too distant Kew on the coming Sunday. If Eileen, as he now knew her, wished, she would be most welcome to make up a foursome with his friend Ray, Ray's girlfriend and of course himself. The bait was accepted without pause or scruple, assured as it was by safety in numbers.

The search for the cat was instantly abandoned, Eileen returning to her home around the corner, Jim, hurriedly, to Ray's house around several corners to remonstrate with Ray not to make conflicting arrangements with his girl-friend for the coming Sunday – they were destined for an afternoon at Kew, all expenses covered, negligible as they were.

Fortunately the bright intervals promised by the sun's appearance on the day the plot was hatched were validated. On the days leading up to the weekend the skies were cloudless. To those living in this sceptred isle who complain the weather cannot be relied upon, he could but suggest they had never stood in his shoes. Success in the conspiracy with Ray rested upon the weather at the venue conjured up for the foursome. A cinema could so easily have been chosen, but primeval instinct dictated otherwise. In puberty, cinemas were only entered in pairs.

Sunday dawned full of promise. The morning newspapers forecasted unbroken sunshine. Kew Gardens, as the destination was generally known, would be well attended on such a fine day, and those who had arrived in the morning intending a full day of enjoyment would, weary- limbed, be sat upon every bench in the gardens, while, in such areas where the public were permitted to do so, the grass would be completely dry and would present a haven of rest.

Having continually asked the accompanying trio whether they fancied a well-earned rest from the very moment of arrival at the gates of Kew Gardens, they eventually waved the white flag and in the shade cast by a huge sequoia tree they seated themselves on the turf. At first the conversation was incessant, but before long the contribution from each of the males petered out as, in what might wrongly be thought a rehearsed stratagem, they both sank back on the grass, grunting as appropriate when required to respond to a remark. After a while, noticing that Jim's unsupported neck looked far from comfortable, Eileen considerately passed her left arm underneath it. While it was more relaxing for him it could not have been so for her. Compelled to relieve the weight on her arm supporting his neck, she readjusted her body allowing it to lightly rest on the right side of his sprawled torso.

Thus positioned, their eyes were transfixed. Knowing not what she read into his look, hers demanded response. Intent on capturing her heart and quaintly adopting an outrageously romantic role, he recited:

> "Drink to me only with thine eyes and I will pledge with mine,
> Or, leave a kiss but in the cup and I'll not look for wine.
> The thirst that from the soul doth rise doth seek a drink divine,
> But, might I of Jove's nectar sup, I would not change for thine."

With misty eyes, those usually bright, smiling eyes, Eileen lowered her head and tenderly but innocently kissed his longing lips. No longer able to quell her guiltless passion, tears rolled down her cheeks and on to his face. Her heaving breasts beat gently on his chest. So they remained, each giving of themselves for the pleasure and thrill of the other, she comforted by the caring arm he placed around her waist; he, conscious for the first time in his life of the gratification imparted by the closeness of a lover's bosom.

On the homeward train journey it was Ray and his companion who contributed most of the conversation, of course responded to by either Eileen or Jim when words were required; otherwise by a nod or shake of the head. Eileen and he sat hand in hand, transmitting to each other their personal thoughts but whether she was fully able to decipher his ardent wish to share his life with her and, hopefully, to share hers, he could not tell. Possibly, not yet 16 years of age, she might need another day or two in which to decide. He, at the far more mature age of 16, was already certain.

Wishing to lavish on her something more than a trip to Kew Gardens and a little more frequently than just once in her lifetime, there was desperate need for income additional to the sum he earned in the employ of the General Post Office.

His position of boy messenger in the GPO had been instigated by his parents. Having experienced the Depression of 1929 and the slump that followed in which countless thousands lost their livelihood, they were anxious their elder son should obtain secure, pensionable employment. Given the option, his choice would have been a career at sea, to which he had been attracted by a distant relative who had travelled the world on ocean liners, but at the time of leaving school in 1939 war clouds marred that alternative and his parent's persuasion prevailed. In consequence, in July he commenced as a messenger at the age of 14, working 48 hours weekly for the sum of ten shillings (50p). After statutory deductions for unemployment benefit and insurance, the sum paid to his mother for his keep, plus the weekly instalment on the bicycle needed to get to and from work, Jim was left with only one shilling (05p). Concluding it unlikely he could get an advance on the strength of the pension payable at 65 years of age, he worked whatever overtime was available. On the weeks when he worked the early shift, 0645 hours to 1445, he would elect to work on until the delivery of telegrams ceased for the day, that is until 2145 hours. In view of the long bicycle ride to reach home, such late hours of work interfered with his courtship of Eileen.

A most unexpected but welcome source of income came to light and to his rescue. During conversation with a neighbour who worked for the Metropolitan Water Board, Jim learned that extra militia were required by this organisation to supplement their own staff who, in the 39th County of London Home Guard, mounted night guard at a huge pumping station not too far from home. Enlisted in the 39th and required to perform guard duty every fifth night, the subsistence allowance of three shillings (15p) every fifth night encouraged belief the world was his oyster, regardless of the lack of sleep on those seemingly endless nights.

With such wealth Eileen was not actually wined and dined on a daily basis but it did mean they no longer had to walk to wherever they wished to go. What it also enabled and what he found most pleasurable was buying her an unexpected gift now and again, perhaps the most appreciated of which were small items of attire only obtainable on surrender of precious clothing coupons. As the GPO issued messengers with uniforms and footwear every six months, Jim always had coupons which were surplus to requirement, which excess enabled him to provide various tokens of his affection. Sometimes the purchase was of stockings, or gloves or, for a special occasion, perhaps a blouse. Lingerie was never contemplated in case Eileen's parents should suspect a special occasion for which those items were intended. Thoughts of presenting Eileen with a nightdress were especially taboo, and not solely for the same reason nor due to any connection with her.

The origin of the aversion arose when Jim was very young, well before his sixth birthday, he could later vouch, because on that very day he was rushed, unconscious, to hospital following a road accident. On his return home some weeks later he discovered that his parent's bed on which Olive, the younger of his two sisters, and he used to play on Sunday mornings had been replaced. On the new bed, tents were no longer to be erected by use of bed linen supported by a couple of props in the centre, as had been the case on the old bed.

Nearly three years his senior, prior to the ban Olive and Jim used to play together for hours in the tent, sometimes until nearly lunchtime. On occasions his sister would rise from what had been her previous position and, standing upright, commence swaying rhythmically as though to music. When aware of his attention her gyrations became more frenzied, while her hands, which previously had been clasped behind her head, slowly raised her nightgown. Revealing her body, with her eyes she fixed his puzzled attention with mesmeric influence. No words were spoken: no gestures were made. Tantalised but confused, all that he could do was avert his gaze. If such it was, it was the only sex education he ever received, but far from being instructive it gave rise to the riddle of a skeleton's residence, in direct consequence of which visits to lingerie counters in departmental stores were warily given a very wide birth for years to come.

*****

In the same manner that Jim found pleasure in providing little treats for Eileen, so with her now out of college and in paid employment she indulged him. Perhaps tobacconists in the vicinity of where she worked would have a delivery of cigarettes, immediately obvious by the queue which had formed and in which she would patiently place herself, if it was necessary for whatever remained of her lunch-break. Eileen did not smoke so any reward obtained by joining the queue would be pressed into his grateful hand. Often, before she got to the head of the line, the shutters of the kiosk from which the cigarettes were meagrely allocated would be pulled down, the entire stock having been sold, and her waiting in vain. At other times she might propose a day out on occasional Sundays, provided Jim was neither working nor due for guard duty later in the day. Though neither would consider themselves keen cinema-goers, once in a while she would suggest a visit, but whichever was the case she insisted the invitation was on her.

As the immature courtship began to develop, and through their only daughter, Eileen's parents extended an invitation to tea. It was a well known fact among lads of Jim's age and acquaintance that such invites from parents of chaste daughters did not stem from the desire for social conversation, but to enable an assessment of credentials. Unworthy and mistrustful hands on virginal daughters would not be tolerated by anxious mothers and streetwise fathers.

Ray, who had submitted himself to a number of such encounters (without much success it would seem judged by their number) readily imparted advice on procedural matters and on exemplary behaviour. He urged only a small bunch of flowers for the lady of the house: larger bouquets were liable to be considered ostentatious, he warned. Ray was anxious to avoid giving the impression there was any suggestion of parsimony in his recommendation. For the father he advised a packet of cigarettes, or pipe tobacco if he administered the drug in that manner. Should he not be addicted to nicotine, Ray thought a gift of the father's favourite tipple might find favour: but Ray further declared that if the man of the house admitted to no vices whatsoever, then it would be advisable to look for a new girl-friend. And if there was a family pet, Jim's advisor urged him to make a fuss of it. Lacking news of Eileen's adventurous cat, and if the furry creature had irrevocably departed for the cattery in the clouds, Jim hoped that any replacement for it would turn out to be something more endearing than a goldfish.

In addition to Ray's invaluable advice on etiquette, among the other 130 boy messengers at the Western District Office with whom Jim worked there were 130 self-opinionated founts of knowledge regarding sartorial elegance. Nearly all of these advisors considered this would be the criterion on which he would be judged. As to the manner of its achievement there was far less agreement. One school, of somewhat abstract thought, insisted that all women were attracted to all males in uniform. That enabled plenty of scope. The messenger's uniform or that of the Home Guard; the former attire associated with bearers of sad tidings and the latter with elderly survivors of the First World War. Jim, himself, merely wondered whether the reputed allure of uniform was not a recruitment gimmick concocted by the military establishment in order to entice men into the armed forces, and he decided not to make his debut in Home Guard garb. A more down to earth collection of messengers restricted their advice to the comment that, if a complete suit did not hang in the wardrobe, expertly pressed trousers and an immaculately clean shirt fronted by a neat, not flash, tie should impress.

Considering the brevity of their recommendation might have devalued its impact, the advantage of collar and tie over an open-necked shirt was given added weight by the observation that pimply traces of puberty on scrawny necks would be hidden from magisterial judgement.

Expertly enlightened on decorum thanks to his friend and work mates and provided with the wherewithal, accumulated due to guard duties at the waterworks, the snares for Eileen's parents were obtained.

All prepared and with the dreaded moment of truth hanging threateningly above his head, the door knocker was thudded against its rest. Jim had contemplated a different reception to the one with which he was confronted. He had had hopes of a grand welcome at the front door by Eileen's parents and a proud introduction to them by her: with more bias toward him being a knight in shining armour rather than a night in bed amoureux. Instead he was scornfully surveyed by Eileen's younger and only other sibling and, in his spare time, blasted nuisance. Limiting his greeting and the announcement of the guest's arrival, he merely yelled down the hall-way "He's arrived," before retreating into the passage and out of sight, with Jim stranded on the doorstep. Nevertheless, footsteps were heard hurrying to the door and introductions were warmly received particularly by the long term prospective mother-in-law, possibly appreciative of her small bouquet. Jim fancied he detected a little less gratitude from Eileen's father, whose face registered more in the way of suspicion than in pleasure. When previously asked her father's indulgence but without giving hint of the reason for enquiring, which, had she known, Eileen would have been better placed to answer, she only said he was fond of port; omitting to mention after Xmas lunch.

Ushered into the dining room, it was obvious the seating arrangements for tea could only have been arranged by Eileen. She had naturally seated Jim next to herself on one side of the table and her parents on the other, with males and females diagonally opposite each other. On the pretext that head of table represented a position of importance, Eileen's teasing brother was placed at the far end but not so far removed from his father as to be out of reach of a chastising hand. While Eileen had not made prior agreement with Jim, an uncanny telepathy developed between them during tea which gave birth to a clanger avoidance mechanism beneath the table top and out of sight of the others. One nudge of knee required the negative when asked a question by Eileen's parents; two nudges required the affirmative. All went without a hitch until Jim asked a well-meant question of her parents. Underneath the table Eileen's knee beat the devil's tattoo, all but dislocating his knee cap as he innocently enquired if and where their errant cat had been found following its lengthy disappearance. With the same questioning look he had given to the label on the bottle of port and in his pidgin English which had not much improved since he immigrated from the continent, the father corrected Jim with the information that the family had never owned a cat. Eileen's halo looked a little askance, Jim thought.

If the bottle of port was not quite the perfect aperitif to sip with afternoon tea and crumpets, Jim thought it did merit some thanks. When gratitude was ultimately expressed it was not "Thanks for the bottle of port". Instead, and with an unfortunate mixture of ill-chosen words and mispronunciation, Eileen's father said "I am glad for you to your cockburns". Jim sensed that under the table the knee of Eileen vibrated excitedly before it nestled against his in willing surrender.

Following tea, all retreated into the lounge before a welcoming, open fire, the flickering flames being the only illumination. While the parents advanced towards the armchairs situated on each side of the fireplace they motioned their guest and daughter to seat themselves on the settee. It was then, as Peter, Eileen's younger brother, beat them to the sofa and seated himself comfortably in its middle, that Jim firmly decided Peter would not be in the reckoning to fulfil the role of best man, come the day. At that precise moment Jim could not think of any attribute remotely good in the lad. During the evening, topics of conversation flowed between occupants of armchairs and settee and across the great divide on the latter, but by far the most meaningful comment was the announcement by his mother that it was past Peter's bedtime. As he departed it was difficult for Jim to refrain from applauding. Not very long after he climbed the stairs, Eileen's parents excused themselves and retired to the kitchen to wash up the crockery and cutlery used at tea. Then, after a while and with a polite knock on the door of the lounge before re-entry, they stated they were also retiring for the night as they, too, had had a long day.

Comfortably seated on the sofa in front of the blazing fire Jim loosened his necktie which had been a source of discomfort since his arrival. As the top button on Eileen's blouse seemed to cause her the same inconvenience it, too, was temptingly unfastened. Careful not to disturb wearied parents or a young lad in need of a good nights sleep, the lovers spoke in subdued tones: but on that evening actions spoke louder than words.

The restriction of other buttons on Eileen's blouse was also remedied, enabling him with his encircling arm to fondle her curvaceous breast, while with her right hand she explored his body. Slipping the straps of her brassiere from her shoulders with her free hand, it enabled Jim to passionately caress with both hands each of Eileen's entirely surrendered breasts, his fondling touch inflaming his inborn virility, her delicate stroke soothing his sensuous desire. Withdrawing her engaged hand she directed his head and guided his lips, first to one nipple then to the other; tenderly and repeatedly he kissed each in turn.

*****

The two years or more since they became infatuated, as some unrequited cynics dared to view their undying love, flew quickly and happily. During that period there were very few days when they did not spend some time together. Even on each miserable fifth night when guard duties called, either before setting off for the water works or early in the morning before either set off for their place of work, broken hearts were healed with tender kisses and loving gaze. Each of them had become welcome in the home of the other, where they were looked upon as members of the family. At times of celebration such as Christmas or on significant birthdays they rejoiced in whichever abode staged the event. At the wedding of Jim's elder sister in 1942 Eileen was one of the fussy bridesmaids. Jim fondly contemplated how sublime she would seem when, as his bride, she would be cosseted by those in the role she was performing.

During weekday evenings when the hours together were curtailed due to late shifts at the Post Office, it was sufficient to be in the company of each other just wandering around the neighbourhood. As the hour neared for them to part, inevitably their footsteps led them to a nearby mews. Unlit as were all thoroughfares, and shunned after darkness except for one or two other couples seeking privacy or at least a degree of seclusion, in an obscure corner kisses galore and vows of undying love made departure for unshared beds just about endurable.

Their last au revoir before Jim left for military service was bitter-sweet. Eileen's parents were not at home on the Sunday, preceding his enlistment on the following day, as they would be travelling to Kent for some purpose or another, thankfully taking with them their son. In their absence Eileen was invited to lunch by her prospective in-laws.

During the meal, which food was memorable for the lack of any appeal, conversation was animated yet instantly recognisable as forced. When lunch was finished and after manners had been observed by not departing too hastily, Eileen and Jim decided to take a stroll; albeit on an afternoon which was so cold that brass monkeys would not have dared to venture outside. In the well established fashion of past evening walks their feet directed them to the mews where, at short distances, they paused for obligatory rather than passionate kisses. As restrained breath was exhaled after each encounter and hung in the air in frozen wisps, it was apparent the hostile weather would render frozen, fumbling hands unwelcome upon warm bodies. Their feet hurried them to Eileen's deserted house.

She had been instructed by her parents to light the fire in the lounge during the evening in anticipation of their late return, but it was obvious the room would remain inhospitable for quite some time. On the other hand, the gas fire in Eileen's bedroom would warm that room more quickly. She led the way upstairs.

The room, at the front of the house, was of the dimension of a double-bedded sitting room but contained only a single divan. Between the two windows which looked out on a huge bomb-site across the road, a neat dressing table displayed an array of various cosmetics the perfume of which Jim found very seductive; the diaphanous nightdress draped across the divan even more so. From the two half opened drawers of a Victorian chest of drawers, dolls, golliwogs and teddy bears peered out. A large wardrobe stood against the wall to the left of the door and a chesterfield occupied the other side of the room.

As the gas fire increased the temperature in the bedroom, both removed their outer garments and seated themselves on the sofa. Jim's eyes returned to Eileen's night gown. Memories of Olive's antics in the tents erected on their parent's bed came flooding back. It required no effort and little imagination to picture Eileen clad in the transparent nightie resting at the foot of her bed. Acutely aware of his own thoughts on the last night together for some time to come, and surmising her emotions were possibly not too far removed from his own, Jim felt he must obviate any notion of sex, yet cause no hurt regardless of whether his assumption was correct or misplaced. He held her hand tightly, their clasp resting on a cushion well clear of the thighs of each other. His throat became parched as a result of his incessant chatter, deliberately preventing an opportunity for sensual, provocative lips to come together. However inadequate or tactless his words sounded, he desperately wanted to make Eileen realise that because of his truly deep love for her he would not risk leaving her with a fatherless child, should anything befall himself during the war.

He stressed that his overriding concern was not a matter of morality. He told her his desire, his ardent desire, was for them to be as intimate in the flesh as they were in mind. The dominant factor was the stark reality of death's grotesque acceleration in wartime, the duration of which was indeterminable: history left the spectre of one war which raged for 100 years. Ever since danger struck from the skies over England in 1940, he viewed survival in terms of for how long rather than somehow. Throughout the height of the blitz, when night after night whole neighbourhoods were demolished leaving many killed and even more terribly injured, he felt that luck was not without limit. While Jim was perfectly aware that folklore maintained cats' lives were nine-fold, he did not believe there was a cat in hell's chance he should be so lucky. And, on a number of occasions he had been very fortunate during his term.

In addition to brain injury following road accidents when aged five and again when eleven years old, he came very close to electrocution in between those years. Returning from the local street market with an empty wooden box to be used as firewood, from it he wrenched a length of wire binding. While crossing the high street, along which trams ran powered by high voltage electricity drawn from a channel between the rails, he casually slipped the wire into the duct. A blinding blue flash ran along the centre of the channel and a shower of molten metal cascaded around him. While it had been an entirely absent-minded act, it was extremely fortunate he released hold of the wire before it made contact with the current.

Since the outbreak of war there had been other incidents. His father had volunteered for service in a civil defence organisation at the outbreak of war and was appointed an air-raid warden. In that capacity he was issued with a stirrup-pump which was kept at home. As the other member of the team, during air raids and when incendiary bombs were dropped in the area it was Jim's task to tackle the bombs and fires caused by them while his father manned the pump. Once the air raids were launched they did not have long to wait before being called into action.

On the night when the area of London around Fleet Street and St. Paul's Cathedral was all but razed to the ground and, of 47 C of E city churches, 23 were destroyed or so badly damaged they had to be closed, a whole stick of incendiary bombs fell in Culford Grove, where Jim lived. Luckily most fell in the road where no danger would result and were left to burn out. In case those which landed in gardens should set fire to fences or hedges they were prodded or poked onto the pavement where they, too, could be ignored. While so doing, smoke and flames from the roof of a house diagonally opposite indicated one had lodged in the tiles. Totally unaware of his predicament, the tenant answered the thunderous knock on the front door before leading Jim and his father upstairs where he pointed to the entrance to the loft. After precariously balancing a short step-ladder on a table on the landing at the top of the stairs, Jim managed to hoist himself into the smoke filled unlit loft. Directed to the seat of the fire more by the sound of crackling timber than by sight, Jim began to fight the blaze.

Gradually, but how slowly he did not appreciate, the fire was doused. Handed a long pole the fire-bomb was dislodged and what remained of it was propelled into the garden below. Suddenly the saturated loft and ceiling beneath collapsed and, with the joists lacking adequate support the rafters supporting a section of the roof gave way and part of it caved in. Trying to pick his way to the loft trap in the dust and smoke he fell headlong through the gap and tumbled to the bottom of the stairs. While it would be misleading to say Jim could not stop laughing, amazingly he suffered no real damage. Again his head had proved more solid than the surface.

Early the following morning he was patiently examined by the family doctor. Sounding as though the interest of his medical practice was only just below the surface he advised Jim to take a 'little' more care. Even less gracious was the comment of the householder of the burned dwelling. " You made a bloody mess in my house last night", he complained.

When next called upon, the potential for mishap had increased. To deter fire-fighters, the Germans had produced explosive incendiary bombs. When tackling one which had been deflected and was under a lorry parked alongside a petrol pump at a road haulier's garage, the water caused the bomb to explode. By good fortune rather than common sense, to direct the flow of water he had been compelled to lay flat on his stomach, the only spot allowing him to do so being behind one of the vehicle's rear wheels. Though deafened by the blast he was protected from bomb splinters.

While, throughout, Eileen had patiently listened without comment he was unsure how his words had been received. Had he injured her feelings by inferring she had deliberately led the way to her bedroom in order to seduce him? If it had been her desire to make love had his attitude insulted her feminine appeal? Perhaps he gave the impression he was contemplating an end to their courtship, as miles, perhaps hundreds of miles, might separate them.

Rising from the chesterfield complaining she was feeling very tired for some inexplicable reason, thereby hinting he should depart, he wondered whether it was a fit of pique. With tears welling in her beautiful, hazel eyes he placed his arms around her and kissed her quivering lips tenderly, while wondering if that moment would be their last, together. To save both from further pain with the prospect of another embrace at the street door he told Eileen he would see himself out.

On the short walk home he felt sure he had destroyed their love affair.

The note he found still trapped in the clutch of his letterbox the next morning completely banished the after-effect of the night's fragmented sleep. Even more than the words expressed in Eileen's message, the three with which the letter closed were the most significant – 'Ever yours, Eileen'. 'Ever', as the vow ran, was for as long as they both should live: but that was in the lap of the gods. 'Yours', was to the exclusion of all others, and that was entirely in her own hands.

The duty-bound journey to Deansbrook Road via Hendon Central on the Northern Line was more tolerable than he had expected, and ... he may have been mistaken on his first trip, for his medical, but he could not recall the underground train emerging from the dark, claustrophobic tunnel into daylight at Golders Green on that day: it did on this occasion, and the sun was out to greet it.

4

UNTOLD WEALTH

Wealth is a fountain when in need
But thirst is never ending:
'Sufficient until the day'
Our back we keep on bending.

Wealth is a temptress, pay no heed
Her promise ever pending.
Look round about, and see the pain
Of hearts in need of mending.

After more than 100 days of anguished separation, sustained only by nearly as many letters in each direction, the young love-birds were re-united. Life, together, would be resumed, at least for 336 blissful hours. The figure sounded infinitely longer than just 14 days.

A visit to the local photographers for a joint sitting was suggested for the next day, for which Jim was implored to attend in his blue uniform, over which Eileen's hands had to be discouraged – at least while her mother's presence continued at the front door.

Even Eileen's young brother who had joined the welcoming party on the doorstep thought his attire was 'smashing', inducing the belief that, so far as it goes with young brothers of teenage girl-friends, he was not too objectionable: a view which was distorted on account of frequent but forgotten interruptions of cuddlesome moments in the lounge of his mother's house. Be that as it may, if Jim had ever spent the sum of one pound so wisely, memory of the purchase evaded him. The fact that he seldom had as much as one pound to spend also escaped him.

Following the photographic session and striving to give the impression of an impromptu act which in reality he had had in mind for ages, Jim checked step as they were passing a jewellers and drew Eileen to the window where rings mounted on velvet show cards were displayed to advantage. Having asked which of those among the dress rings she preferred they entered the premises where, it seemed, she more closely examined the entire stock from which a choice and purchase was ultimately made. If the money paid for his dress uniform was well spent, the purchase of Eileen's dress ring was without doubt an even better acquisition. Once placed on the appropriate finger she found its attraction irresistible, diverting her eyes for only a split second to register her pleasure with a sweet smile before again feasting them on her band of gold.

Well used to penury and the dire necessity of making a little money go a long way, the accumulated wealth of which he had not been told a single word, and of which Jim was now disposing with gay abandon, was due to the General Post Office and his mother. Evidently those in the employ of the GPO on the date of entry into the armed forces had their service pay made up to the sum they would have received in employment had they not enlisted. While he had no knowledge of this windfall, each week the sum was sent to his mother who paid it into an account opened in his name. In addition to these weekly sums Jim's mother also paid into his account the allowance made to her by him out of his service pay, flatly refusing to accept any housekeeping while he was away from home. The amassed fortune was, by far, greater than any he had previously had at his disposal and his intention was to share it with those near and dear to himself.

While he speedily overcame the remorse, for one fleeting moment (there certainly weren't two) he wondered whether such affluence would place him in a position less favourable than that of a camel striving to proceed through the eye of a needle.

*****

Until moving to London, Eileen had not visited the capital on many occasions, and when she had they were mainly restricted to the precise purpose which necessitated the journey. In consequence she was pleased to be conducted around the fashionable districts and to visit as many of London's landmarks as possible.

A whole day was earmarked for a trip to the West End, for the exploration of which Eileen vainly rummaged amongst her parent's possessions for hours on the preceding evening in search of a pre-war street guide. Challenging her on the bus journey the next morning and in no doubt about one of those worthless nuggets of information which humans happen to stumble across and then store with diligent care, Jim remarked that if during their coming walk-about she could find a road, just one road, in the whole of the West End, more exactly delineated as the W1 postal district, she could choose whichever present took her fancy in any of the large departmental stores in the area.

Dismounted, Eileen noticed umpteen streets. Of squares she also found many, disappointed that in Berkeley Square the renowned nightingales were nowhere to be heard. With aplomb she located lanes, places, rows, crescents, courts, mews, yards, closes and passages. Incongruously named in the heart of the metropolis, she detected Shepherds Market; no more resembling a crowded gathering place for purchase and sale than Piccadilly and Oxford Circuses featured performing animals, acrobats or clowns. But of Tottenham Court Road, the only road, aloof on the boundary with the WC1 postal district, she found no sign.

Observing the custom of all young lovers, they sat on the steps at the foot of the statue of Eros in Piccadilly Circus but Cupid was barricaded by sandbags to prevent further mutilation, his bow having been bent out of shape in consequence of the blast from a nearby bomb explosion. Resuming their spree, in whirl-wind fashion the pair swept through practically every store they came across, though the shares of the various establishments through which they hurtled would not have leapt significantly in consequence. However, mental note was made of the silverware on display in Mappin & Webbs and the furniture on show in Waring & Gillows, the banter being that nothing inferior would grace their post-war home.

In Bond Street they did not dare venture inside the exclusive looking premises, but, relieved of any possibility of pressure and obligation, from the neutrality of the pavement they drooled over the unpriced merchandise and speculated upon the likely cost. Among the gems in the jewellers and goldsmiths proudly exhibiting the royal warrant were a pair of ear-rings and matching necklace together with pendant. Remarking upon how nice the jewels would look worn by herself, to Eileen's amusement and in jest Jim consulted his wallet. In disorderly haste they moved on. They paused and admired the canvas exhibited at one of the art galleries. The subject was simple; its appeal spellbinding. A wave breaking on the foreshore. Along its path, from where the crest was beginning to unfold on its inward surge, the misty spray promoted the illusion of moisture on unprotected faces. As the eye was carried along its approach to where it broke on the beach, ozone seemed to invade nostrils and invigorate lungs. Where spent and tending to flow back towards the next incoming wave, mucky looking spume desecrated the washed sand.

As they were not of one mind in which room to hang this work of art they decided not to enquire of the price. Nor did either have the premonition that, for Jim, waves breaking on the foreshore would not always hold the same appeal.

After a pleasurable but exhausting day mostly spent window-shopping, at the request stop outside D.H.Evans in Oxford Street they waited for the bus which would take them home. Dwelling upon the susceptibility of human nature when tired, Jim remarked upon another weary occasion when he stood in the same bus queue. At the store glaziers were gently tapping out the shards of glass remaining in the upper windows, following an overnight air raid. On the scaffolding hung a well-intentioned but badly misguided sign. Like every person who passed by and read the notice, it compelled Jim to glance upwards. The warning read – DANGER! DON'T LOOK UP.

Well into the evening by the time they reached the doorstep of Eileen's house, she was worn out by the hectic exploits of the day. Before goodnight kisses, unstinted in number, sealed the day's joy, arrangements were made for the following day. Fortunate to have been given permission to take her two weeks annual holiday at such short notice but, she emphasised, prepared to feign illness if not, Eileen and Jim determined that precious little of the fortnight would be wasted in avoidable separation; but, as at the end of that perfect day when the necessity of sleep did part them, each vowed the other would be in their dreams.

Whosoever nightly vision melted first, it was Eileen who arrived at Jim's house on the following morning instead of vice versa. She would love to visit the British Museum. Unperturbed by her unashamed admission of this latent love affair, he would not stand in her way. Off they went.

Wandering around the museum, going entranced from one exhibit to the next, from room to room and floor to floor, Jim relived childhood memories. When on holiday from school, spoiled by wet weather which prevented play in the streets, which was the norm in the neighbourhood, his mother would suggest a visit to the premises with whichever of his friends might fancy the trip. With an eager friend rounded-up and a couple of pennies donated to each by his mother, off would go the junior, budding archaeologists. He had explored the wonders of the vast building on many occasions and well before the age at which he was permitted to travel with a contemporary, when one or both of his elder sisters were guardian for the day.

The exhibits, or those which most impressed him, were catalogued in his receptive mind and pilgrimage was made to these on subsequent attendances. The contents of the Egyptian Room had a particular attraction, especially the spooky mummies. Prominent among the long retired residents and the daddy of all mummies was Ginger. This was the nickname that Sonny Jim had conferred on the perfectly preserved body encased in a sculptured sarcophagus, in turn enclosed within a large glass show-case which professed details of the male incumbent. Apart from the concluded view that Ginger had lived somewhere off the main highway between Port Said and Port Suez a few thousand years BC, the dominant, mesmeric feature was the state of preservation of the body, remains being a completely inept term.

Hair on the head was still relatively abundant, ginger in colour no doubt due to the bleaching effect of burial in the hot, dry sand, while eyebrows were also more than merely discernable. Nails on fingers and toes would have caused not the slightest consternation to the visiting manicurist or chiropodist in the Nile delta. The only feature passers-by in the streets of Bloomsbury might have commented upon had Ginger decided to go walk-about was how well he looked, with head to toe bronze (shading ginger) suntan – not dissimilar to over fried bacon rind.

As Eileen and Jim stood gawking at Ginger's unabashed nude pose, Eileen possibly ruminating upon whether his spouse held a contentious opinion on size being of no importance, Jim reflected on his inner thought of how little Ginger had aged during the course of the ten tears or so since last he saw him. Lacking a nimble wit, it did not dawn on Jim that there was scant evidence of the ravages of time extending over the previous

5000 years since the corpse kicked the ancient earthenware bucket.

Unlike the previous day when amidst the disorderly haste of their West End expedition their undemanding stomachs were content to bide time, Ginger's plight reminded them of the consequence of famine and starvation. Seated before a nondescript meal in an unpretentious restaurant in an obscure avenue leading to the hubbub of High Holborn, a totally inoffensive suggestion from Eileen jarred against Jim's overworked, grinding molars. Shall they go to a dance at the town hall on Saturday evening? With the exception of himself, probably, the entire male population would have been in ecstasies at the lascivious thought of Eileen in their clutches. Jim was a little more guarded.

Ages ago, but fully aware that dancing was a passport which permitted arms around the waist of girls, whether familiar with them or not, Jim asked his elder sister, accomplished in the skill, to teach him. If it was sheer physical agony for his sister, with several trampled toes to prove the point, it was excruciatingly embarrassing for himself.

Try as he frequently and painstakingly did, he failed miserably to exert any control over his feet whatsoever while assiduously attempting to dance. They could be persuaded to accomplish most other demands made upon them, in some cases and without any trace of immodesty, quite well in certain activities, but both left and right lacked all sense of rhythm. Even the widely considered simple steps of the waltz were beyond his mastery when it came to making a change of direction. It never actually came to the point of his sister insisting he should discontinue darkening her doorstep, but it never reached his ears that she had a breakdown in consequence of the termination of her tuition.

Not that it was only his feet that were beyond control when trying to dance, but whether it was inevitable and excusable to be roused by the closeness of a partner's body and the perfume which adorned it, he was by no means sure. Of what he had not the slightest doubt however, was the inhibition he experienced on the dance floor.

Although by no means taking Eileen's affection for granted, with her there was no reticence in any situation, save for that upon which there was now no misunderstanding. Eileen had long ago helped him to overcome his childhood shyness, at least towards herself. Snugly nestled beside him in Kew Gardens (Kewquest, as he liked to look upon the exorcism) had been the beginning of what turned out to be far more than just bearable therapy. Realising Eileen was still awaiting his response, as he unconvincingly nodded his head he hit upon the perfect solution. To avoid dancing with any but Eileen, the instant an excuse me was announced he would find it necessary to visit the loo. It also occurred to him that the meal was not so indigestible after all.

Simply too nice an afternoon to spend in the confines of the museum, they ambled down Sicilian Avenue to Southampton Row thence along Kingsway to Aldwych, the very heart of theatre-land. Wandering past one renowned place of entertainment to the next, two theatres prompted recollection, again from the balmy days of employment as a messenger.

If the job of plodding the streets of the West End of London delivering telegrams with no company but one's own was not the epitome of job satisfaction, there were occasions, though admittedly few, when intense boredom gave way to plain boredom. These highlights were mainly when on express delivery service, which entailed the collection of a package at an address within the district and its delivery at another, often miles away. In such cases there was a scale of payment for fares commensurate with the distance, on which it was not unusual to conjure a small profit. Besides a change of landscape, sometimes one met individuals with more image than other boy messengers. Two such cases involved a couple in the acting profession.

In one instance, Jim had to collect from a pharmacy a remedy for the troublesome throat of Ivor Novello who was appearing in The Dancing Years. Managing to evade the stage door-keeper, Jim made the delivery to the actor who modestly claimed his voice was "at one and the same time irritable, and irreplaceable". In keeping with his modesty he tipped Jim with the measly sum of tuppence. In the other case, from a Mayfair upmarket milliner the consignment was a decorative hat for the actress, Nora Swinburn: she was even less generous. She gave him a smile.

The most lucrative express delivery, in fact it was one repeated a number of times over the months, was for a Polish countess. Admitted to her apartment in Park Street, next to Park Lane in location but second to none of Park Lane's hotels in opulence, the countess instructed Jim. The envelopes handed to him were to be delivered at various addresses in Little Bookham in Surrey. He would be met at Bookham Station on arrival of the 12.30 train from Waterloo by a chauffer driven car which would convey him to the addresses, after which he would be taken to her country residence to pick up a number of packages and then to the station, for the return to Waterloo. From there he was to take a taxi and return to Park Street and take up to her apartment the various parcels which he had collected. A tip was pressed into his hand – a ten shilling note! He was also given five shillings for the taxi fare to and from Waterloo, one half of which, the outward fare, he pocketed with the tip. For a couple of pence and from the underground station around the corner the tube train would get him to Waterloo in good time to catch the 12.30.

Taking him the best part of the remainder of the day to complete the task, he was highly delighted. He was even more pleased when several weeks later, on return from whichever area the delivery of telegrams had taken him, he was handed a familiar express delivery slip. The document was for a messenger to call at an address in Park Street for items to be delivered in Little Bookham and to gather in the village packages for delivery to Park Street. It was of course from the countess; she had requested the same messenger. The routine and the rewards were as before and, at intervals, so matters remained. But ......

In the course of time the calls at the country seat of the countess were discontinued. The letters and the packages were delivered and collected from the same respective address. Although in each case the visits were to private residences, in the small community of Little Bookham it did not escape notice that addressees' surnames coincided with those displayed on shop fronts of a variety of tradesmen – the butcher, the grocer, the greengrocer, an outfitters, and not only of men's apparel. While it was a trifle disconcerting to dwell upon the penalty for 'illegitimate trafficking in officially controlled commodities' (if his growing suspicion was valid), Jim was averse to ending these errands – of mercy for the countess and of prosperity for himself. As a public spirited public servant he consulted the messenger's rule book but found nothing requiring them to be suspicious of countesses. His mind relieved, the journeys to Little Bookham continued, until in the course of time his manna from Park Street dried up, though whether as a result of the arrest and prosecution of the countess, or the shortage of funds to finance the transactions with black-marketeers, he never knew.

Disclosure to Eileen in the course of a few hours not only this possible smudge on his character, but also a scrumping episode, caused Jim to wonder if he had given her the impression he was an habitual criminal; but she did not detach the arm which had found its way round her slender waist.

Keen to spend part of his accumulated riches on other members of each family, theatre tickets were purchased for later in the week: three, in fact. Jim had suggested by way of a surprise for each of them, inviting both Eileen's and his own mother to accompany them to the chosen show, but Eileen thought that as the two mothers had not actually met the occasion might not be appropriate. Instead, with her help, a brooch was purchased for her mother. For the two fathers there were other plans but, for Eileen's, the gift would be of something requiring less linguistic skill by way of appreciation than another bottle of Cockburns. Peter the great (in terms of nuisance) was not in the running for a hand-out in case it was seen as a bribe and encouraged further hopes.

Careful not to walk Eileen off her feet as had been the case the previous day, the young lovers dodged traffic in the Strand and sauntered down to Victoria Embankment Gardens. If other people were present in that small oasis of calm they were not noticeable. Seated on a bench, and hand in hand, Eileen and Jim watched the war-torn world drag itself along. Needing a shoulder on which to rest her head she nestled up to Jim. Neither spoke. Each pursued their own dream.

On the following day the lure of other museums, in South Kensington, beckoned. Briskly passing Harrods, as the temptations on display in the windows would soon have emptied Jim's pocket, the first visit was to the Victoria and Albert Museum, but of the four from which to choose and within walking distance of each other, the Natural History and the Science Museums occupied most of their time.

By the time they were almost indecently ejected from the last building on the day's round it was becoming quite dark. Not at all certain whether Harrods might possibly still be open for business, Knightsbridge was again skirted on the homeward journey. With the advantage of knowing the area like the back of his hand he led the way towards Kensington Gore. Passing the Albert Hall en route, it would have been ludicrous to imagine that during the coming months he would actually be taking part in a nightly performance in the celebrated arena, though by no means completely hogging the limelight.

On the darkening evening, worsened by the blackout which was still in operation despite the considerable decline in air raids, they entered Hyde Park making steps towards Marble Arch in order to board a bus which would convey them to within a short distance of home. In order to relieve an urgent call of nature he made for the public convenience, unfortunately found to be securely locked. Leaving Eileen on the path Jim hastened for the cover of a large tree. Up against another huge tree, dim though the vision was, there was little doubt as to what the pair were engaged in. Nor, he found, was that tree the only one concealing the same activity. Dashing back to the path where he had left Eileen and where shadowy images approached, paired and made off, to his alarm he realised those in the oldest profession were touting their services.

Eileen was not where he had left her. He called her name, at the top of his voice, time and time again. He had no idea in which direction he should search, fearing his pursuit could distance themselves. Yet again he shouted and shouted, each frantic yell louder than the last. He attracted no response from her, but abuse from males and females awaiting approach from each other, the voices of some women indicative of nothing more than youngsters, protected from recognition in the evening gloom as being under age. Then, very faintly, as the roar of traffic in Kensington Gore momentarily abated, he heard her cry his name. He tore across the ring road in the park, out of the vehicular access to it and into the Gore, and threw his arms around Eileen. Wiping her tears and consoling her feelings on the proposition made to her, eventually they boarded the bus for home.

The following day the three theatre tickets enabled Jim's mother and father and Olive to enjoy the entertainment. Eileen and he would not have enjoyed it after her ordeal of the previous evening. Nor had she any enthusiasm for the planned dance. That too was called off. Though, as the days passed, she became more composed, she really had been hurt by her experience, her loathing embittered by the thought of men and women, in all probability complete strangers, debasing human decency in a public place in nothing more than a financial transaction.

Though in low key, the second week's leave sped. On the last evening together they talked openly of marriage once the war was over and he was demobilised. Without actually stating the number, Eileen spoke of her preference for the order of arrival of their offspring and of her aspirations for them. Lips which had restricted their ardour to pecks since Eileen's upset, became much more passionate as well as numerous. Hands that had only squeezed the other pair became independent and travelled further afield, yielding bodies emphasising just how much their fondling touch had been missed. Though it was Eileen's wish to sip the last dregs of the remaining minutes of his leave by accompanying him, Jim could not permit her company on his reluctant walk to catch the bus operating the all night service to Waterloo Station.

He would not contemplate her homeward return, alone, after midnight. The scar from her experience in Hyde Park had by no means completely healed. He gently kissed the closed lids of her tearful eyes. He had not realised just how salty tear-drops were until that parting moment. It was many moments later, in a crowded, stuffy train compartment when sleep finally overcame him, somewhere between Basingstoke and Salisbury, before the salinity faded.

5

ANOTHER RAW DEAL & SHADES OF GRAY

Here rests his head upon the lap of earth,
A youth to fortune and to fame unknown.
Fair science frown'd not on his humble birth,
And melancholy mark'd him for her own.

Large was his bounty, and his soul sincere,
Heav'n did a recompense as largely send:
He gave to mis'ry all he had, a tear,
He gain'd from heav'n ('twas all he wished) a friend.

Thomas Gray 1716-71.

If, as some wags declare, it is nicer to travel than arrive, then they haven't been on the 0120 from Waterloo. No ghost train ever inflicted upon those who travelled on it the horrors suffered by the passengers on its counterpart, operated by the Southern Railway Company. Such was the experience on the journey to Exeter, it was sight of Dalditch that was enjoyable.

Back in camp, Jim found three months doing virtually nothing very boring, though light duties certainly provided ample time for the composition of many and in some cases lengthy letters. Seated ostracised around the hut stove, the abundant leisure was mostly spent playing card games for cash of which there was far less abundance. Alternatively, for those so inclined and with the necessary money for the fare, light duties or more explicitly non existent duties did enable the convalescents to catch the earlier of the buses which the local, public transport company provided. The drawback to an evening in Exmouth was the five mile walk back to camp unless prepared to return on the 2100 hours bus, the last for the day. In whatsoever way time was utilised, the deprivation of route marches by day and sentry duties at night was stoically borne.

However, towards the end of the period of excused duties matters did stir when, throughout the length and breadth of camp, loudspeakers summoned all ranks to fall-in on the main parade ground where the adjutant would address them. Even the crocks on light duties could not evade this one. They would be excused marching, in step, to the parade ground with others in their respective squad. They could hobble.

Once assembled, the adjutant revealed the Admiralty had announced a new role for Royal Marines in pursuit of ultimate victory. The long planned cross channel assault on north west Europe was gaining momentum and with it the realisation by the supreme command that it needed to be on a larger scale than was at first contemplated. In consequence, this led to the conclusion the Royal Navy would not be able to provide the manpower necessary to man all of the additional landing craft. Marines were to be press-ganged to step into the breach. Although, as Rudyard Kipling had written, they were "soldiers and sailors too" this would be an entirely new nautical role. While some would serve on the larger landing craft, under the command of Royal Navy officers, many were required to operate the smallest vessels – the landing craft assault and the landing craft mechanical – which flotillas would be entirely crewed by marines. As the coxswains would be responsible for the vessel and its crew, a degree of authority was essential and in consequence volunteers were called for; for training as NCOs at Deal.

Unwise enough to lead with his chin despite very many previously well aimed blows to it, Jim put in and had his application accepted. On arrival in the town and quartered in East Barracks, if he had hitherto looked upon previous training at the other two camps as demanding, he hastily came to look back upon Exton (particularly) and Dalditch with the same affection usually reserved for childhood memories of kindergarten. The instructors were senior NCOs able to discern between potential leaders and the chaff. In what was ironically termed a welcoming address the trainee NCOs were berated with the comment that whereas at Exton or Dalditch they may have been looked upon as the finished product, at Deal they were considered raw material. Discipline, they were warned, would be paramount: not that imposed by fear of external retribution but that which came from within, born of unbreakable spirit and will-power. Simple courage would not do, either: it had to be ruthless. Adding to the bonhomie, the staff sergeant major threatened the course would make them or break them. When finally dismissed, most dwelt upon what the following day would bring.

At first light and with scant opportunity to get into the kit for physical training ordered by their task masters, the new-comers to Deal were introduced to the sea. It was not a lengthy introduction nor was a particularly prolonged one necessary. On arrival at East Barracks they could not have failed to notice it as it was little more than the width of the road away. Brusquely ordered to take a dawn dip in the briny and assured that their appetites would be whet in consequence of the immersion, the dawn intruders departed, presumably for their breakfast.

Later in the day it came to be known the whole affair was a hoax. It was nothing more than a long established initiation ceremony, gleefully inflicted upon every new intake by other, more advanced trainee NCOs, demonstrating the power of command which they had acquired.

Tuition in the exercise of authority and leadership occupied most of each day. In turn, each marine in each of the several squads was appointed instructor for the duration of a specific activity. At first it was taking drill on the parade ground, each trainee striving to be heard above orders given by others and to deliver the command on the correct foot to ensure that the drill was smartly accomplished. Initially and frequently, while resolutely striving to achieve these ends, those being drilled had come face to face with the boundary wall of the barracks or found themselves jostling with other squads as their paths collided. Thankfully and by degrees a semblance of co-ordination was achieved and budding NCOs marched squads between East, North and South barracks in fine style. And so the manner needed to be. Deal was the finishing school for the incomparable King's Squad from whom the holy of the holies was selected – the King's Badge man.

South Barracks was the site of the depot gymnasium and of the church. In the former, bodies were stretched to breaking point; in the latter, a benign padre healed souls. On Sundays, following restoration of the low spirited, the entire congregation formed up behind the band and marched back to East Barracks by a circuitous route which took them through the centre of town. Though the parade had taken place on every Sunday beyond living memory it was still an attraction and admired event.

Besides being a long term home for marines both in barracks and in the surrounding houses where many had settled down after discharge from the corps, Deal was also an attraction for German gunners manning the coastal batteries on the other side of the channel in the vicinity of Cap Griz-Nez. Unlike in air raids, where sirens gave advance warning of the possibility of attack, shells arrived unannounced. Cinemas, public houses and those other places frequented by the public emptied, leaving those ejected from buildings, which gave a degree of protection, exposed to any approaching hardware, and if in time, to duck. It was a ghoulish practice among those hardened to the shell fire to adopt the role of Job's comforter to new arrivals in Deal, advising them there was no danger from the shells to be heard shrieking downwards. Cause for worry was from the ones which could not be heard!

Of the relics of history to be found in the three Royal Marine barracks, a small cemetery in one of them held a sort of morbid fascination. As he read some of the epitaphs inscribed on a number of tombstones Jim believed he understood how Gray felt as he elegized in the churchyard at Stoke Poges. True that in the centre of Deal lowing herds were not in evidence slowly winding their way oer the lea nor was there sight of a weary ploughman; and perhaps bells tolling the knell of parting day, soon after noon on a bright day in August, was a figment of Jim's imagination, but among the graves the solitude was just as melancholy. In fact Jim's pensiveness was probably more sinister. In Stoke Poges cemetery it was more than likely that a large percentage of those interred were elderly citizens. That was most unlikely to be the case of those who met their end while serving in the corps. Equally baffling, if the custom at sea and on land was to dispose of bodies where they fell it was most peculiar to find so many buried at Deal. He pondered their fate. It would be too lewd to harbour the thought that perhaps Hannah Snell or Hannah Whitney had been habitually stationed at Deal. Had the deceased all been trainee NCOs, he wondered. Deciding he might be dispatched to the same resting place if he asked too many awkward questions, he closed the lych-gate behind him.

Whatever had brought about their demise, the prospect of the crematory one to which the intake were introduced during their course was, to put it mildly, not over-popular.

While the sole object of the training was to teach leadership rather than seamanship – that would come later, elsewhere – as though to rekindle perceived flagging enthusiasm for the latter role, a bizarre stimulus was introduced. A demonstration was to take place on the beach opposite East Barracks and was laid on for the early hours preceding the morning's dawn. The trainees were emphatically told this near nocturnal affair was not yet another prank.

On the appointed day the cadre were awakened and merely ordered to make their own way to the section of beach which had been enclosed with barbed wire. The immediate reaction was this was to be even another method of surmounting such entanglements. If it promised an improvement on what they had suffered (not always in silence) at Dalditch, when, in relays, individuals flung themselves spreadeagle fashion on row upon row of the spiky wire enabling others to trample over them to reach the next obstacle, then for such mercy they would be truly thankful. But such was not the case.

On the beach and with the enshrouding tarpaulin sheet quickly removed was a Centaur tank, adapted for use as a flame-thrower. At anchor on the sea, a not inconsiderable distance from the tank, was an old naval cutter. In the eerie morning light and, apart from the gathering on the beach, witnessed only by the disturbed, squawking seagulls, burning liquid was jetted from the tank. Spanning the waves before engulfing the boat, the debris was left half submerged in the flame-licked sea. On return to the haven of barracks, impressed but not altogether joyful at what they had seen, the would-be coxswains did not eat breakfast with much gusto. However, by the midday break the customary banter had restored higher spirit. It was remarked by one that he recognised how a fillet of cod felt when immersed in the drum of bubbling oil at a fish and chip shop.

At the other end of the training spectrum, somewhat less daunting were the chat sessions. At intervals during other instruction, individuals were called to the front of the squad and told to address the others for an allotted length of time on any subject of their choice. Although the object of this exercise was neither explained by those who instigated it nor apparent to some called upon to deliver the talk, the deliberately withheld reason was purely to define the extent to which a trainee could express themself. There was never the slightest tendency to coax or prompt the speaker. For those that did stumble with delivery or who had some difficulty in sustaining their choice of topic for more than a short spell it was rather humiliating. Sometimes the chosen themes were rather dull or in other instances too technical for those not conversant with the subject. Those which raised a laugh were the most appreciated.

One in particular which appealed to Jim's sense of humour touched upon the subject of newspapers and journalese. It also had very familiar overtones. Jim's father, disadvantaged by upbringing and the scourge of unemployment facing those returning from the 1914-18 war, was a newsvendor. From the daily newspapers which he sold, each evening Olive and Jim would scour the copy of each edition which was brought home to see who could find the most unlikely headline.

The other connotation was in regard to the father of the marine giving the talk. The speaker told of his father's occupation and employment with the Hackney Gazette, the local newspaper for which Jim's brother, Bob, also worked. Countless examples were given by the father to his son of the perils inherent in the brevity of newspaper headlines or even more so on the very restricted space on bill-boards and on placards.

The most hilarious example which he illustrated originated in the First World War. Evidently the French army had launched a tremendous attack (push). Although the French had failed to capture the position defended by the German troops, thousands of the defenders had been cut off (bottled up).

Rather tarnishing the success of the manoeuvre (and a shade too unsavoury to contemplate over morning porridge) one prominent newspaper bandied the headline 'FRENCH PUSH BOTTLES UP THOUSANDS OF GERMANS'!!! Jim thought the Germans must have felt completely buggered.

In due course promotion was gained by a good proportion of those who had arrived at Deal several weeks earlier. Certificates of qualification and presentation of chevrons instantly removed nervous expressions from wrinkled brows, chewed fingernails from between teeth, and restored blood pressures to more acceptable levels. As if it really mattered, pay books were requested and increments in pay were entered. Two stripes would also free those who wore them from further sentry duty and from spud-bashing.

Contemplating a celebratory evening, pubs were categorised by those who had frequented them. The choice rested upon the lesser of two evils. A balance had to be made between those pubs sufficiently distant from any of the barracks to ensure raucous, disgusting ditties would not be overheard by the military police, bringing them hurriedly to the premises, and on the other hand not so far removed that those who had supped a little too much could not be propelled homeward by one means or another. Known variations in prices for drinks barely entered the reckoning, now that they were corporals; but barmaids at the various inns did merit careful appraisal. Taking care not to encroach upon the intended space for the fluid intake, empty stomachs were not cluttered with the evening meal, but as it turned out the German gunners across the channel had the last say. Forced to vacate the pub, a quick deal with the host, for as much liquor as the group could carry, rescued the situation.

The following morning, hale and haggard alike, returned to their different bases, there to be granted seven days leave before taking up their newly acquired responsibilities. Better informed for this furlough, Jim made quite sure the rail warrant for the homeward journey was via Exeter, St. David's to Paddington. To pilfer the few extra hours with Eileen the return would be on the overnight train from Waterloo. As the engine hurtled passengers on the train toward the buffers at the terminus, Jim realised that on this leave he would see less of Eileen than he had done on the previous occasion.

Those seven days must have coincided with the most begrudged week that ever was spared by Father Time. Other than at the weekend there were only a few fleeting hours together during the evenings: but how the hours dragged while Eileen was at work during the day. On this leave there was to be no escape from the Saturday evening dance at the town hall. And worse. Jim knew from Eileen's correspondence that she and a party of friends regularly went to the gig and this weekend would be no exception. There would be four girls besides Eileen. He could not hope to get through the evening, without dancing with any of them, on the strength of his weak bladder. Nor did he.

The need for complete concentration, on where the next step should be placed, utterly ruled out all conversation: the result of provocation, aroused by cleavage where oodles of seductive perfume had been placed, by no means ruled out Jim's annihilation. But none of the young ladies slapped his face nor did he ever learn from Eileen that friendships had been ruined.

Possibly to cool his ardour, at the end of the evening Eileen suggested the long way home. Content to leave her to decide their path and intent only in keeping his arm around her, he took little notice of their direction. When it did dawn on him he found they had almost completed a circle and were approaching the water works at which he used to mount guard every fifth night. It was Eileen who reminded him of the well documented panic which befell the duty sergeant and the relieving sentry who found Jim, flat on his face and unconscious.

From seven o'clock in the evening until five o'clock on the following morning, in watches which comprised two hours on guard and four hours off, sentries were posted to safeguard the huge pumping station in Green Lanes, on the borders of Islington and Stoke Newington. On the night in question, in 1942, Jim was on guard duty at the main entrance on the 2100 hours to 2300 hours stint. Evidently, as the escort approached where Jim should have been stationed and from where the relief should have been confronted with the challenge of 'Halt. Who goes there?' there was neither sound from nor sight of Jim.

He was found some distance away, unconscious. His steel helmet, still fastened by the chin-strap was not on his skull but rested at the back of his neck, like a pillow. Over his right temple was a huge bump. On the ground and covered by his prostrate body, the bolt of his rifle was half closed with a bullet partially fed into the firing chamber. The entire guard was turned out and a huge search was made but nothing nor anybody was found about the waterworks. A doctor was summoned who in turn ordered an ambulance and Jim was whisked off, still comatose. Thus he remained until the next morning, in the Metropolitan Hospital for the third time in his life.

He had absolutely no recollection of the incident, nor was any conclusion reached save for the presumption that with the rifle half-cocked and the protrusion on his forehead there had been some kind of skirmish which had been aborted by the marching feet of the relieving sentry. During the couple of weeks he was hospitalised he was visited on a number of occasions by army officers, who, he presumed from their questioning, were from the Intelligence Corps. They never actually expressed the sentiment, but Jim sensed they were peeved the whole waterworks had not been blown up. It would have made so much more sense and would have enabled the closure of another file.

As for the hospital doctor, while he was a nice enough individual he did have one or two minor misconceptions. Invariably he spoke of Jim's head as though it was a shared object. On his daily rounds, it was always "How is our head, today?". The only occasion when the doctor distanced himself from Jim's cranium was when he referred to X-rays and medical notes of previous periods in the same hospital, also following concussion. Obviously intended as a pun, that Jim must be very thick headed not to have fractured his skull in three violent encounters with immovable surfaces, Jim thought better than to jokingly remark that those in the medical profession were not beyond ridicule, bearing in mind how many had died from illness throughout history!

Passing the vast filter beds, around which all-night vigil was kept in the futile hope it would prevent suspect agents poisoning water supplies, the lovers unpardonably entered Clissold Park intending it to be a short cut towards their neighbourhood. Yet further demonstrating the idiotic reasoning of officialdom, whereas firmly locked at each entrance to the park its isolated gates still remained in situ, in between them the entire length of cast-iron railings had long since been dismantled and smelted in aid of munitions.

At the small boating lake surrounding the thickly wooded island which had been the cradle of Jim's childhood wanderlust, they seated themselves. The whole park was theirs. Even the ducks, presumably nestled in the seclusion of the island, respected their privacy. There was no need. Forays purposely halted at the boundary agreed upon on the night before Jim left for Woodbury Road on his enlistment. It was Eileen, herself, who said there would be no violation of no man's land. They kissed and cuddled, they talked and laughed. Intermittently Jim smoked and Eileen coughed. Day had almost broken before the short cut route led them to their separate homes.

Sunday, in consequence, barely happened and the remaining week days of leave came and went in indecent haste. Each striving to cheer the other with visions of their life together after the war, on the last evening they almost succeeded in raising a deposit for a house in a quickly agreed part of England, chose and completely furnished the abode and sorted out the schools for their offspring. Regrettably their idyll was constantly interrupted by the lounge loiterer, in the shape of Eileen's brother. He had again managed to come between them on the settee in the lounge. While she tried unsuccessfully to rid them of his presence with half of a promise that he would be able to come and stay at their house once they were married, Jim viewed Peter's visit, if granted, to be valid grounds for divorce. Coming within an inch of his life with his petty annoyance, he lived to tease on other days by the timely intervention of his mother who considered the hour past his bedtime.

The space that Peter had previously occupied was immediately eliminated and minds were put at rest that parenthood was feasible. On the 0120 train from Waterloo on the expiry of his leave Jim consoled himself with thoughts of their idealistic future. All that was required of him by Eileen was for him to keep his head. He promised not to part with it – not for love or money.

6

DELIGHTFUL WALES AND WAILS OF DESPAIR

A life on the ocean wave,
A home on the rolling deep,
Where the scatter'd waters rave
And the winds their revels keep.

Like an eagle, caged, I pine
On this dull, unchanging shore,
Oh give me the flashing brine,
The spray and the tempest's roar

And the song of our hearts shall be
While the wind and the waters rave,
A life on the heaving sea
A home on the bounding wave.

The regimental march of the Royal Marines.

Well before the 0120 got to Woking, the first scheduled stop on the dismal journey, it came to a halt. As seconds ticked the night away, instilling in those whose leave had officially expired at midnight the feeling they might not reach camp before the first parade of the day, a spell of jankers loomed. Or worse.

AWOL (absence while on leave) was a crime construed to fit the punishment, based on the plausibility of irrelevant facts. If, when departing on leave an individual took with him nothing more than that in which he was attired, he was at a disadvantage to one who took with himself additional items of kit, of which he was still in possession when apprehended. The fact he had not disposed of the kit gave credence to the view he was not a deserter: he who quite innocently left camp empty-handed had no such redemptive tokens of goodwill and was more prone to the charge of desertion.

Following a lengthy diversion which gave the impression of a Cook's Tour of the southern Home Counties, due, it subsequently emerged, to an aeroplane crash on the railway, the train eventually rejoined the main line beyond Andover where it began to make up for lost time – 'and over fist. As it transpired those returning to Dalditch arrived in the nick of time to avoid the charge of AWOL. Those stationed further down the line would need a convincing excuse.

At the conclusion of each spell of leave the future seemed dismal. As was the case on the command 'mark time', when on the parade ground, life was at a standstill: but not the years. Since the war began, precious adolescence had been frittered away in air raid shelters, on fire patrol with his father, and on sleepless nights while on guard duty. Training as a marine had done nothing to hasten the war's end.

However, within 48 hours of returning from leave, instructions posted on orders boards outside the holding company office directed coxswains to parade outside the transport section, with complete kit, at 1800 hours on the day of the order. They were to be posted to Merionethshire in North Wales, to a camp at unpronounceable Ynysymaengwyn. The destination was numerically, though respectably, nicknamed 'Four-letterwise'.

The group numbered only 16. As a result there would be neither baggage party between stations in Exeter, nor reservation of compartments on any of the trains. Conveyed by lorry on the first stage, to Exmouth Station, the succession of changes between stations and platforms were very inconvenient, lumbered as they all were not only in full marching order and with their original kitbag but additionally with a hammock and another, larger kitbag crammed with sea service items of kit. By far the worst leg was the struggle across Exeter from the Central Station to St. David's. Hardly clear of Exeter Central it was obvious they would never make St. David's individually. With two remaining with the kit dumped on the pavement the other draftees took what they could, and left that under the care of two more of the group at St. David's. In such relays that stage was finally accomplished. Other changes of train at Taunton, Bristol and Shrewsbury only involved moving luggage to other platforms, almost a doddle in comparison.

Bleary eyes opened in the early hours of the next morning on the last stretch of the journey. With the engine hauling the train having to wrestle with the gradients of the Cambrian Mountains and the carriages giving the impression of reluctance to follow, the panorama could be leisurely viewed. Having never visited mountainous regions Jim feasted his eyes on the peaks and boosted his circulation with the exciting thought of climbing to the top of them. There was ample time to imprint on the mind the names of some stations past which the locomotive crept, but many of the names were incapable of pronunciation such was the shortage of vowels in the name.

At some stations where the train halted, more, it seemed, to recuperate than for passengers, announcements were in English and in what sounded like gibberish, which vocabulary was favoured by the few who joined the train at a small number of stops. After repeatedly switching from one side to the other of the many tributaries of the River Dovey, soon after settling for the north bank of its estuary, Aberdovey then came into view. At this halt the loudspeaker proclaimed the next stop would be Tywyn.

There the group detrained and awaited the arranged transportation to camp. Situated about two miles from Tywyn Station, their new quarters gave the impression reminiscent of pre-war holiday camps. An open mind would probably accede that the then curtained chalets would have been more lavishly appointed, the current inventory boasting only two bunk-beds. Nor was it beyond dispute the presumed holiday camp would have had the edge in culinary excellence, as the ersatz meal thrust upon the new arrivals would not have guaranteed the return of paying guests. Nevertheless, accommodating only four persons instead of the far greater number crammed into Nissen huts or barrack rooms, annoyance at the inconsideration of others returning the worse for drink after a night out would be considerably reduced.

As the bulk of the trainee crews were not due to join the coxswains until after the weekend it allowed the NCOs to do as they pleased during what remained of Saturday and the whole of Sunday. What seemed to please a number of them on Saturday was to follow up the salacious information passed on to them by the permanent camp staff. They decided upon reconnaissance in depth of a large army camp at nearby Ton-Fanau, which was affectionately referred to as 'tons of fanny' on account of the considerable contingent of ATS girls who were stationed there. For others, Jim among them, conquest of a different kind was sought. Visible from the camp was a dominating feature at Bryncrug, known as Sugar Loaf Mountain: Jim's group decided they would tackle that. When, that evening, everyone returned, it was difficult to guess which group had had most success.

On Sunday, the coxswains planned a night out together. They would have a few drinks in Tywyn, there being no pub in the village. In fact there was hardly anything. Removed to baffle the foe when invasion threatened in 1940, even the signpost was devoid of directions. The group left camp well after what would be considered opening time for the Sabbath but, being unable to gain entry at any of the hostelries, they enquired of a passing citizen the time at which the pubs opened in the evening. Reproachfully, they were informed that public houses never opened doors at all on Sundays, sanctimoniously adding "There is the chapel". Glasses of beer were not lifted with the toast of 'iachai da' that evening. It was back to camp, and a mug of cocoa before lights out and 'nos da'.

It was not until well into the evening on the following day that the crews arrived, and then it was only the deck hands. The stokers would not join the others for a number of weeks. Their training took place at Hayling Island. Being so late, from the two ranks in which they stood two crewmen were picked at random and led by their future coxswain to a chalet.

In the unmistakable dialect of Somerset one of Jim's crew introduced himself as Sandy, obviously nicknamed on account of the colouring of his hair. In terms of age he would be considered in his middle twenties: in build, regarded stocky. The other occupant of the hut, Paddy, although not two paces short of his graveside, gave the impression of being much older, in fact beyond the age of military service. A tall Ulsterman, his greying hair had begun to recede, possibly prompting his perceived age. From the very beginning the trio bonded well. Despite the fact that Jim had not then reached the age of 19 they generously bestowed a greater measure of deference upon him than he thought two stripes warranted.

The preliminary course of training and at the next two camps in the circuit, Llanegryn and Llwyngwril was rather humdrum, but the latter was at least in sight of the ocean waves. All manner of knots and their specific uses were demonstrated and practised but did little to excite. Aircraft recognition was another cause of widespread boredom and yawns, so repeatedly and laboriously was it rammed home. Jim reckoned he was so familiar with the Luftwaffe that he would probably recognise the pilots as well. Satisfaction was found by the majority in learning, transmitting and receiving Morse coded message by use of Aldis lamps, but none of the yeomen of signals in the Royal Navy had reason to feel insecure. Similarly and notwithstanding the fact the exercise was only on paper, navigation was liked by most coxswains.

At Llwyngwril the final phase in training took the form of anti-aircraft defence. Many sessions were spent in a building referred to as the dome, on the revolving cupola of which different German aircraft made simulated attacks from various heights and different directions on the position occupied by the trainee, who was harnessed to a modified Oerlikon ack-ack gun. When the mock aim at the attacking plane registered a hit it was obliterated and was replaced by another aircraft. Once the required standard of proficiency was acquired, action moved outside. From an impressive display of Oerlikon guns mounted close to the beach, live ammunition was fired at a drogue towed at a safe distance from an aeroplane flying over the sea.

The concluding stage of training in North Wales was at Barmouth. The quarters were in a row of requisitioned private dwellings aptly named Panorama Walk which overlooked beautiful Mawddach Estuary, at the seaward extremity of which was the railway and, alongside, pedestrian bridges linking Llwyngwril and Barmouth.

Looking down from a second-floor window of the room he shared with Sandy and Paddy, Jim was captivated by the beauty of hills and lofty mountains, among which the peak of Cader Idris majestically held court. The river, its gentle source in those remote, wild surroundings, now more bold in flow in the estuary was exasperated by the bedded pillars supporting the bridges which impeded its almost frantic discharge into Cardigan Bay. Across the railway bridge, steam hung as the engine hauled its carriages northward towards Harlech; but of sound, none was audible across the distance. Jim was besotted with Cymru, his Celtic seductress. Equal but totally different in their allure, Eileen was responsive and compliant, till death them should part: Wales, assailed but unconquerable, defiant till eternity: Cymru am byth.

In training, secure in life jackets coxswains and crews boarded the small landing craft moored to a windswept jetty in the upper reaches of the estuary. Under expert instruction from naval personnel supervising the launch, ropes securing the vessels fore and aft were cast, following which procedure some of the virgin sea-farers virtually felt obliged to look sea-sick. In line astern, the upstream progress against the strong current was so slow that it was hardly discernible, but as confidence gradually increased and throttles were gingerly opened the speed increased. On instruction from tutors keeping careful watch over their protégé, speed was reduced and the landing craft were turned about. Several of the coxswains, believing engine revolutions should be increased to the level immediately prior to the turn did so, mindless of the fact they were running with the current against which they had previously had to struggle.

Near chaos resulted. For all the effort which had gone into teaching navigational skill it was perfectly clear next to nothing had been gained from such pains. Parrot-fashion they had chanted the couplets which governed the rules of the road to which they had been introduced, but the majority of minds had long since discarded them. The only lasting inclination towards rhyme was restricted to obscene limericks, the most recent of which revolved around 'a young lady from Leeds'. Frantic resort was made to the klaxon on each vessel milling about in the estuary, but persistent efforts by each coxswain to make their own horn heard above similar warnings from others neutralised the attempts of all. Adding further to the problem of steerage, since leaving the sanctuary of the jetty a crosswind had developed, which eased in ferocity every time action was taken to rectify its effect.

Where the rate of knots had been increased since making the turn, ramps barged into the stern of those ahead or, attempting to avoid collision, coxswains violently swung the steering wheel to port or starboard, narrowly missing other landing craft and small boats tied to buoys in the estuary. The supervising sailors were not especially impressed by the rabble under their tutelage, but they all refrained from leaping overboard to relative safety. After what seemed like eternity, line astern formation was restored and the flotilla retired to the jetty, much to the jetty's cost.

Coming alongside almost required the wisdom of Solomon, the strength of an ox, the four arms and for all round vision the four faces of Brahma, or, lacking every one of the attributes, belief in life hereafter. In the enclosure for coxswains, akin to an up-ended coffin but providing less respite, two nigh immovable levers operated port and starboard engines – up for for'ard and down for astern. Separate throttles governed the speed of each engine, while the steering wheel required at least one steadying hand. In addition to the steerage obtained by permutation of any of these five devices, effect had to be given for strength and direction of current and the force of the wind. Eyes required 360 degrees of vision, not only to check or alter one's own approach but also that of other craft. Finally hove-to alongside the battered jetty, the not too badly traumatised crews lurched back to billets, while the cadaverous hoped for sufficient strength to get to a pharmacy for tranquillisers.

Solely because there was no other option, ability did improve. Upstream the formation was often line abreast, reverting to line astern on their return when running with the current, seaward. Ultimately and riskily they sailed downstream in line abreast, narrowly avoiding the pillars supporting the bridges. Christmas was approaching encouraging the instructors to pray Santa Claus might produce their discharge documents.

Inevitably the festive season's deluge of Christmas greetings was delaying receipt of letters. It was some little time since Jim had last heard from Eileen. He hoped, he was sure, the delivery of mail in the district of London where she lived, not very far from the Northern District Office, would not be subject to the same delay as in the wilds of Merionethshire. From the replies he was receiving from relatives all of whom resided in the same postal district as Eileen, it was evident his own letters were not much delayed.

A couple of days before Christmas he was relieved when, at the customary assembly outside the orderly room awaiting issue of the day's mail, his name was called. The not inconsiderable batch he was handed gave vent to the attitude of long suffering queues of people at bus stops when several vehicles arrived together. But from Eileen there was just the one envelope. Turning it over to rip open the sealed flap, he noticed she had forgotten to inscribe on the gummed edge the acronym

'SWALK' which was so commonplace between wives or girl-friends and their menfolk serving in the armed forces. Nevertheless he had not the slightest doubt it had been 'sealed with a loving kiss'.

As his eyes progressed from one line to the next he felt the elation at hearing from Eileen drain from himself. The content of the letter devastated him and to such an extent it was not read in its entirety. He was wholly deprived of his senses. No doubt there was sight, but he saw next to nothing. Presumably ear drums continued to function, but he heard no sound. Had he possessed the inclination to pinch himself it was unlikely he would have experienced any sensation. His world was not merely turned up-side down but also inside out. Previously the most brilliant star in the Milky Way, like a shooting star it had utterly burnt out.

Ultimately reinvigorated with the vitality of a zombie, he glanced at her words again. Eileen wished to cease their relationship. She had met another. Jim could not face reading again as much of the letter as on the first occasion, but was of the belief that it mentioned the chap was an American soldier. With more certainty, he recalled she was 'expecting'. And should she return the ring, to Jim.

That ring, he remonstrated with himself. Why on earth had he not bought Eileen an engagement ring. Had he proposed marriage to her once the war was over and had his proposal been accepted, then, actually engaged, he was sure she would have remained faithful and this liaison would not have occurred. Eileen was not that sort of girl: she must have been plied with strong drink, otherwise she 'wouldn't have'.

As he silently fumed at himself, in his anguish Jim knew his mother's teaching of years ago was orchestrating his attitude. Whenever one or another of her offspring came to her in tears, hurt physically or mentally by blows or unkind words, she would give comfort and lessen pain by suggesting that perhaps the damage so inflicted had not been intentional. Pain was abated and reconciliation with adversary was enabled, perhaps not immediately but sooner and with much more certainty than otherwise may have been the case. Perhaps during a period in her simple life she had read from a book which advocated neighbourliness and forgiveness of trespass.

Not that his mother nor any in the family were particularly religious. While it was undeniable all of the children had attended church regularly, it was not upon the insistence of pious parents. The siblings were expected if not actually compelled to do so by virtue of their membership of the Girls or of the Boys Brigade. Sure and steadfast they were required to be, at least in accordance with the motto of the organisation. Concerning attendance at church by his parents, Jim could only recall one isolated instance throughout the whole of his life and that was upon the occasion of the wedding of their elder daughter. Yet, as his jumbled mind dwelt upon it, in the same manner regular attendance at school during the week was insisted upon by his parents, for religious instruction their children were also rigidly dispatched to Sunday school. Though there might have been an alternative and less altruistic motive for ridding themselves of their brats for an hour or two each Sunday afternoon, Jim preferred to think otherwise.

Though still not completely aware of the world about him, apathetically Jim returned to the billet and sank on to his bed. After ages of retrospection he stirred from his reverie and, too late for the Saturday midday meal, he decided to walk into the centre of Barmouth for a bite. En-route, to his left, the pedestrian bridge over the mouth of the Mawddach beckoned. He wasn't really hungry. Such desires as still persisted within he would satisfy on Cader Idris, where he would find solace in its wilderness.

Pausing on the bridge to watch a small boat passing beneath and enter Cardigan Bay, he remained transfixed by the wake created by the boat's passage lapping against the stanchions supporting the foot-bridge. Standing hypnotised, he felt something brush against his legs, the approach of which object had been unseen and unheard. It was a collie of some description; Welsh Border, possibly. Deigning to succumb to the animals obvious wish for attention, he bent and patted its back. Approaching footsteps heralded the owners of the collie, the unattached lead swinging in the man's hand.

Halting to fasten it to the dog's collar, the accompanying lady remarked the water below would be very cold on that December afternoon. Passing the harnessed lead into Jim's hand it was suggested he might like to stroll into Barmouth with them. Jim hesitated. Then concluding it would probably be almost as cold on Cader Idris he walked back across the bridge with them. On the way they were soon on Christian name terms. She was Angharad, he, Desmond; and would Jim care to return with them to their home for a cup of tea. Even more than the kind offer, Jim was struck by their names. Desmond and Angharad. To him the names seemed almost biblical. Certainly their concern was divine. Subtle though the act of placing the dog's lead in his hand had been, he was aware their motive had been to coax him from the brink, but he politely declined the invitation knowing full well that despite Eileen's decision to end their love affair she would be concerned about its impact on himself. He would drop her a few lines.

If a more bitter pill did exist, Jim prayed circumstance would never prevail upon any person to swallow it. In pretence he claimed he was not aggrieved at her letter. In cowardice, at the memories it would stir, he thanked her for the offer to return the ring but felt it better she should dispose of it in any manner she wished. Callously, every, single word which drained ink from his pen drained him tenfold, but wishing her every future happiness he finally managed its completion.

Resigned to a sleepless night, nevertheless he turned in during the early evening. Forlorn and unable to look upon their love affair as at an end, he took the leather covered, hinged frame containing a photograph of each of them from the shelf above his bed. 'Ever yours' written by Eileen on the photo of herself was not as specific as he had previously thought. Jim placed the snapshots under his pummelled makeshift pillow. In his sleep they had that one last night together.

Christmas arrived and passed with little cheer or reason to celebrate. Training resumed and consisted almost entirely in better control of self-willed landing craft, less inclined to respond to rudder and acceleration or deceleration than to changeable tide and wind: but Jim was not much bothered what degree of improvement he attained. He was even devoid of his sense of humour which in the past had been his salvation when in the doldrums.

Then, toward the end of the training schedule in North Wales, a novel event boosted his flagging spirit. A national newspaper, the *Daily Express*, had commissioned the impresario, Ralph

Reader, to direct a show portraying more than 800 years of naval history, commencing in the period of Alfred the Great, the founder of the present day Royal Navy. The show, titled 'Hearts of Oak', was to be staged at the Royal Albert Hall and would run for two weeks. There would be a few professional actors and actresses the best known of whom was Flora Robson. Each of the Pros would portray prominent figures in or connected with the Royal Navy, the reprobates as well as those of good repute; but the vast majority of the performers were service personnel, among whom were a sizeable contingent of Royal Marines, of which Jim was a member.

In charge of the baggage party, which baggage incredibly included dozens of large rolls of barbed wire, Jim and his cohorts were not regarded with a great deal of affection by the many people literally hooked on it on its transit from North Wales to the Albert Hall. For a start, on the first leg of the train journey there was no luggage van. It is doubtful whether many people can be adept in getting into or out of narrow compartments of trains where barbed wire occupies much of the space; nor were the passengers travelling between Barmouth and Shrewsbury on the day the marines rode into town. It was decidedly worse in London. No transport was provided to convey the rolls of wire from Park Lane to the Albert Hall. In a measured straight line the distance is one and a half miles. On foot it is about two and a half, sufficient for some of Jim's party to board buses with their luggage. For probably the only occasion in its chequered history, employees of London Transport and passengers spoke with one voice, their blasphemy as barbed as the wire they were obliged to go along with.

In London, accommodation for the group from North Wales was at the Piccadilly end of Park Lane and was most conveniently situated opposite a public house. For the entire duration of the stay in the capital, morning parades were discontinued but at the appointed hour for afternoon and evening parades, prior to setting out for the Albert Hall for the matinee and evening performances, the dignified atmosphere in the pub was disturbed when the bellow of 'Fall in' practically emptied all bars.

The show was quite impressive and had a good write up, at least, in the *Daily Express*. Glimpses of life aboard ships of war throughout the centuries, of naval victories, customs and ceremonies were all very well portrayed. Coercion of seafarers by press gang gave little consolation to those conscripted for the affray with Hitler, nor were the conscripts disposed to think pay and conditions had much improved. The scene in which Jim took part illustrated a commando raid on an enemy fortification, when the barbed wire so tenaciously negotiated across two hundred miles was cut to shreds – making its disposal even more challenging though within walking distance. After completion of the mock operation and as the marines withdrew from the floor of the arena via the aisles, a sudden and unexpected fusillade of dummy cartridges gave the impression of actual accident among the audience seated nearby.

Performances always ended with the observance of 'Sunset', surely the most moving of all ceremonies. Following the hymn 'The day thou gavest Lord is ended', when the white ensign was gradually and spectacularly lowered and the piercing notes of bugles resounded in the vast building, it never failed to cause a tingling sensation in the nape of Jim's neck.

But, for the baggage party each evening was still young. The shredded barbed wire had to be removed from the premises. Once it had been gingerly removed from the arena, and costumes of artists disentangled as the wire was dragged around the circular passage towards the main door, Jim decided the only place to dispose of it was in Hyde Park, just across the road from the concert hall. There, in the park, in a war department compound alongside the Albert Memorial and all but dwarfing it, was a mountain of coiled barbed wire! Precisely for what purpose he knew not, but he was well and truly aware of ripped garments between Barmouth and Kensington.

Few constables can have asked for assistance with their inquires from a felon in such a precarious position as occurred in Hyde Park. For those disinclined to swell the coffers of the Albert Hall, on most mornings members of the public could watch the antics of the marines negotiating an assault course which they had erected in the park. It involved much use of ropes suspended from or linked to rows of other trees. The many rope bridges consisted of a single length of rope along which boots could be eased, while at shoulder level and at arm's width two other lengths enabled hands to drag their owners forward. At intervals the higher and lower ropes were fastened together with toggle ropes.

While perilously hanging upside-down, by means of upward turned and outward facing feet, barely lapping the two upper ropes, and while refastening the toggle ropes from them to the foot rope, the police arrived. Evidently they had been alerted by a telephonic message that boys were climbing trees in the park, an activity forbidden in the by-laws displayed on notice boards throughout the park. The sergeant/physical training instructor showing no intention of unhooking his feet and descending, and the police even less determination to apprehend him at his altitude, stalemate was unavoidable.

Dismissing all belief that the constabulary regarded discretion the better part of valour, outnumbered though they over-whelmingly were, or were somewhat intimidated by thought of gun boats assembling on the Serpentine, following the exchange of firmly held views the police disconsolately withdrew. As the piratical element in Penzance will be fully aware, a policeman's lot is not a happy one.

Though each of the Sundays they were in London was entirely free, Jim decided against going home on the first one. He did not want to risk running into Eileen. Aimlessly he drifted around the metropolis. When at a spot they had often frequented, his feet were tempted to go in search of her. His mind deterred them, but granted thought of how to react if she was encountered. At a request stop he boarded a bus for Richmond on Thames, a place which had not entertained them. The intention was to keep away from the river and spend the day in Richmond Park. He'd have the deers for company: but en route it commenced snowing. That may not have bothered the deer, accustomed as the species are to the annual trek in knee deep snow to deliver Christmas gifts, but for himself the shelter of a cinema was preferred.

The following Sunday he did go home, the long way round to avoid passing Eileen's house. He learned Eileen no longer lived with her parents. He was relieved that on his next leave, at the end of the course in North Wales, each of them would be spared possible embarrassment. He neither saw nor heard of her again.

At Barmouth the course was completed and trainees were drafted to an East Anglia backwater, at St. Osyth.

7

CLOSE OF PLAY
AT CRICKET

There's a breathless hush in the close tonight
Ten to score and the match to win- -
A bumping pitch and a blinding light,
An hour to play and the last man in.

But it's not for the sake of a ribboned coat,
Or the selfish hope of a season's fame,
But his captain's hand on his shoulder smote
"Play up! Play up! And play the game!"

Vitai Lampada
By Sir Henry Newbolt 1862-1938

Though throughout history there has never been unanimous agreement among eminent zoologists as to the migratory instincts and winter habitats of brass monkeys, none have ever categorically voiced the opinion that any remain on the east coast of Great Britain.

Whether in more equable quarters of the year, when sub-zero temperatures no longer endanger procreative apparatus they reappear in St. Osyth, Jim couldn't say. For virtually the entire period he languished there he formed the opinion winter was perpetual.

Nor, for one single moment, was he convinced that the surrounding natives in Clacton-on-Sea and in Brightlingsea spoke the same language as the new arrivals from Barmouth. Undoubtedly in the hope of attracting holidaymakers, in the resort of Clacton the residents described the air as bracing, not completely in tune with the verbal tirade the marines used; and whoever flippantly cooked up 'Brightlingsea' encouraged the return of the rack for false pretence. For the recently arrived, the only aspect of the place which was bright was the prospect of departure from it; while the sea thereabouts was a treacherous expanse of mudflats on which landing craft regularly ran aground and where on too many bitterly cold nights crews were stranded.

Before the commencement of the advance training programme the seven days leave due to the trainees was granted. For Jim it dragged and dragged. He was not miserable, as such. His despondency had diminished appreciably, but leave without someone with whom to share it was a bit meaningless. He hoped his mood was not adversely viewed by members of his family, but over seven days and with each person in the household having demands on their time the house seemed a bit empty.

On one such blank day he took himself to where, on leaving school and for practically the next four years, he had plod the postal area served by the Western District Office. He reminded himself how, from those upon whom he called with messages of gloom or of joy, on days of glorious sunshine their expression was one of envy, but there was little clamour for an outside job when the rain was incessant, or when snow had turned to slush and had penetrated the gap between leather gaiters and boots.

Appreciating that he would find among the messengers a considerable number whose employment commenced after his enlistment, as he went down the flight of rickety steps leading to the delivery room he shuddered to think of how many fatalities he would learn, among those he had known. From the innermost recesses of his mind came recollection of the sorrowfully long Roll of Honour commemorating those who had previously worked at the district office and who had sacrificed their life during the First World War. Displayed behind the counter at which members of the public queued to purchase stamps, and standing in the line to pay in the excess charge on a pre-paid telegram, Jim aimlessly determined between which two names on the list his surname happened to fall.

That was on the very first occasion on which he caught sight of the Roll of Honour, during the few months between the commencement of work and the outbreak of war. At that time, his attitude was not that of an individual liable to face addition to the recorded names. Conversely, acquainted with the casualties among his former associates, recollection of the list was a stark reminder he was now in the firing line. One name mentioned in the casualties hit Jim particularly hard. Although the person tragically killed was very nearly two years Jim's senior he would still not have attained the age of 21. He had joined the

RAF and had risen to the rank of flight sergeant. He had been killed on a mission when his plane was shot down.

The person Jim had most wished to see was on Special Investigation Branch business. As the hour was approaching noon, Jim knew his return was not likely to be far off. He decided to wait.

The job which his friend was carrying out occurred every morning. It was not delegated to any particular lad but to whoever was next in line for despatch with telegrams, when the requisition from the SIB was received. From the outer office of the department the messenger collected a sealed package which was further secreted in a large satchel collected on the way to the SIB. Provided with the necessary fare from Oxford Circus to St. Paul's underground station, and return, the contents of the satchel were taken to the headquarters of the General Post Office in St. Martin's le Grand. There it was handed through a scarcely opened hatch, on the other side of which was the inner sanctum of the branch. Seated in an adjoining waiting room, usually for hours, messengers awaited the return of the package they had delivered, occasionally, the weight suggested, deplete. Then the return journey and delivery to the office from which it had been issued. Messengers arrived at the headquarters building every morning and from every district in the London postal area which extended far beyond the boundary of the county of London. It was reputed it also happened in every large city, thereby providing nationwide surveillance of suspect mail.

Whether investigation into certain correspondence was purely a war time measure in the interest of national security or whether it pre-dated the war and was directed against known criminals, Jim had not the slightest idea. For that matter, it was never established the contents of the packages were suspect letters. As with the scarcity of information in the rule book on impeachable countesses, the regulations were no more forthcoming on other dodgy clients.

Returned from his task, the two chums took lunch in the canteen during the course of which air- raid sirens blared, most unusual in daylight hours at that stage of the war. In the customary manner and to the place staff knew only too well, everyone on the upper floor entered the spacious lift and descended to the basement. From there they cautiously picked their way down the steep, seemingly endless spiral staircase which wound round the parcel chute, ultimately emerging on the platform of the small underground rail system operated by the post office.

The remarkably efficient manner in which this little known arm of the post office operated was a credit to those who spent so much of the working day in the bowels of the capital. The engines which pulled the trucks were electrically driven and were not much bigger than dodgem cars seen at fairgrounds. They had no driver but were sent on their way or, on arrival from elsewhere, halted by buttons on a control box on the platform. If the height of waists from ground level can be considered more uniform than their girth, the trucks towed by the locos were waist high, and were a little more in length than an average bath.

Although the air raid alert was of short duration, allowing postmen, messengers, telegraphists, sorters, clerical staff, and canteen workers to vacate the subterranean refuge and resume their more earthly existence, the event rekindled many memories. Of whole nights, sometimes successive nights, spent down there with many others, they not knowing how members of their household had fared and families praying their absent ones were safe. Of princely sums, hard-earned trudging the streets in all weathers, gambled and too often lost playing solo whist. And who among them would possibly ever forget the ghastly inadequate toilet facilities.

Resembling a tortured soul stranded somewhere between heaven and hell unsure as to whether his onward journey was in the lap of the gods or in the palms of Gog and Magog, Jim spent most mornings wondering where to go or what to do during what remained of each day. Those of his age and acqaintance who were not absent in the armed forces would be at their place of employment or, if on night shift, would be in their bed, either fast asleep or for sexual enjoyment. Misleadingly described in newspapers as 'Forthcoming Attractions', the next days' flops at local cinemas failed to budge him – so the remainder of leave dragged on.

On return to St. Osyth at the end of the most uninspiring week of his life it was good to be constantly occupied, though handling ill-disposed landing craft in the open sea, in gigantic swells, was a vastly different proposition to serenely drifting along in the calm Mawddach Estuary, as those episodes now seemed. The sheets of ice-cold water which saturated crews as ramps crashed into huge waves certainly could not be regarded as spray, or even 'effing' spray. At times, as much of the frigid North Sea as the vessel displaced, seemed to swill about in its well. Techniques were developed in the skill required to beach landing craft laden with the vehicles of war. The propulsion of wheels or tracks on the deck exerted a corresponding reverse thrust on the buoyant vessel, which effect coxswains were compelled to compensate by engaging slow ahead on port, or on starboard, or both engines depending on the tide and current, at the same time ensuring the power employed did not result in the landing craft becoming badly broached, side on to the beach.

Instruction was received on an item of equipment which, whatever its technical or descriptive name, was only ever referred to as 'it'. 'It' had only very, very recently been developed and perfected and was classified as top secret. Strict orders were that in the event of impending capture coxswains should throw the apparatus into the sea. Substantially weighted at its base it would remain secret in Davy Jones's locker. At first glance, it resembled an elongated box camera and similarly had an aperture on the top and another on the side, with a lens in the front of the box. In use, where it differed was that if the relayed beam appeared towards the top of the aperture in use, instead of tilting the lens upward towards the object it was turned away from it in order to centralise it. Comparably, if the object was to left of centre the lens was turned to the right. Although the instruction was simple enough to comprehend, so contrary to instinct was the required alignment that compliance required the utmost concentration. Jim clearly remembered how instinctively he and all the others around him reacted to the sign outside DH Evans, not to look upward. Therefore, if the navigational benefit of the gadget was to be achieved then, prior to D Day, coxswains had to learn to master impulse when intercepting spasmodic signals.

The advance training was by no means the only visible indication the cross channel strike was drawing near. The Luftwaffe made persistent reconnaissance missions and a heavy bombing attack on St. Osyth. For lengthy periods during many evenings and winging there way in the opposite direction, huge formations of Allied aircraft filled the sky. Each following morning, newspapers proclaimed 'Thousand bomber raids on Germany'.

On conclusion of training at St. Osyth and with not a jot of regret, the crews were posted to Westcliffe-on-sea, there to await formation of the flotilla in which they would see active service. Seaward of the railway station and spread across block after block, the base was a holding unit for landing craft crews of the Royal Navy and Royal Marines, which personnel were billeted in houses, hotels and other buildings requisitioned by the government. Many in the crews also virtually commandeered the railway station at weekends. By train, the lure of London was only about an hour distant and an attraction for not only those who lived there but also for those who sought pleasure outside the domestic scene.

Only there was a snag, as newcomers found. The fly in the ointment was, with the progress of time towards the invasion, the powers that be had gradually imposed travel restrictions in the areas of build-up. London was far beyond the permitted boundary for those stationed at HMS *Westcliffe* and, to enforce the curtailment, military and naval police were constantly present in the booking office at the station. For those of suspicious mind, the multitudes who queued for a railway ticket to Chalkwell, the next station along the line in the direction of London, beggared belief; particularly as the intending passengers could have reached Chalkwell on foot in less time than they spent in the queue. Who is to deny that the lengthy wait may have caused the passengers to fall asleep before reaching Chalkwell.

Awakened with a start from their heavy sleep by the porter's cries of 'Fenchurch Street', at the London terminus, it was to be expected that in their consequential semi-conscious state they could not instantly call to mind the station from which they had travelled. None the less, at the exit barriers, ticket collectors readily accepted that whatever fare was proffered was commensurate with the journey made. Fortunately for the railway company, this loss of revenue was arrested when the emergent 606 Landing Craft/Mechanical Flotilla were moved closer to the south coast, though they were still without their vessels. They were also without Brighton, at HMS *King Alfred*.

Outside the resort they may have been, but a short distance along the coast at Hove, and billeted in Courtenay Gate, yet another requisitioned property, they were almost afloat at high tide. The small number of officers required to make up the complement arrived and together they did little, except wait. While production of every type of landing craft needed had been stepped up, because the initial plan for the assault had been increased from three to five divisions, sufficient vessels were still not available. When in the vicinity of Brightlingsea, they had seen for themselves the frantic race there was to repair or patch up an enormous collection of minor craft and had wondered whether any of those salvaged vessels would be pressed into service with the flotilla. In the meantime and though stationed close to the sea, crews could only stand and gaze at it in anticipation of a life on the ocean waves.

An alternative interest was provided at the rear of their quarters where from windows on the upper floor they could watch naval ratings practice their anticipated role in the task ahead. On an empty stretch of waste land the matelots hurled themselves at a series of obstacles strewn on the site, perhaps overstated as an assault course. Those gingerly negotiating the obstructions wore a shoulder flash denoting them Naval Commandos. Ah well. If the marines were pretending to be seaman, why should the matelots not usurp the role of the 'boot necks', as the sailors scornfully regarded marines.

The period at Hove was very short-lived and, toward the end of April, 606 moved to a makeshift camp named HMS *Cricket*, situated between Portsmouth and Southampton. To conceal where troops were being marshalled for the approaching invasion (the concentration to an extent indicating the direction of the attack) letters were no longer headed with geographical locations but with army post office box numbers. Letters to those at home were also subject to censorship to combat any information which might be helpful to the enemy if, somehow, the contents became known.

The woodlands at Bursledon in which the camp was located provided ideal camouflage and led down to the River Hamble. Here, on arrival of the crews, were moored the 16 landing craft which constituted the flotilla. Several hundred years previously and when not on the high seas, the tidal creeks of the Hamble were also utilised as anchorage for the nation's ships, many of which were left to rot and vanish from sight in the thick ooze, but the traces of some were visible at low tide. One such remnant was that of the Grace Dieu, by far the largest ship commissioned for Henry the Fifth. Equal in size to Admiral Nelson's flag-ship HMS *Victory*, it began to leak alarmingly while in tow on the way to repair and refurbishment, in the process of which it was struck by lightening and set ablaze. More recent connections with warfare were sight of midget submarines and inflatable cockleshell boats, such as used in the attack on the blockade-running ships on the River Gironde at Bordeaux.

During the day the routine was mainly in the nature of messing about on the river and, too often for comfort of mind, visiting the small boatyards further down the Hamble for replacement of defective components. Evenings allowed all ranks to do as they pleased. For a large proportion in the flotilla that pleasure was sought in a canteen established in the church hall of St. John's in the village of Hedge End, frequented as the canteen was by many ATS girls from the nearby army camp at Botley. At weekends, when personnel were free after the mid-day meal, longer excursions to Southampton or to Portsmouth were possible where a greater variety of diversions were to be found.

It was in Portsmouth, on the third Saturday in May, that Jim and a couple of friends went to a cinema during the late afternoon. The main feature in the programme was 'For whom the bell tolls'. Though none of them had an inkling how close was their baptism of fire, it was extraordinary that as the plot unfolded it did not occur to them how ominous was the title. After the film they made their way to a YMCA canteen for a meal, during the consumption of which Jim became conscious of an inflamed and obstructed throat which made swallowing solids mildly painful. By the time they got back to camp he was feeling decidedly under the weather, and by morning very feverish.

Attending the early, Sunday morning sick parade, on double-checking his temperature some concern was raised while inspection of his throat indicated tonsillitis. There being no facilities within the base for the sick, he was driven to the naval hospital at Warsash, further down-river from Bursledon. In fact the ailment with which he was stricken was diagnosed as

Vincent's Throat. Jim was confined to bed for ten days during the course of which his throat was liberally daubed with a tincture applied with a long, softly bristled artist's brush. Within 48 hours of being allowed out of bed he was on his way back to camp.

Jim was discharged from hospital on the first day of June. On the return journey to camp he was flabbergasted at the colossal build-up of troops, vehicles and equipment which had taken place. It was not fanciful to believe that apart from the centre of the road which had been deliberately left uncluttered to allow passage, every single yard of space was occupied, bordering on encroachment on unfenced gardens. Where clearance allowed, beneath parked vehicles soldiers rested on ground sheets which covered the cobbled roads. Some were busy playing cards. Tarpaulins and camouflage netting bedecked lines of tanks which stretched out of sight around bends in the roads. In the open turrets of some tanks, looking at their lathered faces in small, propped-up vanity mirrors, members of the crews shaved. Kindly civilians from houses overlooking the accumulated ordnance stood talking to the servicemen, waiting for the latter to finish the cup of tea which they had provided. Expectantly hanging about for either chocolate or boiled sweets from rations issued to the troops, children were excited by the actual apparatus of war as distinct from the miniscule replica with which they imitated battle.

Approaching the camp perimeter, activity was no less frenetic. Passing a line of stationary vehicles extending to the entrance, barricades of barbed wire had been moved aside to facilitate off-loading from the foremost lorry. The supplies debussed were large jerrycans which, judged by the heave it needed, were full of either fuel or water. A can in each hand was carried by each marine in the party along a precipitous and slippery path to where the landing craft were moored. After reporting himself discharged from hospital and fit for duty he joined the throng of marines from whom he learned of developments during his absence.

For reasons of security the camp was sealed. Evidently there were avenues of escape for a night out but, with military police abounding outside both on foot and on motor cycle, freedom was precarious. To protect rifle muzzles and to keep wristwatches waterproof, condoms had been issued. The hand-outs had been eagerly grabbed with the chorus that the mission in France was not in order to fight, after all.

On Saturday, the third of June, kit bags were packed not only with dire necessities but also with such personal possessions as each individual thought desirable. Photographs of those held dear, and cherished letters in which comfort was to be found were given loving kisses before being enclosed. Those of excessive superstitious inclination who owned a talisman either lodged it about their person or stowed it with their kit. Many wrote last words to those closest to themselves, not in morbid vein but in admission of previously held but unvoiced feelings. These letters were entrusted to camp staff who would not be taking part in the invasion but who would duly despatch them in the event of the hapless correspondent not returning to reclaim the envelope.

Sleep didn't come easily that night and when it did it was not for long, nor deep sleep. Some indulged in chance of their own design and played cards until well into the early hours. Though the stakes gambled were vast, there was little enthusiasm, and its absence naggingly eerie. The next morning, the day of departure, probably resulted in more helpings at breakfast for those who did attend the meal than had ever been known. The hours laboured on without any clear indication of departure, insidiously gnawing away at the excitement of sorts which had been building up for days. The anticipation was palpable. Towards mid afternoon crews were paraded and both identity discs fastened around necks were verified, following which crews made their way to their moorings. But no sooner had the ropes securing the landing craft been slipped and the voyage downstream commenced, than they were turned about, the craft secured and crews stood down. There had been a last minute postponement. The crossing to France was on hold for a further 24 hours.

To all concerned those 24 hours were unbearable. Having been hyped up for the big occasion everyone felt utterly drained by the anticlimax. Jim felt sure that for everyone the 24 hours between Sunday the fourth and Monday the fifth of June would be the most tantalising day they would ever experience.

A new day did dawn, and on that occasion there was no turning back.

8

THE SINKING OF THE
SVENNER

*Though German leaders were in accord
That, snug in harbour, their ships should hoard
Sure, that in such weather, no foe would sail –*

*Yet, from Le Havre, Heinrich's boats did speed
Crews with knowledge they could not but heed
Nor their captives' silence completely veil.*

Following the ritual of the previous day but speculating on another aborted mission, cables securing the landing craft to their mooring were deftly slipped and, line astern, the small vessels secretly left the tranquillity of the River Hamble and headed for war.

The presumed secrecy of their departure was, alarmingly, misplaced. The bridge which spans the river on the arterial road which links Southampton and Portsmouth was thronged with well wishers and silent witnesses. From those bystanders sufficiently in control of pent up emotions, cries of encouragement and good luck together with wishes for a safe return solemnised the gravity and the knowledge of the mission. The silent spectators waved farewell in automatic fashion but doubtless with equally well intended compassion. As it passed beneath the congested bridge a few onlookers sprinkled petals upon the disappearing flotilla. Most members of the crews returned acknowledgement of the various gestures from above by means of an upturned thumb of a clenched fist, while with fixed gaze on the object of their passion the more demonstrative blew kisses in the direction of attractive girls lining the bridge rails.

Once beyond the acclamation from the bridge, near silence prevailed among Jim's crew. Not painstakingly constructed with comfort first and foremost in mind and with little to occupy themselves during the long voyage ahead, Paddy and Sandy sought what creature comfort there was on board. That extended to little more than a matting fender for each of them. Still damp from when last lowered over the side to lessen impact when coming alongside other ships, nevertheless they provided something better sprung upon which to seat themselves than the steel deck. While the stoker spasmodically popped head and shoulders out of his stokehold, he didn't add greatly to the conversation between the other two deck hands.

At the helm in the stern, Jim was very largely left to his own thoughts – of the abundance of relayed messages there had been in recent days from the higher echelons of command, quite apart from the crop of personally delivered speeches from more junior officers at unit level.

Resulting in different levels of ridicule from those at whom they were directed, some of the entreaties gave the firm impression they strove more for literary excellence rather than inspirational leadership. From one commander came an undisguised attempt to surpass Shakespeare's narrative regarding those a-bed in England on Saint Crispin's day. Another, among the senior staff officers, adopted an historic theme, boldly claiming the assembled fleet would accomplish that which the Spanish Armada had miserably failed to achieve; what Napoleon had contemplated and what Hitler feared to attempt. One supernumerary officer evidently considered that Admiral Nelson's brief reminder, regarding the nation's expectations of every man, to be too brief. Instead he launched into long-winded sermons and the art of gentle persuasion. Howls of uncouth derision rejected the presumption that all concerned should feel fortunate and honoured to be taking part in the coming crusade and eventual liberation of the continent. Sarcastic remarks from some listeners suggested they would be able to hide their bitter disappointment and swallow their pride.

Almost without exception, those hell-bent on introducing an element of sanctity to the approaching battle took the opportunity to preach that the Almighty was on the side of the Allied forces, which sermon would be found to conflict with the inscription of 'Gott mit uns', displayed on buckles of waist belts worn by German prisoners rounded up on the beaches by the crews of landing craft, who then ferried them to ships for transportation to the UK.

Perhaps because they stated the obvious, the most recent batch of dire warnings from a number of sources (that not all would go according to plan, that at times there would be confusion, even utter chaos) provoked very little response. Nor could any in 606 flotilla have even the slightest inkling of the catastrophe that would strike before an angry shot had been fired.

The landing craft in which the crews were to make the arduous voyage to Normandy only arrived at HMS *Cricket* a few weeks before D Day. The vessels were not, by any means, newly commissioned: as a matter of fact none were fully equipped. Not one of the 16 were furnished with the machine guns with which they should have been armed, and some lacked a winch or kedge anchor, or both. Recurring mechanical defects resulted in some needing overhaul or repair at one or another of the many shipbuilders dotted along the banks of the River Hamble. As the flotilla steadily made its way downstream to join the many hundreds of different ships massing in the Solent for the channel crossing on the eve of D Day, it was from the slipway of a shipyard where it had been undergoing test that the first ill-fated craft in 606 joined the procession, with which it was, ultimately, unable to keep in touch.

It would seem there could be only two explanations as to why, the next morning, in the first grey light of an eerie dawn some few miles off the coast of Normandy, this particular LCM was not among the innumerable ships awaiting H Hour. Either it was adrift, a ship less than 50 feet in length lost in the vast space of the English Channel, or some fault had developed causing it to sink.

For whatever reason contact with the convoy might have been lost, if it was still afloat, but lacking even the most basic navigational aids of compass or charts, the landing craft and crew of four would be completely at the mercy of providence. Rescue would depend upon being sighted by friendly aircraft once daylight appeared but before they were sighted by the enemy. If, on the other hand, it had sunk it was not inconceivable that, prior to the perilous crossing when, in heavy seas, every on-coming wave would pound against the ramp, the structure may not have been fully hoisted and secured, allowing the sea to rapidly rush in.

Unquestionably there had not been any attacks on the convoy either by aeroplanes or by surface craft which could account for the disappearance. More open to question were the snatches of overheard conversation and other snippets of information which gradually emerged with the passage of time.

It was perfectly obvious the enemy were unaware of the colossal armada steaming towards the five designated beaches. In fact in one newspaper cutting provided by one of the follow-up troops who arrived soon after D Day, the German high command were reputed to have completely dismissed all belief an invasion could be mounted in the prevailing inclement weather. Another report, seeming to confirm the conviction the invasion was not imminent, alleged that Rommel's staff car had been strafed while he was being driven back to Normandy on D Day, having been absent in Herlingen, in Germany, in order to celebrate his wife's birthday; but there was no mention as to his condition. Though his vehicle was not attacked en route, he did not reach Normandy until well into the evening of D Day. There was even more irony in the absence of several of Rommel's distinguished commanders who were in Rennes, very nearly 100 miles from the nearest beach-head. Even as landing craft were preparing to run the gauntlet of murderous fire and the menace of the mined underwater obstacles, his generals were attending counter-invasion exercises!

Much later, various enemy documents revealed that, prior to embarking upon a journey even further afield, the Admiral in Command of the Western Fleet convinced the Field Marshall commanding all troops in the west that the Allies would not risk a channel crossing in the prevailing conditions. To illustrate the courage of his conviction, Theodore Krank, CIC Navy Group West, made it quite clear he had ordered all patrol boats based between Cherbourg and Le Havre to stand down until further notice.

In the immediate aftermath of the tragic loss of the crew from 606, even had they been known, neither the disclosure of the prediction the invasion was not remotely feasible nor the decision taken on that assumption would have aroused very much deliberation. But ......

*****

Though, from the beginning of the invasion of Normandy, newspaper reports which subsequently reached the beachhead spoke of 'Everything proceeding according to plan', by far the greater number among those at the sharp end of events failed to recollect prophecy of the situation in which they found themselves. In addition to the overnight disappearance of one of the flotilla's vessels, the commanding officer of 606 had been grieviously wounded on the first day of the landings and died en route to England on the following one. Since then, and due to the combination of enemy action and the unprecedented storms which raged for days in succession in the Bay of the Seine, only a small number of the original 16 LCMs which left the River Hamble were operational. It could no longer be looked upon as a viable formation and in consequence during the month of July the flotilla, or what remained of it, returned to England.

The survivors from 606 returned to the refuge of HMS *Cricket* where they remained in limbo while awaiting deployment to other units elsewhere. Unlike the unfortunate ones who had not returned and whose letters had been forwarded as requested to their next of kin, the survivors retrieved theirs. Quickly surveying the words he had previously penned for his parents, Jim, his life spared, had a feeling which approached that of guilt.

Free time permitted abundant spells of leisure, especially in the evenings, most of which were spent in the church hall at Hedge End, considerably under a pleasurable hour distant at leisurely pace. In the church hall the attractions were tea, table tennis and a bevy of ATS girls, this being the ascending order in which the delights of the church hall were esteemed. Along with nightly mugs of tea and mugging at table tennis by Vera, one of the delights, romance bloomed and in September he was rewarded by her acceptance of his proposal. A few days later a jeweller in Southampton prospered from his sale of an engagement ring, but his gain was not nearly as great as that of his customer. The vendor had obtained a few pound notes but, as Jim slipped the ring on Vera's outstretched finger, he well knew he had secured the love of a beautiful young lady.

Unfortunately their idyllic evenings together were numbered. But, before their respective postings which separated them for more than two years, happily Jim obtained and spent seven days leave where she was stationed: sadly, they flew by.

Vera's draft took her first to liberated France and, as the allied advance progressed, to Holland and finally Germany. Jim resumed commando training, returning to north Wales for the initial stint. All training was conducted from the camp at Llanegryn, the other bases having been moth-balled or, in the instance of Barmouth, the private dwellings derequisitioned. During a night exercise in the area of the Mawddach Estuary his thoughts went back to his initial torment upon receiving Eileen's letter the previous Christmas. With the prospect of sharing his life with Vera after the war he was able to look back on that sorry episode as water under the bridge – reminiscent of the water which raged around the pillars of the bridge from which he stared down on that melancholy occasion.

During the time at Llanegryn there were two other, far more significant occurrences. The first was most unfortunate. Besides Jim there were just a couple of others from 606 on the commando course, the two, his long established friends. Having survived Normandy, one (Johnny) had a particularly serious accident in training and was returned to unit. The other incident, while manifestly a cause for jubilation, was a matter for considerable speculation.

While in charge of a group of marines on fatigue duty, tidying up in an annexe to the canteen used as a library and reading room, from the pile of litter Jim rescued the remnants of an old issue of *The Globe and Laurel*, the journal of the Royal Marines which was published at regular intervals. Idly browsing through its crumpled pages his glance was arrested by details of a letter sent in by the mother of a serving marine. Jim could hardly believe what he read.

The letter was from the mother of the coxswain at the helm of the landing craft which had vanished during the channel crossing on the eve of D Day. She revealed that her son and the other three members of the crew were in a prisoner of war camp in Germany. The letter made no reference to the manner of their capture but, like all other coxswains involved in the frantic struggle to avoid collision with the stern of the vessel immediately ahead, as periodically the entire line of shipping came to an abrupt halt, undoubtedly he veered too far to port or to starboard and, disorientated, lost station entirely. Whatever may have caused the problem, off course and without means of contact with the convoy, he had little choice but to plough a lonely furrow in pitch darkness, eventually sighting land as the sky lightened with the approach of dawn. With absolutely no indication whether the coast ahead was that of France or whether he had completely wheeled about in the mayhem and darkness and now faced the shore of England, it goes without saying he had no other option than to make for land. In point of fact it must have been France but unfortunately many miles from where the landings were shortly due to take place.

The five chosen beach-heads for the invasion were spread along more than 50 miles of coastline. Each sector had the protection of separate naval forces, all of which were obviously beyond the horizon visible by the hapless crew. Beyond the horizon, to the west and at the tip of the Contentin Peninsula was the port of Cherbourg: to the east and in closer proximity was the port of Le Havre. He read the account again, but still the significance of what he read failed to register.

It was not until several days later, while continuing to dwell upon the good news the four were alive, that he recollected the newspaper cuttings which found their way to the beaches by one means or another soon after D Day. One article reported that in the only naval engagement which took place before the assault, a Norwegian destroyer, HMNS *Svenner*, was sunk in an attack by a number of E boats which ventured out of Le Havre. Yet the emphatic order from the Admiral Commanding Western Naval Forces had been that no ships were to leave bases.

Discipline throughout all branches of the German armed forces was renowned, especially with regard to obedience of orders issued by seniors. Yet a relatively insignificant commander of a small force of patrol boats took it upon himself to order a few E boats to leave the sanctuary of harbour. Jim, as was his want, pondered. What could have possessed a mere Lieut. Commander, Heinrich Hoffman, to deliberately defy a direct order from an admiral – surely a court-martial offence.

Without any doubt the captive crew of the LCM would have been subjected to exhaustive interrogation, but assuming each of the four restricted the answers they gave to details of name, rank and regimental number, and nothing, more, how would the captors have viewed the mission on which the quartet were engaged?

The fact they were in a POW camp was evidence they had not been considered to be on a commando raid, otherwise they would have been shot, out of hand. The rumour of a punitive commando order issued by Hitler had proven to be more than hearsay and the threats had been carried out in sickening fashion on a number of occasions.

Alternatively, although the Germans expected that whenever and wherever the main assault might fall it would be preceded by a diversionary attack, four marines with a rifle apiece hardly fitted the expectation. Appreciably more likely is the surmise that the captors saw the solitary landing craft for what it was. A vessel which had strayed off course, and from what it had accidently veered demanded immediate investigation.

What the foray from Le Havre did discover, as the line of Heinrich's E boats penetrated the dense smoke screen in the Bay of the Seine, some 25 miles from harbour and a few miles off the coast at Ouistreham, was a formidable array of warships which stretched out of sight towards Cherbourg. Before returning to Le Harve as urgently as they had departed and with news of what had been sighted, torpedoes were hurriedly aimed at the armada. Most of the missiles were evaded by prompt and skilful action of those on watch on the bridge of the other attacked vessels, but one, the *Svenner*, was hit twice amidships and sank almost immediately but defiantly, the severed fore and aft sections forming a V as though signalling the victory sign as she went down.

Further to the west four other battle groups lurked, in position off their allotted beaches. That of which 606 formed part was G force, lying off Gold beach, the furthest west of the British sectors.

9

DER TAG

Troops came, they saw, they conquered too:
They came in ships which were not few.
The sky was filled with 'ours' not 'theirs'-
Glory to him, whose life he dares.

In din, with carnage all around
The fortress yields: they gain some ground.
For those to come, in times less grave,
Tender in years, their lives they gave.

Quite apart from the landing craft and crew which mysteriously disappeared during the night, the channel crossing was far from plain sailing for the rest of the flotilla.

Having set sail from HMS *Cricket* at 1600 hours, and having made steady headway except for the short halt at the shipyard for the ill-fated craft to join the rest, at the confluence with Southampton Water progress was severely impeded. Ignoring all the nautical niceties of rules of the road, the larger vessels making their way downstream from Southampton showed no intention of giving way to tiny LCMs.

Ultimately compelled to take hold of the horns of the proverbial bull and gingerly edge forward, passage into the mainstream was gained during a slightly longer interval between the line of ships from upstream, but well before all of the flotilla managed the manoeuvre, four irate blasts on the horn of a fast approaching tank landing craft warned 'Get out of my way – I can't get out of yours'.

Among the smallest craft faced with the 100 mile channel crossing under their own power, upon entering Southampton Water it was found to be decidedly choppy and the strength of the wind more noticeable, an ill-omen for the crews of 606 indicating not merely an uncomfortable voyage but also a treacherous one, once on the high sea.

With several halts for no explicable reason the endless line of shipping finally entered the Solent and, passing the northern shore of the Isle of White to starboard, into Spithead. Though the light of day had diminished considerably, keen eyes were able to detect the awe inspiring sight of vast numbers and types of shipping, from huge impressively gunned battleships down to the pathetic size of their own frail craft picking a way through the anchored fleet. There were ocean liners, no longer engaged in exotic cruises for affluent passengers but lined with tiers of assault landing craft suspended outboard on davits. The crowded rails of the merchantmen were bedecked with the regimental colours of those units aboard: from the stern of the warships fluttering flags displayed the colours of different nations. Ears were assailed with a cacophony of music. From one direction, the faint sound of bagpipes. The monotonous drone not nearly faint enough for Sassenach cousins. From elsewhere (the pit of purgatory sprang to Jim's mind) a morbid, struggling virtuoso rendered 'Stormy Weather' on a wheezy mouth organ, and confirming the belief the world tolerates people of every sort and kind, over a tannoy system one of its jesters facetiously played a recording of 'For those in peril on the sea'! Preceding the Mexican Wave, Spithead cheers increased and decreased in volume as they passed along the line of ships.

The streamers, the competing melodies, the whole pent atmosphere of the big occasion reminded Jim of his childhood participation in jamborees organised by the Lifebuoys and Boys Brigade, but his nostalgia was suddenly cut short. Well inshore of the majestic fleet, rather like unkempt urchins banished to the nursery out of sight of visiting well-to-do relatives, 606 were circling in flotilla formation while awaiting direction to their position in the convoy which was slowly being marshalled. In the gloom of late evening, none noticed that the hypothetical axis around which they rotated was drifting ever closer to the shore, towards the protected entrance to Portsmouth harbour. Mercifully an alert look-out manning the defences of the naval base did notice their plight. From behind one of the harbour forts a motor-launch appeared, blaring over a loud-hailer as it approached 'Ahoy, there! Ahoy, there! You are steaming into danger. Follow me, line astern'. In the wake of their saviours, 606 were led clear of the under-water devices safeguarding the port and were ushered to their position in the assembled convoy.

Departing from the area of near disaster, in almost impenetrable dusk they sailed past the Isle of Wight. Leaving the shores of England for the very first time in his life, perhaps never again to see them, Jim found the occasion heart-rending. Fear was not the dominant factor. Of course all were aware they would be facing danger: that was accepted, but it did not generate fear. The impression he gained from those with whom he had spoken on the subject, and those occasions were few, was of quiet resolve. Most had experienced helplessness when bombed or anguish when told of the loss of relations or friends; now was their chance to strike back. As fear was not their foe, nor was bravery their companion: what was required by circumstance would be done to the best of their ability – and the sooner it was over and done with, the better. At 19 years of age he had never before felt so much love for his parents and siblings nor for the country he was leaving behind.

He stole one last, backwards glimpse toward the land of his birth. Clear of the shelter of all land, the strong wind and heavy seas caused havoc for the LCMs, their shallow draught and high freeboard causing them to slew from side to side in menacing fashion. Coxswains striving to regain station were at times swept into the path of other craft struggling to achieve the same end. Frequent and totally unexpected pauses ahead jeopardised all who followed astern. If the resultant diminishing distance from the vessel immediately ahead was not quickly realised, ramps slammed, domino fashion, into the sterns of those ahead. The consequent pile-up was like a mammoth encounter between dodgem cars at a fun-fare, but the horrendous knowledge was, the fairground was that of Davy Jones. On occasions during exercises and immediately prior to departure from England it was stressed the convoy could not be halted for the sake of rescue. Life-jackets incorporating a small red coloured bulb wired to a small battery was the sole hope of attracting succour from ships, on the following day.

Throughout the nerve-racking night the hazardous conditions prevailed, fully concentrating minds and entirely exhausting the bad language of weary coxswains. Stokers, too, were at least partially occupied. Both groups were fortunate; but for the two unoccupied deck-hands who squatted in the violently jolted, spray-drenched well of the LCM, and for whom no sleep was remotely possible, they had only their inner thoughts upon which to dwell.

Adrenalin sustained determination enabled coxswains to accomplish the crossing, and, in the very early hours of D Day 606 was among the huge number of vessels lying several miles off the coast of Normandy. On that dismal, grey morning was the sombre realisation one of their craft had been lost during the night.

Too weary to attempt scaling the scrambling net draped over the side of the flotilla's mother ship, crews tied up alongside or, once all available space had been taken, alongside other craft which had found room. A mug of tepid tea and something to eat prior to the run in to the beach was not worth the effort entailed in the climb. Instead, the contents of 24 hour emergency ration packs were opened and considered, but few were tempted. Most of what the packs contained was dehydrated in form and the occasion was not one for reconstituting them. Some of the crews made do with sucking a boiled sweet to ease salt-caked throats, or urged teeth into very chunky slabs of chocolate, persuaded that it provided energy.

For the little time crews were at rest, yawning was the prime occupation. There had been no sleep during the night, and precious little the previous one with minds concentrated on what the following day would bring. Slumped in whatever position comfort was to be found, eyes and, to a lesser extent, minds closed out the surroundings: but paradise was not long-lasting. The call to stations at about 0500 hours preceded the loading of the implements of warfare, vehicles and the embarkation of troops – easier described than accomplished. Several among the descending soldiers only narrowly escaped very serious injury, or worse. With the rise and fall of each wave causing landing craft to pitch and toss severely, ill-judged steps from the scrambling net nearly resulted in some troops becoming crushed between the side of the landing craft and the parent ship; but, safely boarded, the laden craft took up formation line astern and headed for the beach.

Separated by a few miles from Omaha, one of the American beaches, the section of Gold beach towards which 606 launched themselves was Jig/Green which stretched eastwards from Le Hamel to the quiet peace time holiday resort of La Riviere. Of the type of fortifications which awaited them the crews were only vaguely aware. History has provided a more detailed account.

*****

From the moment he assumed command of Army Group B, Field Marshall Rommel had insisted the invaders must be repelled on the beaches. He was in no doubt the war would be won or lost on the foreshore. Very close to the point of causing ill-feeling among contemporaries, he constantly insisted upon outrageous supplies from the high command. He argued that every piece of equipment and all items of arms which were available should be deployed on the coast to destroy hostile landing craft. It was imperative the foreshore should become the watery graveyard of all who came to scale the boasted, impregnable Atlantic Wall.

For various levels of the beaches between high and low water marks he devised a complex system of obstacles which would destroy or repel landing craft. Stout, steel capped beams firmly embedded in the sand were intended to pierce and impale lightly armoured hulls of oncoming vessels causing them to sink or flounder, sitting ducks for the guns. Lines of underwater obstacles of reinforced concrete buffers were intended to halt progress towards the shore compelling coxswains to alter course and search for other channels, thereby extending their vulnerability to defensive fire. Steel tripods, securely anchored, were capped with Teller mines which would cause ships, at least the smaller craft, to sink. Fence-like entanglements were festooned with shells detonated to explode if struck by shore-bound vessels. On land, machine guns and artillery of differing calibre were situated to pour fire enfilade. Likewise, flame-throwers were placed to contribute their deterrent, and, from the demonstration on the beach at Deal, Jim was fully aware of the problem they posed.

The pill boxes and larger strong points in which defending troops awaited the onslaught were built of reinforced concrete and were practically indestructible except for direct hits by huge shells, such as those fired by the warships anchored off shore.

*****

At a little after 0500 hours the battleships commenced the attempt. The term ear-splitting is hopelessly inadequate to describe the effect. Not only were ear drums all but shattered by the noise which erupted: nostrils were invaded by the smell of cordite following the blinding flash which belched from the gun barrels. As the salvoes from HMS *Orion* passed overhead the vibration played havoc with the nervous system. When the barrage lifted as the assaulting landing craft came closer to the shore, it was superseded by what could only be described as saturation fire from Landing Craft/Rocket. Positioned broadside on to the beach and only a few hundred yards off shore, from row upon row of mortar barrels welded to the deck of these adapted Landing Craft/Tank, hundreds of rockets were hurled upon the beach, the smoke from the discharge completely blotting the vessels out of sight. If the assaulting troops who witnessed the withering fire were not altogether overcome with remorse for those on the receiving end, who presently would be trying their utmost to blow out the brains of the approaching invaders, the sight of the complete obliteration of an entire area of beach did elicit the murmur of "poor buggers".

Venturing as far as they could with the assault wave, destroyers and Landing Craft/Gun joined in. Landing Craft/Flak, surplus to the requirement of defence against air attack, also used their might against the beach defences. The bombardment was incessant and unmerciful. In some of the attacking force it fostered hope the landing would be only perfunctorily opposed: it encouraged the illusion of cowed defenders hurriedly hoisting white flags. Meanwhile, overhead and with wings and fuselage boldly painted with broad black and white bands to distinguish them as 'ours', countless fighter planes patrolled the sky ready to repel any enemy aircraft which came to molest. Unloading their cargo to the rear of the beach defences on radar stations and on other lines of communications, massed formations of bombers crammed air space, their similar means of establishing identification giving the impression of huge winged zebras, rather than of Flying Fortresses. The obscenities from Jim who recalled countless, wasted hours spent on aircraft recognition scorned the challenge of even the most gifted blackguard.

Towards 0730 hours the signal was given for the flotilla to alter formation from line astern to line abreast for the final leg. All was then down to the individual coxswains, aided by a slice of good luck. In none of the flotillas were there sufficient slices to go round.

Crushing the optimistic hope those manning the Atlantic Wall who had survived the pounding would resort to some form of insurrection, all hell was let loose by the defenders. Flashes from the shore followed by ever encroaching spouts of water warned that German gunners were perfecting their aim. Although the din hid the tell-tale sound of discharge from numbers of Nebelwerfen, the clusters of mortar bombs which rained down left little doubt as to the weapon which lobbed them. Anti-tank gun crews, awaiting the debut of their natural prey, contented themselves by directing fire from their PAK 38s at anything which moved. Deafening as was the barrage, talk was in whispers among those aboard the land-bound vessels, and was of the relief they would find anywhere, other than on the 'effing' LCMs.

In the last few yards of approach, as coxswains strove to make themselves heard with the yell of 'stand by to beach', fire of even greater dread leapt from a flame-thrower located in a heavily defended strong point. From hidden though unmistakable Spandau machine-guns, burst of bullets noisily rapped against the hulls of landing craft, the ricochets persuading all who could to keep their head down, and coxswains, who couldn't, to offer a silent prayer. Out of view, the mined underwater obstacles which had not been rendered ineffective, by Royal Navy and Royal Marine Landing Craft Obstruction Clearance Units, waited to wreak their carnage. Whether it was caused by an underwater explosion or as a result of shell-fire, the first loss in 606 due to enemy action resulted in the tragic death of the C.O.

For quite some time many in the flotilla were unaware of the tragedy, such was the chaotic pandemonium. Eyes were compelled to focus exclusively on the immediate vicinity: ears were deaf to more distant noise. Minds were occupied with the assortment of problems which were apparent. The solution, less obvious, was subject to amendment as reasoning fluctuated between conviction and doubt. To prevent craft being swept broadside on to the beach by wind and surf, or astern by momentum of vehicles driving forward over the lowered ramp, minds were kept fully concentrated. In the idiom, Jim swore to "keep this effing flat-bottomed pleasure boat steady even if it k......." – to conclude he searched for an expression which entailed a little less grievous bodily harm.

When his mind finally became less absorbed with the task in

hand his thoughts wandered from one recollection to another, from the most mundane event in early childhood to the position in which he then stood. He meditated upon the degradation of war: that those who had been mown down or who had been drowned trying to reach the shore had been deprived of even the dignity of status. However small their personal part, each had been an actor on the stage of history. Now, in the Normandy theatre of war, all were just remains; debris, to be gathered up like so much litter left behind by day trippers on a visit to the seaside.

Undoubtedly with similar anguish indelibly etched upon the memories of all participants, with troops, vehicles and supplies disembarked, and more in hope rather than by nautical skill, coxswains nervously commenced to extricate their craft from the surrounding wreckage, a vast accumulation of capsized craft of every description. Some vessels wallowed about in the undulating waves, liable to detonate mines. Other ships, swept in by the flooding tide, sprawled in drunken- like stupor at the water's edge.

Clear of the flotsam, en route to the anchorage to take aboard another contingent of troops and equipment, unemployed deck hands set about tidying their bespattered floating palace.

It truly was a nauseating task.

It did not require the whole hour or so which it took to return to the anchorage, but it was not an enviable job. After squeamishly tossing the Bags/Vomit overboard, a feat in which the donors failed, the restoration of the vessel to its original unsullied splendour only entailed emptying the ship's bucket, the brimful, galvanised throne being the ship's pièce de résistance. Unwisely decorated with the slogan 'bottoms up', from the very beginning of its admittedly unceremonious inauguration the troops just made a convenience of it. If largely adequate for that purpose, for its primary function, even with the issued sea water soap, it enabled little in the way of personal hygiene.

To stretch a point in favour of gratitude, besides the galvan-ised amenity there was yet another concession to the luxury of mod cons on some of the LCMs. The culinary appliance. In essence the bottom half of a large biscuit tin obtained from the NAAFI prior to leaving HMS *Cricket*, several coxswains had had the sagacity to appreciate its potential. As was found when time permitted the art of cookery, when partly filled with sand well doused in diesel oil and then ignited, it heated mess tins containing water adulterated to individual taste by the addition of crumbled cubes of oats, or meat extract; or sugar substitute with powered milk and tea dust, the principal contents of the 24 hour emergency ration packs. Once the oily film was scooped from the surface of the substance, each of the courses provided an indefinable flavour, any of which might have spawned the term of dish-water.

Adding further to the picture of existence on the minor landing craft, aids to sweet repose were also a bit limited. Enwrapped in the spray moistened pile of a duffel coat-cum-blanket, imaginative deck hands sensed warmth. If the desire was more inclined to relief of lumbar discomfort, those optimists folded and placed the coat between the metal ribbed surface of the deck; but whereas board and lodging gave rise to endless light-hearted if unrighteous comment amongst crews, in retrospect perhaps historical records present a far more sober version of conditions: 'The crossing of the hundred miles of channel under their own power completed, the LCMs began their task of bringing in supplies, and for weeks they worked in the worst possible conditions of weather, discomfort and exposure to attack. It was a battle for the delivery of supplies, and on the outcome depended the success or failure of the invasion. The landing craft were in the thick of it, for it was these which the Germans sought to destroy'.

Similarly another account relates 'For the landing craft crews, there was less glory, more discomfort and more acute danger than for any other men in the seaborne task forces. Although the Luftwaffe possessed no power to impede Allied operations seriously, it was still capable of causing acute danger among men living and working on the principle targets – the beaches'.

*****

Previously and frequently briefed on the onerous task of ensuring the flow of troops, vehicles and supplies outstripped the speed with which the Germans were able to reinforce their

[1] From *The Marines Were There*, by Sir Bruce Lockhart, KCMG.

[2] From *Overlord*, by Max Hastings.

troops, landing craft personnel laboured without respite. Reputed to be true maids of all work with the capacity to separately ferry 100 troops/6 jeeps/2 Bren gun carriers/a Sherman tank/a cargo of 30 tons or 2 37mm guns and their tractors, throughout the day and at the maximum number of knots which could be coaxed out of the LCMs, (eleven when light but only eight knots when loaded), they surged backwards and forwards from ship to shore with their complement. Despite the calculated sheer length of daylight, from before 0500 hours to 2300 hours, the determination was to press on until complete darkness compelled a halt. But, as with the best laid plans of mice and men......

Round about 2100 hours, with the mass of debris becoming more widely dispersed as the in-coming tide flushed the expanse of beach, a highly pitched screech and instant loss of power indicated to Jim that the propellers on his craft had been fouled, which could not be rectified until the tide receded in the very early hours of the next morning. Once the forward impetuous of the ship ceased to have effect, a line was attached to a larger craft stranded further up on the beach. Not altogether furious that an early night had been imposed upon themselves, before turning-in the biscuit tin was pressed into service. With open mouths and anxious gaze the table d'hote slipped out of view, but with the fear that was not necessarily the last that would be seen of it!

For the time being, drained of all physical and mental vigour, conversation between the four was only spasmodic and petered out altogether as the light of day began to fade. Sheltered out of sight of all surroundings except the sky above, one after another of the crew selected a spot where, they must have prayed, sleep might be obtained, and where, as like as not, thanksgiving was rendered. Although the prospect for either prolonged or uninterrupted slumber was not remotely likely, Jim did enjoy a spell of oblivion. Unfortunately it was ended by a vigorous nudge from the stoker. Perhaps having managed a measure of sleep in the shelter and warmth of the stokehold during the crossing to Normandy, laying wide awake and watching the (illusory) erratic movement of the clouds it gradually dawned upon him it was the LCM which was careering about.

Joined on the gunwales by the two deck hands who had also

clambered out of the well of the vessel, it was clear they were well and truly adrift, with the rope which had moored them now trailing behind. As is invariably the position when negligence is attributable, each of the deck hands exonerated themselves, both insisting they knew full well how to secure a line. Making it abundantly clear the predicament required remedy not blame, Jim elected to swim for the shore with a line to attach to another stable object, towards which the crew could then winch in their own vessel.

Previous training at Deal having firmly demonstrated the considerable disadvantage of swimming when clothed, off came everything and with an arm through the eye of the rope (which was found to be another impediment) he swam towards the shore. The sudden shock of plunging into the chilly sea gradually wore off with the exertion of each stroke and concentration on the problem of the trailing rope, which continually became entwined with thrashing feet and which erratically slipped from flailing arms. Out of breath but at last able to wade and clumsily stagger to a completely wrecked LCM, broached-to and high and dry on the beach, the rope was made secure. Vigorously he tugged it three times – the pre-arranged signal for the crew to winch in.

Signifying the LCM had been hauled to within hailing distance, stark naked, again shivering in the night air, Jim detected Paddy's unmistakable cry of "Corporal", but the vehemence which followed was not blarney. The line had parted under the strain.

Another rope; another swim. To obviate the difficulty experienced with the rope during the first, aborted attempt, the noose was less restrictively draped around Jim's neck with dire threats and strict orders to allow plenty of slack. Also opting for the breast stroke, progress was significantly easier. Then, almost necessitating a backward somersault under the water, the rope forcibly dragged him through the waves. Frantically he struggled with the taut line jerking him along. Fazed by what was happening, he had none but himself to blame for stupidly placing the rope around his neck: but who would have anticipated the likelihood of the passage of another vessel in the dead of night and amidst so many hazards, assured as he was that the line had become ensnared in such transit. Suddenly the noose became limp and as he surfaced, gasping for breath, he removed the sisal stranglehold from his throat. Mercifully, this line too had been severed.

Although the trauma had seemed prolonged, judged by his insignificant distance from the LCM when he surfaced, the duration of the tussle to free himself could not have lasted for more than a minute or so. It required relatively few strokes to reach the craft but to clamber aboard he needed assistance. While the concern expressed by the crew regarding yet another attempt was unquestionably genuine, a third and provisionally final try was put into effect, during the course of which a lone German aircraft came in at low altitude and raked the beach area with machine gun fire. Attracting a heavy barrage of anti-aircraft fire from the warships anchored offshore, the tracer projectiles wove an eerie pattern in the heavens and shed a cascade of shrapnel on earth. Before being driven off by the ack-ack, and certain to hit some form of target cluttering the shore, reversing its flight-path the pilot released a whole stick of bombs along the beach.

In comparative peace and safety, the immobilised LCM was eventually and indisputably made secure to a cleat on another wrecked and immovable LCA. Practically as motionless, in fact frozen to death would have been only a slight exaggeration, the crew speedily came to Jim's aid with towels and warm clothing. Perhaps lacking the maternal instinct of tenderness, they soon had his blood circulating through veins nearly deprived of the protection of an outer layer of skin. While helping him into his clothing, from the top of his head covered by the hood of his duffel coat to toes snugly cradled in thick, woollen knee length sea socks, a decision which would brook no argument deemed he should be settled in the stokehold where a few degrees of warmth from the two Thornycroft engines still lingered.

When awakened with a mess tin of almost scum free, luke warm tea, Jim felt he had been granted the sleep of the just, however inappropriate the simile which entered his mind. In like delirium, he felt none awoken with breakfast at the Ritz could have experienced comparable room service. Further revived, despite the futility of going through the motions of washing and shaving with the useless sea water soap which was unable to produce the slightest lather, he joined his crew who, since first light, had toiled with the difficulty of freeing the propellers.

The entanglement was a length of wire hawser, almost certainly part of a demolished Element C, one of the underwater devices strewn between high and low water marks, and which had not been removed following the work of the obstruction clearance unit. The restraining cable was so tightly wrapped around the propeller shaft it was impossible for bare hands to loosen it. Considering the ingenuity which had gone into the planning for the invasion it seemed ridiculous no apparatus had been provided to deal with such an obvious contingency. Two Mulberry Harbours had been constructed and towed across the channel, tanks had been modified to float on it, and an oil pipe line was laid on its bed, but neither implements nor instruction had been given thought in order to deal with fouled propellers. The absence of instruction aside, something as uncomplicated as a marlinspike would have been a godsend.

Castigating himself for his lack of imagination, it slowly dawned upon him each had a gadget which would be ideal for the purpose. Their winkle-picker. In addition to rifles, each of the four had a bayonet. Not the outmoded flat blade of steel well over a foot in length but the newer type. Rounded and with a very sharp point and measuring roughly eight inches, it was sufficiently long to firmly grasp with both hands and utilise to gradually prise apart the separate strands of wire which formed the hawser. Working in pairs on each of the propeller shafts, all but confining themselves to gentlemanly language as the bayonet of one 'effing' partner slipped and gouged layers of flesh from the hands of the other, the job was completed with plenty of time to spare before the rising tide refloated the LCM and enabled its crew to resume their mission.

Though an hour or two earlier room service had been on a par with that at the Ritz, the breakfast menu at the hotel conceivably had the edge on choice. To fortify themselves for another day on the ocean waves the selection was between rehydrated oats or rejuvenated beef extract, each served with diesel dressing.

10

THE HIDDEN COST OF SLIPPED DISCS

O Christ, whose voice the waters heard
And hushed their raging at thy word:

Who walkedst on the foaming deep
And calm amid the storm didst sleep –

O hear us when we cry to thee
For those in peril on the sea.

Wm. Whiting 1825-78

Watched over by their vigilant escorts, as on the previous day the enemy troops who had been compelled to surrender awaited evacuation from the congested beach-head.

In all probability they were unaccustomed to the sight of prisoners of war being transported by ships instead of by lorries or by trains to areas in the rear of the battle zone.

In some of the younger captives there were indications which suggested an inward dread they were to be taken out to sea to be mercilessly shot and then cast overboard. Initially a small number of them ignored the gesture to step on to the lowered ramp of the LCT which would transport them to the British Isles, but were swiftly persuaded to comply when guards angrily removed rifles slung over their shoulders and menacingly pointed them in the direction of the fracas. Outstretched hands of some prisoners willingly offered a variety of souvenirs while questioning looks betrayed fears their bribes might be considered hopelessly inadequate.

Awaiting high tide for the opportunity to set sail and resume duty, within earshot of many of the captives Jim slowly began to realise there were various nationalities among the group. He had not the faintest idea of the languages in which considerable numbers of them conversed but he was quite certain it was not German.

Like a sizeable number of his generation who had only

received the scant benefit of an elementary education, prior to leaving school at the age of fourteen in 1939 he was strongly persuaded by his headmaster to continue schooling at the local evening institute, an opportunity which was completely free. Particularly urged by the headmaster to learn a second language, to assist in which he was rewarded with a phrase book in French and in German, Jim found the nasal tone of the former more difficult to imitate than the guttural sounds of the latter and in consequence he decided upon German. For several months, after work and twice weekly, he attended the course and made rapid progress, primarily due to the fact that as he trudged the streets of the West End of London delivering batches of telegrams, his mind was completely free to swot from the text book and perfect his vocabulary and pronunciation. Most unfortunately, as the months passed the approach of war brought about the end of evening tuition, but he had acquired and retained enough of what he had learned to realise many of the captives were not German.

Once again it was from sources far removed from the beachhead, in the form of extracts from news bulletins as related by reinforcements arriving on subsequent days, that details of the foreign elements in the Wehrmacht were established. Evidently, in the countries which had been occupied by the Nazis, guileful persuasion was continually brought to bear to induce men of military age to accept service in the German armed forces as an alternative to abject slavery in labour camps. Whether and to what extent broadcasts by the BBC may have been embroidered for purposes of propaganda, it was announced that numbers of the mercenaries claimed they felt more at liberty as prisoners of the Allies and subject to less domination than in the ranks of the German army.

Still with ample time to spare before casting off the rope which secured their craft to the overnight makeshift mooring, the crew carefully picked their way along the beach to inspect a particular strong point which had previously held out for hours, causing severe losses of successive waves of vessels and troops. Once inside the deserted bunker it was obvious that it was all but impregnable and clear why it was bypassed by the advancing infantry. Such damage as had been caused on the outer casement by naval gun-fire or by aerial bombardment had failed to penetrate the immensely thick, reinforced concrete. Neither were there apparent indications of adjacent skirmish. Perhaps by nightfall, short or out of ammunition and with no hope of re-supply, the position had been abandoned under cover of darkness.

Paraphernalia abounded. Remnants of food and wine bottles only partly emptied littered a small table. Assuming that the few words at the bottom of each page entitled the magazines to come under the heading, literature was prominent; as were the breasts of the models above the footnotes. Conceivably the action of the last soldier to vacate the bunker, scribbling defaced and obliterated official-looking memos fastened to a notice board. The nail from which it hung lopsidedly was adorned with a length of toilet paper, possibly adding emphasis to the scrawl. For any member of Jim's crew seeking souvenirs of the taken for granted victorious invasion, there were plenty from which to select. The choice in headgear was between steel, bucket-style helmets and cloth peak or forage-caps. To one side of the bunker was a small line of highly polished jackboots. Ersatz leather waist-belts and one or two personal items (fountain pens and hinged photograph frames) had been overlooked by the departed owners – so, no doubt it was hoped, the bait would be considered.

Fortunately, as a result of repeated reminders during training, the snare of booby-traps had been thoroughly digested. None of the crew were tempted, not even to painstakingly probe with their winkle-pickers to see if the objects were primed to detonate if grabbed. Sadly, as they later heard, a member of another crew in the flotilla was less wary and picked up a device which exploded in his hand causing horrific injury. .

*****

Other than the nightly bombing attacks by small numbers of aircraft which were considered more of a nuisance than a serious hazard, after a short period of time and in terms of actual combat the days were largely uneventful.

Food and sleep, or, more accurately, the lack of each in satisfactory quality as well as quantity was the chief bugbear.

Whatever may have been the scheduled date for its function off Jig/Green sector of Gold Beach, when, in despair, it was located by Jim's crew, the Landing Craft/Kitchen only made marginal improvement to the lack lustre diet: certainly the cuisine would not have found favour in the good food guide. Although the benefit of invigorating calories was, without doubt, thoroughly researched and developed, the hectic scramble to get alongside and then away from the vessel probably expended more nervous energy than the food provided. Like birds of prey wheeling above disembowelled carrion while awaiting their turn to scavenge, in disorderly manner and in anticipation of the command to collect supposedly heat retentive boxes containing a once hot meal, landing craft circled what later came to be known as Anaemics Anonymous.

Because hands holding the heavy, cumbersome hay-boxes prevented grasp of required support when clambering back across rows of pitching and tossing vessels alongside the LC/K, the mere effort frayed nerves and ruined appetites of those performing the task; but seldom did other members of the crew clamour for a share of an unwanted portion.

However, when the gap between American forces on Omaha Beach and British troops on Gold Beach was closed following the capture of Port-en-Bessin by 47 Royal Marine Commando, and once the United States Navy commenced the disembarkation of some of their forces at the port, an unexpected but highly welcome improvement came about in the provision of rations. Far more lavishly supplied in quantity as well as in quality, from time to time a considerable amount of US supplies of enviable food was tossed into the sea, sometimes the entire contents of the box – the assorted selection of nourishment marked on the wooden case obviously not to the liking of the litter-lout. History has not recorded the extent to which victory in Europe was delayed in consequence of the minor landing craft fraternity pausing to clear the English Channel of such jetsam, as they diligently ploughed backwards and forwards; but, on the reverse side of the coin, perhaps it could be suggested the improved diet did manage to keep body and soul together.

It was a matter of considerable regret that in some fashion sleep could not also be supplemented. War has taught those who have participated in them many truths but, of all the lessons learned by each and every combatant since war was first waged, none can be more incontestable than the fact that continuous and refreshing sleep is very difficult to come by on unsteady, open, chilly, stubbornly rigid and often spray drenched decks of LCMs.

Beneficially for some, as the proverb implies, an ill wind blew. A very cantankerous wind and throughout several days. The minor landing craft were contemptuously tossed about, as though to demonstrate they had no rightful place on the open sea. Those close to the shore were violently swept on to the beach well beyond the water's edge – an irate warning not to chance their luck again. Further out to sea, vessels were treated with less tolerance. They were swamped; a ghastly reminder to those craft paralysed on the beach that, if not utterly wrecked and beyond repair, they again ventured out, they too would suffer the same fate. When, over distance and if in time, fortunate crews reached shelter, prevented from delivering supplies for three consecutive days while the storm raged, they redeemed themselves with the knowledge that those forced to run away lived to fight another day.

Jim and his crew were among the fortunate number to make fast alongside their mother-ship. Once aboard the matriarchal vessel, a number of matters soon became apparent. Enjoying the rapture the prodigal son must have experienced on his return, below deck the food was vastly improved, added to which it was sheer luxury to clamber into a suspended hammock – even though the body odour of the throng was hardly agreeable. Notwithstanding that unfortunate state of affairs, by far the greater cause for concern was the plight of the crews not aboard. Though a gaping line of scuttled merchant ships which made up the 'gooseberry', a form of breakwater, did offer the possibility of salvation, they by no means provided a haven for those in peril.

It was during a frantic tussle with unruly elements en route to the haven of their mother-ship that one crew plucked a bloated and mutilated body from the cruel sea. After great difficulty and at times undignified methods the corpse was transferred to the parent-ship of 606. Attired in the ragged remnants of blue dungarees, the torso and pockets were searched by the officer of the watch for clues of identity, but with little success. The only objects found which might have been of any relevance were two or three Kroner, the coins perhaps indicating the deceased was from the sunken Norwegian destroyer. A type of coarse blanket was produced and, weighted, fastened securely around the body. Following what had struck most of the burial party as an indecently short service the remains of the never to be known individual was returned to the sea.

Lighting a much needed cigarette after the congregation drifted from the scene, Jim was deeply saddened to think of the endless grief of families who would never know what happened to their loved ones nor where they were at rest. Of a child, perhaps, who would never have known its father, nor ever be able to place flowers on his grave..

*****

After three days, its ferocity spent, its havoc cruelly wreaked, the storm passed but, as is usually the case following storms, in its wake a very heavy swell developed which greatly exacerbated the problems which beset the LCMs. Lacking a pointed bow to cut through the heaving, unbroken waves and drawing very little water, a fitting comparison was with a cork in a mill-race. When allocated the untried task of towing Rhino ferries, it was ultimately found that it could better be done from alongside rather than from ahead. Quite apart from the reduction of strain upon the tow rope, there was considerable relief at the stabilizing effect the Rhinos had on the landing craft.

In uncomplicated terms the ferries were floating platforms which consisted of a series of large galvanized-iron tanks bolted together. At one end were two largish outboard motors which propelled it. Whether the engines had seized up, or whether they were inadequate to the task in the pulsating swell, none in 606 had the faintest idea, but for some appreciable time the flotilla was assigned the roll of tug-boats. With one LCM tightly lashed forward on the starboard side, and with another also firmly tied aft, to port, the shuttle-service operated well and resulted in the delivery of more supplies than the two landing craft could have transported between them. This was nothing more than was needed. While crews were aboard their parent ship they learned that for each of the three days the gales lasted there was a shortfall of nearly 50,000 tons.

With the artificial Mulberry harbour in the American zone completely wrecked due to the storms and the one in the British sector severely damaged, the speedy extraction of many fingers was essential. But, once more plagued with pre-invasion predictions from some quarters that not all projects would proceed as planned, in the long run the advantage of towing Rhinos secured alongside turned out to be counter-productive.

No matter how tightly ropes from the landing craft to the Rhinos were fastened, unavoidably and due to inevitable strain on the hawsers, in time a certain amount of play developed in the line, which continually allowed the LCMs and Rhinos to separate a little before jerking them together again. Despite the fact fenders were placed between the sides to reduce impact, lines of small holes became apparent along the side of landing craft, the symmetrically perforated rows unquestionably caused by the bolts on the side of the Rhinos.

Thus pierced perilously close to the water line, Jim discovered his vessel to be, but fortunately the craft was also close to the shore. Once the vehicles had been driven off the Rhinos and arrangements made with the Beachmaster's staff for their return to the anchorage, Jim propelled his LCM as far up the beach as the tide permitted. He also satisfied himself that it was securely moored, with no possibility of it drifting again. For him swimming had lost much of its appeal.

Adhering firmly to the belief that if a job is worth doing it is worth finding someone else to do it, Jim went in search of the naval artificer who had been appointed to 606 a few days before leaving England. It was his job to advise on, help with, or carry out repairs and maintenance of disabled vessels. Whereas he had often been seen about the beach in the early days of the invasion, on reflection it seemed there had been appreciably less evidence of him in the recent past. Ultimately Jim was informed that since the capture of Port en Bassin he had acquired a small workshop close to the harbour, where he could be located when not actually working on damaged landing craft. After a long trek along the shore the makeshift building was soon traced, but the only trace of the artisan was his scribbled, bedraggled note announcing he would not be available until morning. Pausing to wonder upon just how many dawns might have greeted the message, Jim trudged back along the beach, determined that the next morning he would return before the elusive Pimpernel could make another get-away.

In fact as early as was Jim's return visit the craftsman was already hard at work, and judged by the number of memos impaled on a metallic spike situated on a window-sill it was likely to be some time before he could attend to Jim's LCM. The promise given was to the effect he would get along to where the vessel was moored as soon as he could, but stressed it would certainly not be on that day. Nor, for that matter, was the next day guaranteed.

With plenty of time to fritter away and the disinclination to yet again scramble along the coastal path towards the east he followed the line of Jeeps, larger wheeled vehicles, tanks and the tracked carriers, all making their way from the harbour area towards an obscured highway. At the junction with the road and despite the fact the two American sectors were to the right, all traffic turned left in the direction Jim needed to go. Patiently waiting to cross the minor road leading from the beach, a lift on a tank, an American tank, was offered and was gratefully accepted. Sprawled on the outside, with each hand firmly clutching and both feet jammed against whatever support was in reach, he was precariously whisked towards Arromanches.

In conversation with a member of the tank crew who was leaning out of the open turret, Jim failed to notice a change of direction at a fork in the road. The diversion was inland. It was only when open countryside gave way to houses and other buildings that he realised the beach must be in the opposite direction to the one along which they travelled. The head and shoulders disappeared from the turret of the tank only to re-emerge in next to no time with a map and with brief information they were now at the approaches to Bayeux. Another voice from within the tank urgently announced that beyond the town their route would be towards the west, away from the direction Jim wanted. With wishes to each other for the best of luck in the struggle ahead he briskly leapt down from the vehicle and watched it trundle away, dust quickly obscuring sight of it.

From large scale maps which had frequently been poured over prior to the invasion, he realised that although in terms of distance the lift on the vehicle had been of no benefit whatsoever, it had only marginally increased his return journey. From where he found himself placed, progress along the road's surface would be more swift than on either the undulating coastal path, or along the sandy beach on the last stage. He figured that a little time spent in Bayeux would not greatly delay ultimate victory, nor would he be in any position to speed its end aimlessly seated on the beach alongside his holed landing craft.

He was quite surprised how normal everything appeared in the town. Not that he would have expected to find the jubilation there undoubtedly was when the place was first liberated. That was more than a fortnight earlier. The Germans had been driven out of the town within the first 24 hours of the landings, although looking around he gained the impression the town's defenders had not put up much resistance, so little damage did there appear to be.

The number of flags displayed wherever facilities made it possible were probably more than the average to be seen throughout several, recent years, and it was hardly likely that on a daily basis those wearing a uniform were besieged by so many children in the hope that bars of chocolate or other sweets might be in the offing, but otherwise there was little of note.

It only very gradually dawned upon his mind just how many horse drawn carriages were about in the main square. It may well have been the case that consciously the number failed to register because so very few were mobile. Once his mind did become more aware of their presence it was obvious the couples who mounted the steps of the carriages, and disappeared from view inside, were quite content to rest within. Conveyance seemed not to be the reason for their hire. The indolent coachman only stirred from where he was perched on high and at the front of the carriage either to collect the cost of the hire or to place a replenished nosebag on the head of his patient, un-bridled horse.

On the saunter back to the beach Jim gave completely free rein to his imagination.

During the course of the next morning help of a kind did arrive to enable repairs to the LCM. A carpenter arrived from the articifer's store with a supply of wooden bungs. Nothing with which to hammer them home nor, if too thick, with which to pare them, but more than generous in quantity. The beach thereabout yielded a few pebbles, adequate in every respect for the first task except for the essential quality of weight. The remedy was soon obtained in the revisited German strongpoint. It was recalled that on the original survey a number of pickaxes had been noticed. Luckily they had not been removed. In precautionary fashion, a coil of rope collected from the landing craft was carefully looped around the tools. Protected by the thickness of the walls of the bunker (in the event of a booby-trap among the pickaxes), from outside the rope was tugged. The tools were heard to clatter to the floor, but there was no sound of an explosion. Elated in the certain knowledge the sturdy handles had not been blown to smithereens they were retrieved and the crew returned to the beached vessel to hammer home the plugs.

Accomplished with far more speed than perfection, the protruding ends of row upon row of the bungs gave the landing craft the weird appearance of a huge spiny lobster. Reporting back to their parent ship for the next task, the crew were replaced by one of the several, surplus ones, whose own original craft had been put out of action due to one reason or another. There were no protests among Jim's crew at the deprivation. Nor did any materialise as June gave way to July and breaks in duty became more frequent, thanks to the excess of crews over operational landing craft. Though losses of the latter had been considerable, mercifully loss of life had been far less.

Sleep was the first and most sought relief, hardly remarkable bearing in mind there had been precious little of it throughout the whole month. Once again dining became a regular habit, and without need to trawl for it in the bountiful area of the channel in the American sector, or to risk life and limb to obtain it from Anaemics Anonymous. Not requiring a great deal of endeavour nor ability to surpass the printed correspondence on postcards issued to service personnel on active service, conveying to those to whom they were sent the fact that the sender was safe and well, part of the newly found spare time was devoted to a little more detail. Still intent on denying the enemy knowledge of the whereabouts of the naval force, should correspondence be intercepted, letters continued to bear only post office box numbers for replies and the correspondence was still subject to censorship. Some of the more astute aboard the parent-ship were of the opinion that, having hit upon a pretty shrewd idea of where the fleet might be, the wily Germans were hardly likely to be in need of written confirmation.

With far more free time on their hands days passed less

rapidly. Less occupied minds began to dwell upon what was likely to be their next mission. There was thought to be little prospect of further sea-borne invasions; at least, not in the European theatre of war.

Among lowly, other ranks in 606, wishful rumours began to persist that before the month was out the flotilla, or what remained of it, would return to the UK.

On the day preceding the fall of Caen, when 606 did leave the shores of Normandy, Jim and his crew were involved in another ghastly brush with disaster. Following their latest 24 hour break and with confirmation that within the next 48 hours they would be in England, everyone was in the highest of spirits. At first light the crew was instructed on their tasks for the day. Overeager to get the jobs done and hardly bothering to descend the scrambling net one rung at a time, the stoker had the engines running, the deck hands had cast-off the ropes securing the vessel fore and aft, and with the wheel amidships Jim slowly eased the landing craft astern.

Clear of the mother-ship, with the steering-wheel swung hard to port, and slow speed astern on that engine but with the starboard engine on half speed ahead, Jim swung the LCM around. Changing to full speed ahead on both engines they headed for the distant merchant ship from which they were to collect their first load of the day. The sea was choppy, but not exceptionally so.

Suddenly and alarmingly the ramp crashed down, the forward motion of the vessel practically scooping aboard the crest of each oncoming wave. Urgently switching one of the engines into reverse and whipping the steering wheel hard over on the same side in order to turn away from the oncoming menace, the inrush was lessened but not sufficiently to give hope of reaching the safety of the shore. Hampered as they badly were by the faulty ramp it was also doubtful whether, under their own power, they could reach the nearest ship. With such scant chance the remaining hope was for assistance to reach them before the well-deck filled and the landing craft sank. Never was a klaxon resorted to so frantically nor its hooter pressed so repeatedly. In time, but only just, and thankful for the greater speed of an American Landing Craft/Personnel which was in the British sector, the crew were taken off and carried back to their parent ship. Their return was cause for considerable consternation.

A brief enquiry into the mishap was immediately launched and pertinent questions were put to the crew who had manned the LCM on the previous day. It was hesitantly revealed that what was, euphemistically, described as a glancing blow by a bulldozer working on the beach may have contributed to the weakened ramp.

All items of clothing and equipment lost by the crew when the vessel went to the bottom of the Channel were replaced without the slightest hesitation or penalty. That is with the exception of the crafty deduction of tuppence from Jim's service pay on the next pay parade, for the replacement of his two identity discs.

He was not in the least slow to appreciate the paradox – that had the discs slipped to the bottom of the sea while in the approved position around his neck he would not have been put to such expense.

FOR THE FALLEN

They shall grow not old,
As we that are left grow old.

Age shall not weary them
Nor the years condemn.

At the going down of the sun
And in the morning …
We will remember them.

Laurence Binyon
1869–1943

PART TWO

PER TERRAM

11

A GENUINE SMASHER

As every person well knows,
Nature's creation, the rose,
Is stated 'beyond compare'.

But a lady perceived by Jim
Exquisite in looks and slim,
Such beauty did also share.

Delightful face to behold,
Tender body to enfold –
For him no greater pleasure.

Throughout each day it may be said,
Thoughts of her filled his head.
At night he dreamed – beyond measure.

Derisively dubbed 'la Normandie' by the survivors from 606 Flotilla who were due to sail home aboard her, the nickname was not in connection with the land they were leaving behind, but with the pre-war, blue-ribbon, luxury, ocean liner.

Their ship must have known far better times. Of rats there was no trace aboard. Without having been sunk, they had abandoned the shabby vessel.

Stability-wise, stood astride a massive sheet of steel which spanned the quarter deck one could distinctly feel two different surges through the waves – the result of detonating a mine earlier in the war: but it had not gone to the bottom of the Med.

The mess deck did live up to its name, both with regard to food and accommodation. There was an abundance of the former, which very few fancied, and an insufferable shortage of sleeping accommodation, wherein even fewer enjoyed sweet dreams. In hammocks fastened above mess tables, on mess tables, and under mess tables, cheeks faced cheeks at opposite ends of the anatomy.

Unprepossessing as was the ship, its bows were pointed in the direction of Blighty, and providing the steel plate prevented fore and aft from parting company on the voyage, none aboard her complained too much: though it must be said a higher rate of knots did elicit a twinge of regret.

Nobody in 606 flotilla was of the opinion any continental break could have terminated as jubilantly as the one off the coast of Normandy. Forgoing some of the accumulated trivia gathered in, and for which there was insufficient space in kitbags, other, treasured souvenirs were crammed in or stowed about themselves.

With the return voyage across the English Channel not half accomplished and visions of England only in the imagination, nevertheless those not specifically appointed for duty on the lower decks lined the ship's rails for the first glimpse. Even those individuals most addicted to the vice of gambling had stowed their packs of well-thumbed playing cards into the pockets of battledress tunics, some no doubt contemplating on what they might otherwise have expended the sums which had been lost: the winners, perhaps, constantly revising the type or level of enjoyment their ill-gotten gains would provide, yet knowing it to be far more likely it would all be lost in the next card school.

When, at long last, the cliffs of the Isle of Wight came into view on the distant horizon, gritted teeth relaxed their pressure and vocal cords abstained from their customary activity. Words had no place. In the strange silence each onlooker was aware only of their own sober thoughts. On the crucial eve of departure for Normandy there had been so much festivity, Jim recalled. Was it merely that none wished to appear to have no stomach for the fight, he wondered. Now that those marked to die had perished, was there that pang of indefinable guilt known only to those who had been spared in battle. Fewer in number than when they departed, did they really experience a greater share of honour.

As 'home' drew closer the ship's speed seemed to decrease and did, in fact, come to a complete halt at one stage. When it became clear on which side the ship would eventually dock, everyone on board flocked in that direction. The list which ensued was quite alarming and was emphasised by an immediate and distinctly irate order to trim ship. Instantly! Officers in command of the various units returning to England quickly arrived on the scene and took control of personnel under their authority. Once the list was rectified the ship was finally berthed; but, oh, how torturously long it was for the gangway to be wheeled into position and made secure at the opening in the bulwark of the moored ship.

As undoubtedly would have been the case whichever detachment was the first to be allowed ashore, and regardless of whatever priority was given to those who followed, among the units forced to wait remarks veered between tolerable indignation and inexcusable vilification. The legitimacy of the sequence of disembarkation and of the procreation of those who decided upon it were expressed with equal derision. Had Wally B.....d been present he would have felt he was among relatives.

There was further irritation at the length of time which it took to unload and to sort out ownership of personal belongings and equipment, but that was as nothing compared to the astonishment which greeted the order to assemble with possessions in the huge custom-shed. From where was it the authorities thought the ship's passengers had returned, it was intentionally, loudly voiced. And which dutiable luxuries were conjectured to be crammed into bulging kit bags. What magnificent sum was anticipated in respect of the pathetic bundles of luggage belonging to the bedraggled personnel mustered outside the shed, it was vociferously and contemptuously remonstrated over and over again and not entirely without obscenities.

The irascibility was possibly indicative of the mental exhaustion which had set in since being withdrawn from active service. For a considerable part of the return voyage a goodly number had sat quite motionless, their chin propped up on an upturned hand which in turn was supported by an elbow placed on their thigh, everything around them of negligible interest. Each one of them had given their all: time was now their greatest need.

The procession through customs was, in fact a mere formality. None were required to open the bundle of belongings which they so resentfully dragged along nor were any of them even asked whether they contained items liable to duty. Instead the customs officers made them welcome with kind greetings and congratulations on the part they had played in the invasion.

As the boat-train slowly picked its way over a number of cobbled level crossings where traffic had been bought to a complete standstill in the vicinity of the port, the earlier felt weariness among some of those seated in Jim's compartment eased a little. Although the remarks expressed now and again seldom generated copious conversation, from time to time response was provoked as familiar landmarks came into view, of which that of Bursledon Station was the most eagerly awaited. The journey did not take long to complete and, in keeping with the improvement in organisation since disembarkation, a number of lorries awaited their arrival and transported them to HMS *Cricket*.

In camp, what remained of the day was aimlessly spent. Items which had been carefully packed and placed in store for safe keeping prior to leaving for Normandy were retrieved. Had he not been lucky enough to return, Jim's last letter to his parents would have had a purpose. Not only did that note now have any significance, but what, he wondered, was the importance he had attached to the several other items now also repossessed? He tired his mind completely with his incessant introspection but failed to obtain any release from the burden. He wearily slumped onto his unmade bed, his night attire remaining what it had been throughout the day. His last thoughts dwelt upon the possibility that a man's job had been demanded of mere boys.

It soon became abundantly clear there were no immediate plans for the redeployment of the survivors from 606, and after a few days resettlement in camp leave was granted. Initially Jim found it far more exasperating at home. Not surprisingly, family and neighbours who knew of Jim's involvement wanted to know what it was like 'over there', as though all circumstances were identical. However the question might have been handled by others who had returned, he knew his own account was hopelessly expressed. Or was it that his mind shrank at the prospect of resurrecting the events which he had encountered?

As the days slipped by and fewer people asked the same question, matters became less strained. It was also undoubtedly the case that quietly speaking with members of his family regarding the ordeal had helped to alleviate the tension. Conversely, as he became aware on the very first day of leave, he had to accustom himself to the sound of doodle-bugs, the name given to the unmanned flying-bomb the Germans had developed. Upon cessation of its droning engine, when its descent commenced, it created a nerve-racking interval as it plunged to earth. Its ultimate explosion, elsewhere, brought relief; but death and injury and destruction where it landed.

A couple of days before he was due to return to camp he ran into Eileen's mother. Hoping his look did not divulge an incompletely healed wound, he thanked her for her kind expression at seeing him safe and well, but believing his voice would betray his innermost feeling he refrained from asking after her daughter.

Back at camp and reflecting upon the chance meting with the woman he had previously begun to look upon as his future mother-in-law, Jim's longing for feminine company was rekindled. He yearned for someone, a sweetheart he would cherish and devote himself to. He could not possibly anticipate how soon nor how entirely his ardent wish would come true.

Although while at HMS *Cricket* he had passed through the village of Hedge End on many occasions prior to D Day, he had never set foot in the church hall, but from the nightly boasts of affections won and of conquests made by his mates, he knew the canteen was popular with many ATS girls from the nearby army camp at Botley. Less fanciful than the amorous claims of hut-mates were accounts of one girl who at table-tennis was said to be almost unbeatable.

On an evening which was devoid of any particular inclination, far less the actual intention to play table-tennis or even visit the hall of fame, with the sudden onset of a shower of rain he drifted into the canteen. As the net had not been erected for table-tennis his mind was not focussed in that direction. Sat quietly drinking a most modestly priced cup of tea, his thoughts were still mostly preoccupied with the traumatic events of the past couple of months. After a while he became aware of the sound of the notes coming from a piano, the unmistakable talent of the person at the keyboard significantly more melodious than the voices of the throng of service personnel surrounding and hiding the pianist from view. Several of the ditties being lustily sung by the soldiers had had the original words replaced by lines composed by barrack-room baritones but, as the premises permitting the entertainment were an annexe of the Church of St. John, the blasphemous words which had been inserted were reverently slurred.

Regardless of the fact there was no table-tennis in progress, depriving him of the opportunity to see if he could spot the acclaimed champion, he called to mind the comments of his hut mates. Though their descriptions were imprecise they covered the entire spectrum of men's appreciation of the opposite sex, and always followed the format of appearance before ability. 'She' (none seemed to know her name) was a smasher who was a good table-tennis player.

There may well have been many others, not present on that particular evening, who frequented the canteen and also possessed good looks but Jim was quite sure none could surpass the exquisite features on which his eyes came to rest. Without the slightest exaggeration he could not keep his gaze from the face which he found so attractive, nor did he make any attempt to conceal the look of admiration which he felt sure must have been apparent on his face.

He did not analyse her attractiveness. He felt it would have been clinical and unpardonable to verify the colour of her eyes and hair, and whether the latter was arranged in curls, in waves or was lank: to determine the shape of her nose and lips, and the excellence of her complexion. He did not consider a feast was enhanced by going into detail about its ingredients. As with innumerable objets d'art he had had the opportunity to contemplate in a variety of exclusive establishments in the West End of London, yet without resentment at the knowledge such treasures would ever be his, his mind lingered upon the charm her presence would bring into the life of whoever shared hers.

As it turned out, Jim's goddess was the 'smasher'. Two ATS girls took up the small bats and after a gentle, preliminary knock up serious play commenced. Most fortunately, during the course of the exceedingly one-sided game, a mis-hit ball landed close to his table. Retrieving it, Jim asked to play the ultimate winner, having not the slightest doubt as to who that would be. So it turned out, and after he too lost by a considerable margin due to his opponent's savage backhand smash, tea was suggested and accepted, during the sipping of which conversation hardly stalled between those seated around the table.

Towards the time the canteen was due to close for the evening they left, Vera, as by that time he knew her, permitting him to walk back with her to the camp at which she was stationed. They did not walk arm in arm, kiss on parting nor make any definite plans to meet on a future evening. Whether the absence of such an arrangement was due to the presence of Vera's companion, Alison, another ATS girl who had accompanied her throughout the evening, Jim could only surmise as he made his way back to camp. But he was far more certain he would not flinch from suffering another virtual whitewash at table-tennis on the next evening, if his hopes materialised.

The reluctance with which the next day progressed gave vent to the feeling there must have been more than the standard quota of minutes to each hour, but the drag before afternoon began to slip away was by no means due to the fact there were very few duties to perform in camp.

Mindful of previous occasions almost spoiled in consequence of the curse of his laboured eating habit, he knew full well he would miss the first liberty boat if tea was taken, and he was equally aware the next parade would be as much as an hour and a half later. Without doubt, a couple of slices of bread with scrape of some unrecognisable substance and a mug of tea was scarcely the equivalent of 90 minutes additional shore leave; even though most of that duration was likely to be spent retrieving a ping-pong ball which his bat had failed to return over the net. That was, of course, provided Vera turned up at the venue; and fervently hoping that if she did his prospects might be improved by appearing in his blue uniform, he enthusiastically set about polishing the several brass buttons and badges on his jacket, as well as improving the crease in his trousers.

Of course, his arrival at Saint John's was far too early. The doors of the canteen were still securely locked. There was little doubt that the earthly saints, who poured the tea and served the chosen biscuits and buns to the hells angels who frequented the church hall, were otherwise occupied tending the more deserving needs of their own families.

Even when the massive doors were eventually unbolted and swung open, Jim continued to bide his time. He decided to remain outside to allay all possibility of becoming involved with anyone, at table-tennis or merely in conversation. In due course he reluctantly arrived at the conclusion Vera would not be putting in an appearance at the canteen that evening but, in the course of retracing his steps to Bursledon, she came around the corner with two or three companions; thankfully all girls. Striving to demonstrate surprise at running into the group while unnoticeably shuffling his feet to coincide with the direction of theirs, the party made for the hall. Magnanimity costing very little on the premises, tea and an assortment of biscuits were lavished on the circle of friends, thereby artfully securing his inclusion in the party.

It had been a fine, summer day. From very first light the sky had been cloudless. As the day progressed the temperature increased gradually, but from late afternoon the weather turned decidedly sultry. Despite the fact each of the doors were ajar and the upper, hinged section of every window in the church hall was in an open position, at floor level very little air circulated to any noticeable degree. Practically everyone in the canteen, men and women alike, had removed their close fitting jackets or their somewhat more loose fitting battle dress tunic, which consequent shirtsleeved-fashion Vera and her friends soon adopted.

In the minority among the sexes seated at the table, with the further disadvantage of being a complete stranger to Vera's associates, it was with a feeling of relief that he looked forward to the pleasure of a game of table-tennis with her. Though almost all that it would allow by way of conversation would be the muttered, one-sided score, each of them would have the undivided attention of the other. Once they did obtain a game, in which he soon fell hopelessly behind, he came to appreciate that defeat was partly of his own making. Instead of relentlessly keeping an eye on the ball as Vera treated it to her vicious smash, both eyes were transfixed by the effect on her bosom of the backhand stroke.

At the final close of play on that highly impressionable evening and when they returned to the table they had occupied, Jim was delighted to find that Vera's friends had departed. As the conversation between them ranged from one subject to another throughout the remaining hours Jim increasingly took the view that she probably had a more refined background than he. That was not to infer she adopted airs and graces or for that matter because he believed he typified a downright cockney: but he did come from Hackney which was not quite as salubrious as Sutton, from where Vera came. He had been there, once. On an express delivery service. At the end of the Northern Underground Line, Morden, he had boarded a bus for a particular road in Sutton, but the conductor forgot to announce the destination as had been promised and Jim finished up on Banstead Downs: still, the walk back across the downs to Sutton left very pleasant memories. Another matter which set her apart in his estimation was in having three Christian names – VJM were the initials she gave, together with her surname and regimental number. It was a precautionary measure in case either were moved to another location. They would correspond.

On the walk back to Botley that memorable evening, just the two of them, he was nonplussed. After knowing Vera for only two evenings, in total amounting to only a few hours, would it be tantamount to a kiss of death to their newly forged relationship to place an arm around the waist of a Sutton girl who had three Christian names. He decided neither to chance his arm nor push his luck with a parting kiss, but a date was made for the following day.

Of the shrewd opinion a more enticing setting than the church hall together with a more potent aphrodisiac than tea and doughnuts might produce more rapture, when next they met Vera was asked if she would prefer to spend the evening elsewhere. The fact that she did not mind where they went was unfathomable in terms of enthusiasm. It did not rank in the couldn't care less category but neither was it an indication of what she would like to do, which preference, whatever it may have been, was what he had hoped to provide. While waiting to cross the main road which ran from Botley to Woolston she made a decision. Vera would like to go to The Kettle.

Although Jim had often walked along the road in which the premises were situated, he always wishing to discover what was round the next corner and the one after that, he had never before noticed the little café, set well back from the road as it was. Viewed from outside it was quite an unpretentious establishment but inside it was very neat. Vera and a number of her colleagues had visited the place on many occasions, as was clearly evident from the warm welcome extended to her by the proprietress, a kindly, rotund lady who would have been an invaluable asset in any business. Their choice decided and accepting the suggestion from the owner that perhaps they would prefer it to be served in the garden to the rear, Vera and Jim seated themselves.

No matter where they might otherwise have chosen to spend the evening it could not have been more enjoyable. After they had eaten and the table was cleared of crockery and cutlery Jim produced his cigarettes and a box of matches, placing the latter on the table while he took the wrapper from the cigarette packet. Reading the little joke printed on the label of the match box, Vera realised Jim was awaiting their return but instead of doing so she thoughtfully struck a match and extended her arm toward him. She did not need his guiding hand but he took the chance to gently grasp her wrist as he drew on his cigarette, very nearly causing the lighted match-stick to burn down to her fingers, before hastily blowing out the flame. He did not release his hold nor did Vera try to withdraw her hand. Instead, between the tips of his thumb and forefinger, she allowed him to soothe imaginary burns on each of her fingers.

On the walk back to Botley Camp his arm was lovingly placed around Vera's waist and his stride was carefully adjusted to hers. During the long pause before she had to pass through the gates, in the shadows, a little further down the lane, his arms drew her to his body while each pair of lips responded passionately to the demands imposed by the other's kiss.

On the solitary walk back to Bursledon Camp he was ecstatic to have discovered that having three Christian names was not an impediment to snogging.

Although the church hall continued to be the place most frequented by Vera and Jim, within its four walls the ritual of tea and table tennis lacked variety. To add spice to the routine, life was in dire need of a splash of romance, for which the setting was far from ideal. In the canteen, but under the tables, if at all, masculine hands might have wandered slightly and nervous knees of nubile ATS girls may have been affectionately nudged, but none who were intent on greater intimacy made the premises their love nest. The only connection with love of which Jim was aware, perhaps more accurately stated – was party to in the canteen – was in the score of three games to love, the margin by which Vera usually beat him and most other opponents at table tennis.

For those intent on different pleasures in different

establishments the choice was only marginally better than Hobson's. The only other amenity within an evening's compass, but outside a pocket's affluence, was the local public house – too public for the purposes of necking and petting. Though high on the agenda those activities may have been, another keenly felt deprivation was the basic absence of privacy. Of a dwelling with a room of their own, or some other sheltered den to which they could retire with their companions, there to daydream and fantasise about all manner of things once the war was over and the future more assured. To ramble on and on, without being overheard and told by those of an older generation that, one day, they would grow up.

Annoyed at themselves they had not considered the potential sooner, and while they would not have the place entirely to themselves, there was the cinema; but that would only be feasible on a Saturday, when they were both free from duty soon after midday. That would enable them to get to Bitterne, see the film and return by bus, which was not possible in the course of an evening. On the following Saturday they made the journey.

Bitterne only boasted one cinema and judged by the length of the queue they joined, which wound round the corner from the entrance, they would be lucky to get in for the afternoon performance. And what a large proportion in the queue were children. When their position in the line of people cleared the corner the reason became obvious. The main feature in the programme was Snow White and the Seven Dwarfs. Though Jim was not a big, burly marine, nevertheless he felt a little out of place and hoped against hope none of his hut mates would come along. However, having made the journey they decided to stand their ground, and as close as possible to the children immediately in front of themselves. It would give the impression of dutiful parents: but how young the couple must have looked, to have so many children of such ages. The darkness once inside the cinema was a mighty relief. At first, it was also very noisy within.

As was to be expected, not to pretend it was not also hoped, the unaccompanied children had commandeered the seats as close to the screen as possible. Other youngsters, obliged by their parents or guardians for the afternoon, had to make do with the rows removed from the gathering pandemonium caused by those on parole from the kindergarten. Vera and Jim, deferring to the preference of both groups, were quite prepared to resign themselves to the very back row to which they were guided by the usherette, a person only a little their junior. It is conceivable she had concluded that the ATS girl, revealed by the beam of light from her torch, had not come to swoon over any of the dwarfs or even Prince Charming, nor the marine to drool over the vital statistics of Snow White. Heaven forbid the thought, also in courtship and dated by another marine she may have been introduced to the advantage of more subdued lighting at the rear in this or other cinemas, where she may have found out that her boy-friend appreciated the worth of a 'bird' in the hand compared with two, or any given number, on the celluloid screen.

As the fairy story unfolded, the longer the enthralled children remained mute the more quietly Vera and Jim conversed; and the more they whispered the more necessary it was to incline the head. In the forward attitude this entailed, Jim's arm was slipped around Vera and threaded under her arm, without causing apparent discomfort to her. During a prolonged murmur close to her ear, a just audible gasp revealed the stimulating effect of his warm breath and lips upon Vera's lobe. Envious of the beseeching notice hung at the end of the bed of Sleepy, Jim also hoped Vera and he would not be disturbed.

Whether it was due to the temperature in the cinema or because it was less restrictive, Vera had unbuttoned her tunic before she sat down. By lowering the arm which he had round her waist and taking hold of one of the lower buttons, Jim drew her jacket open. Under it and through a thin, cotton blouse he gently fondled her breast. The nipple, swiftly aroused, stood proud. Leaning just a little further forward to enable each of his hands to deal with the fastening, Vera's brassiere was unhooked. Very careful not to sweep aside her hand resting upon his thigh as he withdrew one hand from under the blouse, he placed it above Vera's knee. Instinctively, each pair of legs yielded.

Until the programme ended and lights flooded the auditorium their whispers ceased. The attention of each of them was completely engaged with the sensation of touch, experienced in equal measure in the willing deed of submission and in the tender act of bestowing thrills.

Waiting for the bus to take them back to Botley, conversation flowed almost without pause. Each in turn introduced the other to details of their past and to members in their family. Was it, Jim began to wonder, an omen for an eventual, permanent link between the two households. Vera came from quite a large family. There were eight children, giving her five brothers and two sisters. Very sadly the eldest brother, a submariner, had been reported missing earlier in the war. His wife was expecting their first child who turned out to be a boy. Another sad case of a young widow and of a child who would never know the love of his father. While Jim dared to hope his courtship of Vera would bloom, that each day, regardless of its demands, he would return home to her, he inwardly vowed that during the war he would never place her and a child by him at such disadvantage.

By the time they got to their destination it was raining quite steadily. Fortunately the stop at which they alighted was right outside The Kettle. Although the time was getting on, the open sign was still displayed. They dashed inside. With profuse apologies the owner told them she was on the point of closing as there was not a scrap of food left on the premises, but in her northern accent told them they were welcome to a brew. They were not hurried by the proprietress and took their time over the pot of tea, but it was still raining when they left. The only cover close at hand was the bus shelter.

Though Jim knew there was no obligation to board any bus which came to a halt at the fare stage, he thought the disinclination to do so would raise a few eyebrows. On the other hand, for the time being they had the refuge entirely to themselves which was all they wanted. Having largely disposed with the subject of their separate past the conversation turned to the future. The present was forfeited. Neither of them resorted to 'our' future but spoke of what they would like of 'the' future, rather as though a benevolent Father Time was on hand to take note of whatever was yearned.

It must be said that Vera had some very specific desires but was far less precise as to how they were to be achieved. Omitting to declare or even give the hint she wished to marry, she wanted to have four children. Almost giving Jim the jitters that she was about to conceive in the bus shelter, necessitating his gormless intervention as obstetrician, she had already carefully decided upon the name of Virginia Margaret for the first infant: rather as though a scan had predicted it would be a girl. Not having been told it was he who would be called upon to assist in the procreation of the child, he felt it would be entirely wrong of him to criticise Vera's choice of names for her daughter. There was nothing about the name of Margaret which was likely to be objectionable to her offspring, but he knew full well the taunts poor Virginia was likely to encounter as she grew up. When from time to time it became known among the messengers with whom he worked that one of them had a girl friend or sister named Virginia, the chorus was always one of "Virgin for short: but not for long".

Stemming from the widespread manner in which names or initials become mill stones around necks of the unfortunate ones, or which attract jibes and pet names, Vera's first two initials (VJ) landed her with the pet name of 'Vidge'. Due to it being misheard, subsequently and affectionally her nickname became Widge.

12

CONTENT WITH GOOD HEALTH

Good health may come
In many guises.
Firstly, to he
Who early rises.

Or, content in
Cottage with mine host,
When refilled glasses
Pledge the toast.

Every morning, standing orders were scrutinized at HMS
Cricket but apart from notification of camp duties or times
of parades, presumably to make quite sure nobody had
absconded, the marines were unoccupied throughout day after
day. In the evenings time was more pleasurably spent; but for
some time it had become increasingly obvious Widge had
something on her mind. She broke the news immediately they
met one evening towards the end of the week.

She had managed to obtain a few days leave and was to return
home. Though she made no reference to it as such, her
comments suggested that it probably was compassionate leave.

She spoke of concern regarding her father but gave no
indication of the cause for her upset. While she spoke Jim firmly
held her hand hoping it might convey his wish to do whatever
he possibly could to alleviate her anxiety. Effectively it turned
out to be next to nothing. When they took leave of each other
on that melancholy evening their kisses expressed less desire.
Compassion was the greater need.

If the following evening was aimless the weekend was
infinitely more depressing, spent as it was within the largely
deserted confines of HMS *Cricket*. Jim was disinclined to visit the
canteen over the weekend knowing for certain Widge would not
be there. When Monday turned up, several days late it seemed, it
was not on account of a Monday morning feeling that he could
not make up his mind whether to go there – he had suffered the

beginning of the week feeling on each day since Widge went home. He was torn between going, and risking the inevitable disappointment if she was not there, or refraining, only to subsequently learn she had returned. He could not decide which would cause himself the greater pain…. He had to go. He did go. And she was not there. The tea and biscuits (or was it a doughnut) refused to make a smooth journey down his gullet. The hunger which required satisfaction was not due to the lack of food.

Three of Widge's colleagues in the ATS came in together and seated themselves on the other side of the church hall. Two of them he recognised. He had met Allison on the evening when he first met Widge, and on a few nights since then. She was married to a soldier stationed elsewhere. To any other male appearing to give her the glad eye she made it quite clear she was not interested. She was not actually rude to any who made approaches but her body language delivered the message instead of her tongue. The other person he was able to identify was one who had accompanied Widge on a couple of occasions. Jim believed the girl had said she came from a place in Yorkshire, not far from Ilkley, but on the evening in question his unswerving attention was upon Widge. It was the girl from Yorkshire who gave a little wave. He crossed the hall to enquire whether any of them knew when Widge was due back in camp, but none did. Of a fashion they invited his company, so he accepted the kindness and drew up a chair.

Together with the girl he had not previously met, Alison arranged a game of table-tennis. By the pair whose game soon came to an end they were offered the bats and commenced play. Passing close to where he was seated with the remaining girl, on their way out of the church hall two mates from 606 jokingly remarked they would not breathe a word of what they had come across when they next met Widge. With the head of his companion at the table slightly turned, Jim could not be sure if her eyelids gestured somewhat. If it was a wink and to give the impression it had not been noticed, he arose telling her he would get some more refreshments. Waiting in the long queue with his back to the table he had vacated, and the one on which the game of table-tennis was coming to an end, it was not until his return with the drinks that he realised Alison and her opponent had departed.

Between sips of tea the Yorkshire lass chatted animatedly, much of which fell on deaf ears. Jim was consumed with other problems. It was one matter to have his leg pulled by his two friends, but what view of his association with the girl might reach the ears of Widge, from the lips of her friends, might not be a laughing matter. The absence of a response, to what had obviously required one, led the girl to bemoan she might as well return to camp. Knowing offence had been taken, Jim's attempt to console with the offer to walk back with her was rather eagerly accepted.

If, at that particular time, reason or defence of his offer had been demanded, lacking any better explanation it could be said he had caused umbrage and wished to make amends. Maybe it could also be said he had cause to amend his concept of the feminine species of the Yorkshire tyke.

It would have been harsh to claim she drained her mug of tea at one gulp like a parched camel slaking its thirst at an oasis in the Sahara, but it did not take much time before she was bursting to depart. Hardly had the second pace on their journey been completed before the young lady reached out and, under her other arm, firmly clamped his arm in position around her waist, or thereabout. It would have been improper and incidental to ponder whether on the days she tramped the area of Ilkley Moor she was 'bar t'hat', but in the area where his hand was pinned Jim soon became aware there was little else of which she was deficient. Even as his biceps stirred to withdraw his trapped arm he recognised the insult it would inflict. He was conversant with the phrase of talking oneself out of difficulty but her armlock compelled submission, and try as he struggled to do with mere words they had no effect. The 'tykess' smiled throughout the contest, seductively.

When on previous occasions he had walked back to camp with Widge he was always surprised and dismayed how quickly they arrived at the gates. On the evening when he was dragged in that direction he felt they would never be reached. Even when they came in sight the clinch remained inescapable. His hand was prised up to her chest and his feet were propelled past the entrance. All who were stationed nearby knew full well what was further up the lane. A spot commonly referred to as the lay-by. Jim spoke just one word, "No!", and stopped. He wrenched his arm free and walked away.

On the walk back to Bursledon and during the whole of the next morning Jim was in a quandary. The most pressing concern, of when to put in another appearance at the church hall, was happily solved when he went to collect the mail for the occupants of his hut. Among the pile were two addressed to himself, one of which was from Widge. The handwriting on the other envelope he could not place. It would have to wait. Among a number of most pleasing matters contained in the correspondence from Widge, the specific mention of her return on the following day dispensed with the decision of whether to visit the canteen on the evening of that day. It also extended the indecision for a further 24 hours on two other concerns.

The girl from Yorkshire had been Widge's friend for some length of time. Jim reasoned that if Widge and he had been engaged it was more than likely she would have told her close friends. It was also reasonable to believe, or at least to allow the benefit of the doubt, those friends would not have played fast and lose with her fiancé.

While Jim was not an authority on bedtime conversations in girl's dormitories, unlike men returning from shore leave with revealing details of their conquests he preferred to think the gentle sex were less explicit. That being the case, the ATS girl in question may not have had reason to think there was anything between Widge and Jim, and was therefore free to make whatever advances she chose. Jim could not think it would be in the interest of anyone to mention the episode, hoping none of it would be related to Widge causing her to suspect his fidelity. That solved the first dilemma.

By far the more ticklish problem was whether to put to the test the affection he believed had developed between Widge and himself. He was fully aware they had not known each other for a lengthy period of time. Nor was he quite so naïve as to pretend to himself they were 'made for each other'. He knew full well that but for the outbreak of war it was extremely unlikely they would have met. Nevertheless, from the commencement of her leave and increasing in effect as each day passed without her companionship (even if only of a few hours) he came to fully appreciate just how deeply he loved her. While he believed their courtship would resume on her return to Botley, a posting elsewhere for either one or the other would again interrupt it, perhaps for ages. Unless betrothed the outcome would be unpredictable.

Convinced he needed no further period of time in which to assess their compatibility, he was also disturbingly aware that if the question was not popped by himself, another might do so. He would feel shattered by a second, broken love affair. He would take the plunge. He hoped to have the insight to judge when would be an opportune moment, as well as the manner most likely to gain Widge's consent.

By her smile when they met on the following evening he knew the troubles which had beset her had evaporated. Even at table-tennis she was far more tolerant, permitting Jim to accumulate a few points, but he decided against pushing his luck too far on the first evening together. During the course of that reunion, when Widge returned to the table with refilled mugs after a lengthy conversation with one of the ladies serving tea in the canteen, she informed him they had both been invited out at the weekend. On Saturday. Widge had got to know the person who was a voluntary worker at the church hall some months previously. Widge also knew the helper's grown-up daughter who came to stay with her parents in Hedge End from time to time. Evidently the daughter was born with cerebral palsy but nevertheless largely lived an independent life. On Saturday her mother was to drive her back to the hotel at which she resided. En route, in the New Forest the foursome were to stop at a splendid restaurant for afternoon tea. Completely convinced the afternoon would set the perfect atmosphere for the evening performance, once back at HMS *Cricket* that evening Jim practiced his lines. Ceaselessly.

When they got back to Hedge End in the evening following the outing Widge and Jim were invited into the beautiful home of their hostess. The lady's husband, a successful businessman, produced a potent but delectable whisky liqueur. Their stay at the house outlasted the generous tipple, so glasses were replenished. A further offer, which would have been bound to result in the most slobbered oath of love and proposal of marriage implored by a young man, was politely declined. After a further hour or so of total abstinence, they took leave of their kind host whose hospitality was well known and so much appreciated by many service personnel who frequented the canteen.

As they approached the church hall, on their way to the junction of the Botley and Bursledon roads, it struck Jim it would be an unkind though unintended snub to the place in which the seeds of their love had been sown not to pop the question there. Not actually in the canteen, which had been closed at the usual time, but in the grounds of the church. There would not be a soul about, apart from those in the churchyard and they had not stirred for ages. Just inside the entrance to the grounds of the Church of St. John, Jim put his trust in the saintly landlord. He must have given his blessing because from whatever position he had made his proposal, and after the Drambuie he may well have been on both knees, Jim distinctly heard Widge promise to be his wife.

If on his walk back to Bursledon on by far the happiest day of his life there was the semblance of a spring in his step, it came from the knowledge the countdown had begun to the time when they would bed down together instead of miles apart.

Until the early hours of the next morning sleep played truant. The alcohol may have had a stimulating effect, but if so it was only contributory. He reckoned he would have been no less exhilarated if each of the noggins had been gripe water. Even to himself he could not properly narrate what it meant that one day, when the war was eventually over, Widge and he would settle down under one roof. Perhaps after all, as a working partner in the project, he would be able to persuade her that Virginia Margaret would suffer less taunts if she was given the names of Veronica Margaret. Thereby prolonging his sleeplessness, his mind strayed to the wedding of his younger sister at which he had been the bridegroom's attendant. Prompted by the vicar, phrase by phrase Frank managed to repeat the wedding vows without difficulty. In his head Jim began to rehearse them. Although he wondered if his vow to endow all his worldly goods might sound begrudging to the assembled congregation, they would not detect the slightest reluctance in his promise to worship Widge with his body.

Facetiously hoping the current crop of boy messengers employed by the General Post Office were as reliable as they were in his day, he planned to send a telegram to his mother in the morning, asking her to kindly forward his savings account book on receipt of the request.

Awakening from the deep sleep into which he ultimately sank, it was some considerable time before he realised it was Sunday, and yet longer before it dawned upon him it would not be possible to despatch the telegram to his mother until the next day; but the Sabbath was no obstacle to spreading word of his engagement among a number of his hut mates. Without mentioning to which of the engaged couple his comment referred, one of them jealously remarked "lucky sod", causing Jim to contemplate whether the chap considered himself to be far more than just a good friend.

Once in possession of the substantially funded savings account book, on the next Saturday Widge and Jim set out for Southampton to purchase an engagement ring. Except for the occasion when 606 returned from Normandy and were transported from the docks by train, Jim had never visited the place but Widge seemed to know her way around town. In the femininely named suburb of Shirley, where by then cultivated poppies of the same name were as hard to find as needles in haystacks, they scoured windows of jeweller's shops before taking the plunge and entering one.

Like so many commodities, during the war articles made of gold were restricted to a utility standard, that of nine carats being the highest permissible refinement for rings. Although Jim made no comment on the appearance of the trays of rings placed in front of Widge, in his estimation they looked rather shoddy. Not inferior in workmanship but in content. He was fully aware that not all that glitters was gold but, conversely, he did feel that that which was gold should glisten, and those on the counter did not. Whether the expression on Jim's face betrayed his thoughts or whether Widge's apparent lack of enthusiasm prevailed on the assistant's diligence, for one reason or another he retreated to a rear room from which he reappeared with three or four tiny boxes in each of which was a ring of obvious high quality. Those, they were informed, were 22 carat. It transpired that although they were just two carats short of being pure gold they were legitimately saleable as they were second hand. From the rings Widge made her choice and contentedly they made their exit.

Their stay in Southampton was not prolonged, or for no longer than was imposed upon them by the unpredictable, municipal transport. Arrangements had been made on previous days for a few friends on each side to join themselves at the Fountain Inn, a quiet public house in Hedge End – the village of fond memories for the two lovers. The gathering of friends during the evening was not for an organised party but for a celebratory drink. Or two. During the convivial session, with the publican enjoying the proceedings as much as the revellers (though for a more pecuniary reason), Widge and Jim slipped outside. Their kiss was only perfunctory. The real purpose was to symbolise their union with the ritual of slipping the ring on the third finger. As her finger was nervously threaded through the engagement ring his ardent desire was that each of them would find their life together as full of contentment as they did on that especially memorable autumn evening. Before they rejoined their friends in the Fountain, their passionate embrace promised they would.

Whereas each of them knew full well that the good fortune which had brought them together would run out and would quite dispassionately separate them, it did not lessen the impact when it was gleaned, little by little, that draft was in the offing for 606. One rumour, said to have been overheard by someone on fatigue duties in the orderly room, was of a rehabilitation course. Whatever remedy was envisaged for the perceived deficiency, among members of the flotilla the unverifiable report degenerated into lewd discussion of the therapy of which they considered themselves to be most in need.

When a few days later notice of draft appeared in daily orders the posting was to Deal. Had the location been anywhere but Deal, what rehabilitation involved would have been anyone's guess. But Deal ... that scotched all speculation. It would be nothing but weeks of square-bashing, as though need had arisen to teach the ex-crews how to turn left and right again.

Arrival at the barracks did disclose an alternative, of sorts. From a limited number of junior NCOs, applications would be considered for a physical training instructor's course. As the slightly less evil of the two options, Jim once again stuck out his chin. For the first two weeks it was agony, with aches persisting in muscles in places where none were known to exist. Jim was tempted to put in a chit for transfer to the sanctuary of the little cemetery within the barracks. At the end of each day the trainee

PTIs quite literally had to haul themselves up the stairs to their barrack rooms by heaving on the banisters; and to a mixture of applause, ridicule and the sarcastic offer of a helping hand from those who had not been so stupid as to volunteer for the course.

If by the end of the fifth week it could categorically be stated that Jim was not utterly demented, then it could be said he was quite enjoying the training. In fact it had largely been completed. It was never the intention the squad would become fully fledged physical training instructors. That required a far longer period of dedication and, if it was conceivable, made even greater punishing demands on those masochists who went the whole hog. The course in which Jim's intake was involved was merely to teach a properly balanced programme and sequence of exercises, in order to promote and maintain strength and fitness in the comparatively small units in which they were to serve, and which could not support a qualified PTI.

As a break from conducting other trainees in the group in exercises in the gymnasium, on a couple of days during the last week they were introduced to and took part in various field events in athletic sports. It was immensely enjoyable if unproductive of prospective Olympic champions. Neither javelins nor discus could be persuaded to glide through the air in the smooth manner which captures records or, on the two days, even make the qualifying distance. All attempts at putting the shot were shocking. In most cases the heavy ball was hurled not very much further than the contestant's feet; but the event which threatened the greatest disaster, to the largest number of those who merely watched, was throwing the hammer. As the more puny competitors found after managing to swing in a circle a seven kilogram ball attached to the end of a fine steel rod, contrarily the gravitational effect caused themselves to be the object which was swung round and round, in consequence of which all idea of the arc in which it was safe to release hold of the hammer was completely lost. Fortunately all of those watching the event were keen-eyed and swift of foot.

On a number of days in the final week another mental as well as physical distraction occurred, observing others perform in the splendidly equipped gym. While at one end of the building, and in execution of their colleagues commands, several other trainees obediently complied with loosening-up and subsequent gentle exercises, at the other end a team of expert instructors and gymnasts in their own right performed amazing feats in preparation for an inter-service gymnastics competition. Of the acts and physiques of those who performed on the various apparatus, there was nothing but admiration from those who marvelled in awe: of the dedication which the different disciplines required, there was nothing but abstention from such inclination.

As was more or less obligatory at the end of all courses, save perhaps on courses for chaplains in the armed forces, the one for deputy physical training instructors ended with a riotous spree; and riotous it was. Against the better advice of seniors who had supped in every ale-house within staggering distance of the surrounding relics of the Cinque Ports, the newcomers to the inns chose to toast good health in a public house where scuffles or more serious fisticuffs were a nightly occurrence. Jim thought it not improbable that, in years to come, cartographers would mark the site of 'The Cottage Of Content' with crossed swords.

13

FAR AWAY PLACES, WITH STRANGE SOUNDING NAMES

In distance apart
Though not in heart,
Widge's draft came sooner.

To Bayeux, Breda
And Plon went she.
Jim's first stop was Poona.

As the first step in the resumption of training Jim was again posted to Westcliffe-On-Sea.

Widge's notification of draft overseas, in fact to Normandy, came soon after. On her embarkation leave she spent part of the 14 days in Westcliffe but the days passed like lightning. Before she departed for France and to coincide with the second weekend of her leave, Jim managed to obtain a 36 hour pass, from after duty on Saturday morning until midnight on Sunday.

Widge had decided to spend what remained of the fortnight at the home of a friend of the family who lived at Waddon, in Surrey, close to Croydon Airport – in effect within only a few minutes walk. Her aunt (as Widge referred to the lady of the house) along with all the other nearby residents had been canvassed on a number of occasions by the Ministry of Defence, imploring all who had room in their homes to take in lodgers, which boarders were from various regions of the country who were employed on a huge construction project at the aerodrome. Despite the fact Aunt had a teenage daughter and a chronically sick husband to care for, she agreed to take in two of the workmen. In order to additionally accommodate Widge, for the duration of her stay a single bed was placed in the lounge.

At Westcliffe, as elsewhere, the travel restrictions which had been imposed before the invasion of France had been lifted and on Jim's weekend leave he was in London by mid-afternoon. Travelling on the underground network he quickly reached

Victoria Station, from where the journey to Waddon took only a little more than half an hour. Widge was at the station to meet him. Forgoing a lengthy kiss she revealed some good news. One of the two lodgers had returned to his home for the weekend and, in keeping with Aunt's extremely kind nature, she made it known Jim was welcome to the vacant bed if he did not mind sharing the room with the remaining boarder. Jim had no hesitation in accepting the offer. He would have been more than delighted to share a room with Satan in order to spend a further evening with his fiancée.

High tea was provided and was served in the dining-room which looked out onto the back garden. Tapping on the French window before departing, the lodger with whom Jim would be sharing the spare room made it known he would not be joining them for tea, nor returning until late evening. It was thought he had met up with a young lady since taking up residence at Aunt's house, though there had never actually been any mention of her. Though at first Aunt declined the offer of Widge and Jim to clear the table and do the washing–up, believing they would prefer to be on their own, she relented when it was pointed out they would be on their own while doing it. There were no breakages nor did the chore take long. When finished, Widge and Jim joined Aunt and her daughter in the lounge. Aunt's husband, strangely never alluded to as Uncle, retired to his room, perhaps to avoid puffs of irritating smoke from cigarettes resorted to by the others.

Board games were introduced and played by the quartet and conversation was non-stop. All were surprised to hear the door key turn in the lock and the footsteps of the lodger climb the stairs. None had realised the hour was so late. If not with a suggestive stretch, by a ladylike yawn Aunt demonstrated it was past her bedtime. She also urged her daughter not to burn the midnight oil. Fortunately she was an obedient daughter: the dwelling became hushed.

Not to tarnish the golden silence and except for whispers of urgent encouragement or of satisfied gratitude, what else Widge and Jim wished to convey they did by contact. Hands alone could not adequately cope with their extravagant passion. Clothing impeded it; so much of it was removed. Nestled against his bare chest her undraped breasts pounded. The contact was only interrupted to kiss first one then the other. Recklessly, greater satisfaction was craved: fretfully it had to be discouraged. Her guiding hand was gently restrained before penetration. He had not arrived at the house provided with contraceptives in anticipation of sexual intercourse nor, wanting in knowledge, had he any understanding of safe periods.

Although still acutely aware of the previous occasion when emotions were likewise highly aroused, and when on that day it had been thought far better to abstain, Jim wavered on how best to explain his attitude to Widge. His reason had not shifted or weakened one iota. However, conscious of the fact that Widge's deceased brother had fathered a child who would never know his parent, it was unthinkable to labour his opinion. It smacked of pontifical censure.

Not altogether beside the point, Jim was also perfectly aware that Aunt's bedroom adjoined the lounge.

Pathetically, Jim tried to portray the unenviable position in which she'd be placed if anything should happen to himself: the difficulties she would encounter with an extra mouth to feed: an uphill struggle for years, for the sake of a few brief moments of passion. In the little light which stole into the unlit room from the illuminated staircase he believed he detected her under-standing nod.

Goodnight kisses were far greater than the hours of sleep that night.

In an unfamiliar bed, in a room shared with a loud snoring stranger, their joint room fronting the busy thoroughfare of Purley Way and adjoining the room in which slept the chronic-ally asthmatic husband of Aunt, sleep was at a premium. In contrast, Jim's reservation concerning girls with three Christian names was further discounted. Randily.

On Sunday morning, after Widge had voluntarily prepared breakfast for the household, she took Jim to meet her father, from whom it was abundantly clear she had inherited her looks. The meeting was at his place of work, in Croydon. Unfortunately a pressing business matter rather curtailed the time they were able to spend in his company, but he did manage to make time to accompany them to a nearby public house for a quick drink. After making their way back to Aunt's house for lunch, followed by a leisurely stroll around the local park to exercise the family dog, what was left of their time together was spent in the comfort of the lounge. The room was tactfully avoided by those who did not venture out of doors. With no appetite for tea, the pair remained in the arms of each other until mid evening, when at Waddon Station they parted. When the figure of Widge standing on the platform was snatched from view as the train rounded a bend in the line, the morbid feeling it gave was as though his heart had been ripped out.

Throughout the depressing journey back to Westcliffe the torment was of how long it would be before they were together again, hopefully for ever more. Happily it was far sooner than could have been expected. On the very next day, standing orders specified that, among several other flotillas, 606 was to be disbanded and reformed as a battalion. As an alternative and presumably because insufficient numbers were coming forward as volunteers, for those wishing to resume commando training there would be seven days leave. If the inducement was viewed as bribery by an incorruptible few, Jim was prepared to add to his criminal past with corruption and made a bee-line for the orderly room. Unoccupied and locked as he found it, he was determined not to budge until someone arrived to unlock the premises and record his name on the list, preferably at the head of it in case only a limited number were required. His determination was not put to the test for long, but patience, hardly endurable, was still required by virtue of the fact there was no trace of a list of names, suggesting closure of the scheme. It was not the case. A list was not in existence because he was the first to make an application. The notice had only been placed on the board by the orderly clerk on his way elsewhere a few minutes previously.

For the next couple of days, though it seemed much longer, Jim all but slept under the daily orders notice board. Immediate departure on leave would not have been soon enough. Indisputably it would be meaningless once Widge was moved abroad. During the day he swore and fumed at the delay: at night he prayed leave would commence before she did depart. Which entreaty had the desired effect was imponderable, even to he who frequently pondered. As the leave was concessionary rather than an entitlement it did not entail a free rail warrant, but the fare to the holding unit in Bristol, where the apple of his eye was, of all places, billeted in a disused Victorian orphanage, was eagerly surrendered at the booking office when he eventually arrived at Paddington Station. Whether and where he would find somewhere in Templemeads at which to stay had not entered his flustered mind. Had it done so it would have received curt treatment. With Widge incarcerated in a dockside institution awaiting deportation, what cause had he to shrink from the thought of the liberty afforded and the luxury to be enjoyed on a bench at the railway station. Awaiting the bloody whistle from the bloody guard for the bloody train to start, more than a little uneasy in mind Jim gave the impression he was completely unhinged.

By the time the train arrived in Bristol, when either the anxiety or the delirium had subsided, he had conceded to his inner-self that Mullens Orphanage might be miles from any railway station. Harbouring second thoughts, if it was the case then after each night's farewell kiss and by the time he got to his nightly habitat he might well find all of the benches occupied. Just in case, and with plenty of time before the 'orphans' were freed for the evening, he decided to make a few tentative enquires about more enticing accommodation. Shamefaced, he jumped at the very first recommendation regardless of the fact he had no idea whether the abode would turn out to be further from Mullens than even the most distant railway station.

The room at the YMCA was simple but adequate and in the event quite close to the orphanage. The room charge, which was inclusive of breakfast, was pleasingly inexpensive. After the second shave of the day to round up any unwelcome whiskers which may have escaped the morning scrape with the razor, and after a tingling splash equivalent to a deluge of provocative after-shave lotion, he went to comfort the plight of one of the inmates at Mullens.

Except for the occasion when posted to North Wales from Dalditch it was the first time he had been to Bristol, and on the journey he had made all that he had seen of it was from the railway carriage. After establishing the location of the orphanage he decided upon a short stroll around the city.

Due to the loss of the shipment of merchandise since the middle of the previous century when Liverpool began to operate as a major port, and because of the extremely heavy bombing

Bristol had sustained in the earlier years of the war, the area around the docks was a scene of dereliction far removed from the circumstances which gave rise to the saying that 'All was shipshape and Bristol fashion'. That, no doubt, was from the days when voyages were to every corner of the earth, which resulted in the importation of such commodities as tobacco, cacao beans and wine, in which commodities Wills, Frys and Harveys still traded in the manufacture of cigarettes, chocolate and sherry. He learned that as relatively recent as the middle of the 19th century ship building continued in the docks, from one of which Isambard Kingdom Brunel's steamship, *Great Britain*, was launched. In its day it was said to be the largest iron ship afloat.

Jim came across and ventured into the city's cathedral. Imposing though it was to the eye, brought up as a Wesleyan he felt much more affinity with a nonconformist chapel built by John Wesley, which Jim subsequently discovered. Erected in 1739, the plaque proclaimed it to be the oldest Methodist Chapel in the world.

By the time Jim retraced his steps to the orphanage he felt he had got to know Bristol rather well in such a short space of time.

In keeping with widely held (though in some instances rather mistaken) views about orphanages, Mullens was decidedly spartan. The long, bare entrance to the building gave way to a dismal reception area, along three sides of which were a number of rickety-looking, wooden benches. These were dominated by a small platform which was mounted by two or three steps just inside a door, on the fourth side, which led to the interior of the premises. The platform was occupied by one small foldaway table and one folding chair, on which was seated one unbending ATS sergeant adorned with the red-topped cap of the military police. In attitude as well as in appearance she had the appeal one might expect to find in the daughter of Madame Defarge.

Mademoiselle Defarge (obvious as it was that marriage to her was unthinkable) demanded from Jim the cause of his intrusion, and thereby her visible annoyance. Careful to avoid inflaming the unhappy lot of a member of the army's constabulary by use of Christian names, he only gave Widge's surname. He thought the eyes of his inquisitor narrowed somewhat suspiciously as they led his attention to a corner of the room to his rear.

Already on his feet, an American soldier (previously unnoticed when Jim first entered the reception area) took steps towards Jim. Upon assurance he had correctly heard the name given to the sergeant on duty, the American serviceman let it be known that was the name of the dame with whom he had a date that evening.

Jim had read from time to time of the absurd Christian names sometimes given to their offspring by some American parents. He wondered whether the person in front of himself had been christened Lightning and who, bound as he was by dogma never to strike twice in the same place, had descended upon Bristol, far removed from the scene of his previous liaison with Eileen.

The speculation was abruptly ended by the entrance of an ATS girl. To the trio who made up her audience she theatrically and loudly proclaimed her name, rather like the deliberately, exaggerated first appearance on stage of the fairy godmother in pantomime. It seemed odd she did not appear to know that her date was with an American soldier. Concluding the date must have been a blind one, with a jerk of his head to the GI Jim indicated the entrant must be his dame. Without need to introduce herself, Widge appeared soon after.

They spent the precious evening just sauntering around the city. In Jim's freakish mind the leisurely pace seemed to produce the feeling that time passed by more slowly and gave the opportunity for kisses while in motion. On weekday evenings it was all that they did, but it was all they wished – to be in each other's company. At the weekend they went further afield, to the Avon Gorge, where on the Clifton Suspension Bridge they scratched their initials, as was apparent many thousands had.

On the penultimate day of his leave Widge once more seemed to be preoccupied. It was most unusual for them to have such relatively long periods of silence. It prompted Jim to light-heartedly offer the customary penny for her thoughts but she had no desire to share them. He wondered if he had given offence with his banter when they first met that evening. He recalled it had not met with her usual response of a gentle prod to his ribs, and a smile which signified the remarks had not caused umbrage. When Widge ultimately broke the silence it was very difficult to contend with her frame of mind. She spoke of the feeling she had: that she would never be happy. Comforting words were hindered by the fact she did not wish to disclose her reasoning nor elaborate in any manner.

Joy was placed on hold. When they parted company on that evening Jim did not go back to the YMCA straight away. Although he doubted very much that he would quickly fall asleep, he had no wish to attempt to do so. Before they met on the next evening, which would definitely be the last occasion for some considerable while, he felt that he must find a solution to Widge's pessimistic outlook. Though he did not intend to resort to the cliché that love would find a way, with different words he hoped to convince her that by every means he could devise he would manage to provide happiness and security for her and for their contemplated children. He would describe the unmistakable pleasure evident on the face of both of his devoted parents as the result of the abundance of joy which they conferred. If sacrifice was entailed, as it must have been, it would not have been suffered, but would have enhanced the parental pleasure. He would strive with might and main to follow their example. He felt sure he would allay her dread.

Was there anywhere he wondered when he did finally climb into bed that had the same therapeutic air, such as to intoxicate without stupefying, as was encountered in the City of Bristol.

The premonition which he had had that sleep would not come swiftly that night was not at all far fetched. Twisting and turning as he put together his words for the next evening, his bed, like himself, becoming more and more disordered as the chimes of a clock in the vicinity brought nearer the recitation of his contrived conviction, little did he know that the next words to pass between them would be more than two years later.

After waiting outside the orphanage for what seemed to be ages, on what should have been the last meeting with Widge before his leave expired and he returned to Westcliffe, he went inside to the reception area. A different, more amiable red-capped ATS girl was seated in the chair. At courteous length she explained that a delayed notification of draft had only been received at Mullens late on the afternoon of the previous day. Somewhere along the intricate lines of communication the message had been misdirected. Personnel included in the overseas posting were ordered to be ready with kit for departure on the following afternoon. Those like Widge who were not present when the order reached the orphanage were likewise instructed upon their return. Very kindly offering to obtain the army postal address of the contingent, ensuring the earliest delivery of letters, she returned with the coded details of those who had gone to join BLA – the code used for British Liberation Army.

Though for a very different reason, he felt just as he had when Eileen and himself parted company. The inebriating effect of the air less than 24 hours earlier had completely dissipated, leaving him languishing in the dumps. Remarking upon this anticlimax to the military policewoman, with a knowing smile she pointed out that many newcomers to the City of Bristol experienced similar hangovers when the wind blew from the direction where Harveys produced their celebrated Bristol Cream Sherry.

His original intention was to make for the YMCA, collect his belongings and then catch a bus to the railway station where he would take the first train to Paddington. Realising it would be quite late when he reached London, possibly too late to enable him to get another train to Westcliffe, he abandoned the idea. Before another one entered his mind and while waiting to cross a busy road, a bus displaying the destination of Clifton also came to a halt. He hopped on it. If other matters had not favoured him on that day at least the weather was friendly. As though drawn to it at the end of a rope, he stood on the suspension bridge peering down at the silvery thread of the River Avon hundreds of feet below. It really was spectacular. The white cliffs of the gorge through which the river flowed were practically perpendicular. The bridge, a marvel of engineering at the time when it was constructed to span the River Avon, was another of Brunel's remarkable achievements.

Jim had no difficulty in finding where their initials had been scratched. With his finger he traced the grooves they had made. It made Widge seem much closer, which led him to wonder where she might be at that precise moment. Whether she had arrived at her destination and when he would next receive a letter from her. He winced at the depressing thought of how old they each might be before the war was finally at an end. Whereas in Europe, on the eastern front as well as in the west, matters seemed to be going very well, everyone equally knew that when Germany was defeated the battle in the Far East would be a bitter and drawn out affair.

He reflected upon the thought that the Sino-Japanese war was in its 14th year, yet there was no indication whatsoever of any drain on the resources or the will power of the Japanese. It was true that the tide had turned in the Pacific theatre of war, but the advances which had been made and the islands which had been recaptured had been at horrific cost to both victors and vanquished. As terrible as casualties had been, they were suffered in territories beyond the shores of the 'rising sun'. In comparison and horrendous though the death toll had been, it was widely acknowledged that the invasion and ultimate conquest of the islands of Japan would entail even greater bloodshed. The surmise was that the Japanese would never capitulate and the battle would inevitably be to the death. The last evening in Bristol was not Jim's happiest and on the following morning he took leave of the city with far more on his mind than when he arrived.

Within 72 hours of returning to Westcliffe he and others who had opted to recommence commando training were on their way to North Wales for the initial part of the course. Llanegryn, the only camp in the previous circuit which was still in existence, was where they were put through their paces. Since last they were there on the seamanship course it had undergone fundamental modification, and not by any stretch of the imagination for the better.

It was no exaggeration to state that everything that gave even the smallest degree of comfort had been removed, the object of which was to make life as demanding as possible. If memories of the trainees served them correctly, not many of the previous instructors were still in place. Significantly, they had been replaced by officers and NCO's who had been in action with commando units in various theatres of war and who were, therefore, better suited to pile on the agony during the course, and measure its effect on each intake of marines.

On occasions when night exercises did not eliminate the possibility of sleep, it was made more difficult to attain in the first place and less restful once achieved by virtue of the fact mattresses were no longer provided, except of course to camp staff. During a lecture on the art of survival which was of the first order, and with a banal pun which was of the third, it was jeered that the result of nightly repose on the bare wire springs of the bunks would make a lasting impression on 'everybody'.

Within the perimeter of the base, assault courses tensed every nerve and strained each muscle. Various obstacles had to be tunnelled beneath, scrambled through, or scaled, sometimes with the aid of nothing more substantial than a valiantly hunched back of another trainee. Too frequently there was a crop of accidents, in one of which a long-standing friend of Jim came to grief and was invalided out of the corps. Decidedly more welcome was the revelation that the crew of four presumed drowned on the crossing to Normandy on the eve of D Day were alive, albeit as prisoners.

Well beyond the perimeter of the camp, in the wide open spaces of Merionethshire, for training purposes full advantage was taken of the many features which nature provided. Rivers abounded, the muddy beds of which became very familiar with hobnailed boots while the surfaces swirled around the area of heavily burdened shoulders. Towering hills were alive with the sound of gunfire and at Llanberis Mountaineering School, situated almost at the foot of Snowdon Mountain Railway, the rudiments of rock climbing were taught. In the most recently discovered hostile terrain, mickey-taking instructors devised strenuous manoeuvres.

One particular night exercise was in the vicinity of Corris, in a straight line about ten miles from Llanegryn. In foul weather and in cumbersome battle attire the distance was swiftly accomplished with a speed march – alternate and equal periods of marching and running.

Ensuring for themselves a modicum of protection from the weather, half of those taking part in the exercise with the enviable job of defenders did so in what gave the impression of a disused slate quarry. The task for the remainder was to drive the others out and prepare the site for demolition. In utter darkness and completely unfamiliar surroundings a reconnaissance patrol was dispatched to weigh up the situation, hopefully unobserved, to withdraw and report back.

As a result of the preliminary probe, a weakness in the defence thrown up around the quarry was uncovered. A plan was swiftly but carefully devised and put into effect. The only deviation from reality was use of blank rounds rather than live ammunition, requiring the officers appointed as referees the speculative task of deciding which combatants were casualties, with no further part to play in the mock battle.

While those defending and entrenched just inside the entrance to the quarry's stores area were engaged by a large number of the attacking force, unnoticed a small group of the latter withdrew. Clutching the unfastened tail of the jump suit of the person in front to ensure contact was not lost in the darkness, in single file the party clambered over rocks and through scrub until reaching a summit somewhere between Corris and Abergynolwyn, from where to make the steeper and more perilous descent to the quarry on the blind side of the defenders.

With the exception of one marine who slightly twisted his ankle when he slid and dislodged a fragment of rock when beginning the descent, only one other accident occurred but regrettably the injury sustained was more serious. As the demolition party progressed down the mountain side, what must have amounted to a sizeable chunk of scree loosened by the feet of those above forcibly struck the head of someone further down. For reasons which could only be described as pointless bravado, during training steel helmets were scorned. Heads were only covered by cap comforters, which kept the skull warm but provided nothing in the manner of protection against blows. The impact resulted in a serious gash and in profuse bleeding. In the drenched hills in the vicinity of Corris, a short truce prevailed.

The scree was not the only thing that hurtled down from above on that night. During the enforced lull in the exercise the adjudicators went into a huddle. On the battle front friend and foe fraternised and took shelter within the idle premises.

As it turned out, during attention to the more seriously injured individual a truck arrived with the breakfast rations. If the setting in which to tuck into them was not exactly palatial, the lighting was certainly eye-catching. From some niche in the vast quarry dozens of candles had been acquired and gave the occasion the appearance of a medieval banquet within the decaying walls of a castle. To those who ate, the sight of so many candles also gave an uneasy feeling the quarry may not quite have reached the category of defunct.

During the course of heartily demolishing the rations, a thunderous crash, quickly followed by a series of lesser thuds a little distance from the entrance to the quarry, caused a scramble to see what had created the din. Scattered around was the wreckage of what had been a large trolley, wrenched from the body of which each axle complete with its pair of wheels was yards from the main heap of debris. While stood gaping at the heap, a warning shout from an individual who had ventured further outside sent everyone scampering back inside for safety. A second trolley racing down the hillside suddenly zoomed off the rails and came crashing down uncomfortably close to where some in the group had been idly standing. As it hit the ground it too disintegrated. Sorely intimidated by an event which could so easily have maimed for life or killed any person struck by the heavily wheeled axles, after a respectful, cautionary interval just in case other trolleys were about to follow, a party climbed and searched the area around the hill down which the trucks had careered.

It was to no avail. There was no clue as to what had set the two trolleys in motion. It was perfectly obvious from attachments to other trucks, deep inside a cavern towards the top of the hill, that they were meant to be lowered down the hillside under strict control, by means of a cable; but of people their was neither sight nor sound. That of which their was sight in plenty, in other trucks, was bluish-coloured, layered rock, from which it was assumed slate could be split. The debatable status of the quarry again raised its head. With a variety of misgivings on their weary minds the trainees retraced their steps of the previous evening, back to Llanegryn. One of those feelings was to surface a few weeks later, when they were stationed at Achnacarry.

*****

Among more polite persons Achnacarry would be spoken of as remote. Abandoned rather than nestling among endless mountains, it was a place of which even few Scotsmen have heard. Except for Achnacarry House there was nothing. The only road that 'ran past' it did so purely to get somewhere else, and none of the railway companies had been so reckless as to branch in its direction.

The nearest station was at Spean Bridge, some eight miles distant. As at Woodbury Road, Jim distinctly recalled, the platform alongside which the train halted was shunned. The reluctance to permit carriage doors to be opened on the convenient side was hardly because it would have been life-threatening to crowds of passengers waiting to board. There was not a soul about except for a soulless sergeant, to harry the trainees. At Spean Bridge there was no lorry to transport kit and personal belongings. On the shoulders of the newcomers it had to be humped along, though there was consolation in the fact that the NCO sent to welcome them to Achnacarry also had to leg it.

In this far-flung outpost of Great Britain (and whoever flung it made it perfectly obvious they did not wish its return) there was hardly any sign of habitation. Throughout the march to camp they only passed one abode, the lock-keepers isolated cottage at Gairlochy, but there was no sign of the virtual recluse. As the newcomers passed along the western bank of Loch Lochy, the middle of the three major lochs which make up the 60 miles of the Caledonian Canal, there was sight of a small column of people hurriedly making their way north-easterly, in the direction of Loch Ness, possibly in anticipation of catching a glimpse of its renowned monster; but as Nessie had continually done since its first reported sighting in the early years of the seventh century, the monster would probably dodge this column, too.

Ultimately, on the none too bonny-looking banks of Loch Arkaig, the trainees reached camp, at the far from inviting entrance to which were rows of graves. The tombstones did not disclose the names of those in memory of whom they were erected, instead of which they were engraved with the cause of the various fatalities. In one instance, as the result of negligence when priming a hand-grenade. In another case, a matter of failing to ensure that the safety-catch of a loaded rifle was properly applied; yet another, a tragedy in consequence of stupid horseplay with fighting knives. More in keeping with an excess of zeal, one incident occurred during a night exercise when, beneath the barrage of supporting fire, a patrol advanced too far too rapidly.

Actually none of the graves were authentic; nor each of the new arrivals fervently hoped would any of their actions give rise to epitaphs which were.

Apart from the cheerful inscriptions on the tombstones which lined the entrance to what would constitute home for the next eight weeks, there was not a great deal more to gladden the cosmopolitan family, roughly half of whom were from every conceivable unit in the British Army, not to mention some from outside the UK, and half from the Royal Marines. The hut in which the newly arrived were quartered had a roof and beds but very little else. Damp patches on the upper part of the wall betrayed the fact that the waterproof, roofing felt did not live up to its repute. More reliable was the prior intuition felt by trainees that they would not be pampered with the luxury of mattresses – that is, not for the purpose of sleep.

On the other hand, periods were sprawled on them on the seldom tranquil surface of Loch Arkaig. Filled with kapok, water-proofed, and large enough for only one person, the purpose of the floats was to enable silent passage over enemy stretches of water. Other than the use of a hand as a paddle on each side of the mattress, by laying motionless and as flat as possible stability and progress were achievable; but, disproving the pithy saying, practice did not make perfect. Even the slightest attempt to shift from the prone, position to one a little less aquatic invariably ended in capsize. Almost as much time was spent floundering in the water alongside or under the device as on it.

Whereas derisory comment was continually aimed at these painless mishaps, incompetence in the surrounding mountains was far from a laughing matter. Although the incidents were considerably less in number, from time to time there were candidates for whichever civilian hospital could cope with the nature of the injury. Where descent by the trainees was unintended, as when grasp or footing on rocks slipped, bodies arrived with a sickening thump and, if still conscious, an endless stream of profane oaths. While the act of abseiling from the battlements of Achnacarry house was more deliberate and resulted in fewer broken bones, it gave Jim cause to fear that Virginia Margaret together with the intended three other children might have to be adopted.

What did bring about his admittance to hospital was entirely ham-fisted.

Though it could not have been considered either the most likely or quickest way to hasten the end of the war, nevertheless training did involve a few sessions devoted to milling. Rather like reincarnation, Jim supposed, needing to be experienced in order to give accurate account of what is entailed, milling similarly defies concise explanation, or instant appreciation of what is involved. It could vaguely be compared with the noble art of self-defence, but for the fact that self-preservation was artlessly sacrificed in order to pummel opponents into unconsciousness by any means possible. Ignoble or not.

Marginally more refined than gutter level fisticuffs, there was begrudging condescension to the use of boxing gloves during the course of each contest, though the quality of the padding in the ones supplied failed miserably to absorb any impact whatsoever. The short-coming was immediately made clear to Jim as his right fist solidly met the lowered head of his opponent during what seemed to be a never ending bout. As Jim vainly struggled to rip off the glove of the injured hand with the other one, his ruthless adversary took full advantage of the golden opportunity. He unleashed a succession of punches with each fist, undoubtedly leading to a shift of position within the grave of the more sportsmanlike Marquis of Queensbury, whose worthy rules, for boxing, the exponents of milling looked upon as excessively namby-pamby, and inclined to spoil the fun to be enjoyed in milling. It was not a sentiment which had Jim's whole-hearted support.

In the belief he had fractured the base of his thumb he was dispatched to what was referred to as Onich Hospital, presumably so called to save the tongue-twisting pronunciation of Ballachulish Episcopi, the actual site of the building, whereas the village of Onich was four or five miles away. It was obvious that the premises had not been built as a hospital but as a very large house, perhaps in earlier times the residence of bishops, or possibly a small hotel; but whatever had been its original roll it had been requisitioned and converted into a makeshift convalescent hospital. Only the injured or the wounded were nursed within, for which patients a dozen or so beds were available. Cases of illness were treated elsewhere.

X-rays conclusively dispelled the assumption made at Achnacarry but as a precaution against aggravating the injury the thumb was strapped in adhesive plaster, his arm placed in a sling and he was detained. Being one of the walking casualties among the inmates he was allocated a few light duties, of which the daily collection of milk for patients and staff, brought across Loch

Leven on the ferry from South Ballachulish, was most rewarding.

Stood at the slipway awaiting the arrival of the tiny ferry, the views from the loch were really spectacular in each direction. Across placid Loch Linnie, and surrounding Glen Tarbert, several mountains rose to almost 3,000 feet. The map on display in the hospital revealed that the view in the other direction, across Loch Leven, was of the village of Glencoe, the pass of Glen Coe and the Pap Of Glen Coe. Regardless of whether the day was bright or overcast the scenery and solitude promoted total peace of mind. In Glencoe it had not always been so peaceful.

Memory of history lessons were of the perfidious massacre which took place there. Recollection by Jim was of the slaughter of dozens of the Macdonald clan, at the hands of soldiers led by Robert Campbell of Glen Lyon in Tayside. The deed was committed due to the failure of Mac Ian of Glencoe (the revered patriarch of the Macdonald clan), to give up the Jacobite cause and take the oath of allegiance to William III by the end of 1692. In consequence and despite the hospitality provided by the Macdonalds on whom the soldiers had been billeted for nearly a fortnight, in February of the following year the troops carried out the atrocious act.

With the Pap Of Glencoe Jim was less familiar. As it turned out it was not surprising. In conversation with one of the Scottish nurses he learned that pap was the word used by highlanders when alluding to the nipple of a women's breast. In the instance of the geographical term, reference was to the conical shape of the summit of a hill which stood at the entrance to the glen. In the nearby village, the bonny boozer dubbed The Pap allegedly displayed the slogan 'have a wee tipple at the nipple'

Returning from the awesome scenery with the milk one morning toward the end of his stay in hospital, Jim was instructed to report to the small room which was used as a chapel. No indication was given as to why his presence was required or by whom, nor had he the slightest concern. As usual he had retraced his steps after the early morning date with the ferry in a contented frame of mind.

The officer awaiting his arrival motioned to Jim to seat himself at the other side of the desk. From a pregnant looking brief-case the captain produced a thick bundle of papers. Time and again he morosely sifted through them with increasing impatience. Obviously unable to find the particular notes he required, Jim was on the verge of enquiring whether he could assist in any manner with the hand that was not immobilised when, with a relieved sigh and a triumphant flourish, a small sheaf of papers was tossed on to the desk. Throughout the search not a word had been spoken; nor was the silence broken as the officer struggled to cram the larger wad of documents back into the case. Once it was accomplished, and removing Jim's growing belief the meeting had been arranged for games of charades, the visitor to the hospital finally spoke. His voice was solemn.

He had been appointed to investigate a complaint which had been lodged regarding 'wilful damage caused at ......'(Jim did not catch the actual name of the place but had little doubt that he referred to the spot near to Corris, in North Wales) 'on such and such a date' ... the date confirmed his belief. The brief went on to stipulate the cost of merchandise seized when stores were broken into, and of replacing two wagons wrecked by vandalism, plus an estimated amount for the loss of metamorphic rock in the trolleys. He concluded by stating he had obtained written statements from others who had taken part in the exercise on that night and needed one from CH/X113124, but on account of his incapacity he would take down the words under which Jim's signature could then be appended. When it was completed the officer said the statement corroborated those made by the others he had interviewed, returned Jim's cack-handed salute and departed.

Discharged from Onich Hospital a couple of days later and arriving at Achnaccary as the Jeep was preparing to leave for Beinne Bhan with the tea bucket, he climbed aboard to rejoin his squad at the base of the mountain. To the degree required, the bucket shone in near blinding fashion, but its lustre was cosmetic. Overnight its appearance was decidedly grubby.

More to enable mud-splattered and soaking-wet clothing to dry for the next day rather than to provide the luxury of warmth at night, even in the bleak mountainside of Lochaber in the depth of winter, each evening, after dismissal from training and from a bunker at the rear of the quartermaster's store, coal was collected in the bucket by the hut orderly for the day. When duly emptied, in the morning it had to be thoroughly sanitised and repeatedly scoured until rendered fit for the day's tea. If the slightest fault in cleanliness could be found (or imagined) by instructors when the bucket arrived at the training area during the course of the morning, it was declared contaminated and the contents were emptied. As the deprivation of mattresses jeopardised comfort in bed, so the discarded refreshment acted as a gentle reminder not to rely too much on the regularity of supply.

*****

Perhaps because training was almost complete, during the last week the squad were made useful in a most unexpected event. Part of a film given the title of *The Green Beret* was shot in camp. Though none of the troops knew whether the film was being produced as a documentary record by one of the governmental film agencies, or by a commercial company for general release, it was common knowledge that John Mills was one of the actors in the cast. Whatever else may have been required of him in his role of a commando, the only episode in which Jim's detachment appeared with the actor was on the detested speed march to and from Spean Bridge, an overall distance of about 15 miles. Dressed in fighting order weighing nearly two stones and, for effect, encumbered with an assortment of the heaviest weapons available, towards the end of the slog those taking part appeared extremely sweaty and not a trifle dishevelled. Two or three hundred yards short of the camp entrance, at which the sequence ended, the actor vacated the canvas chair alongside the camera crew and with the aid of water splashed on his face to give the impression of perspiration, and untidily arrayed in fighting order, he joined the ranks for the final dash.

None in the squad thought any the less of the actor; but the fit of spleen directed towards the moron who appeared to think there was not sufficient water to splash on their faces, and in consequence sent them 15 miles to work up a sweat, was a little less generous. In good nature, one fatigued trainee suggested that perhaps the actor was paid less for his performance than themselves for their contribution.

There was no passing out parade, as such, but the award of the green beret was a proud occasion. The more or less obligatory drinking session which boisterously marks the end of every course was a little more dignified and without talk of tipping the course instructor into Loch Arkaig. For the first time since arrival at Spean Bridge transport was provided, to take the commandos to the station on the following morning. By evening they were in the holding unit at Wrexham, there to await draft overseas. It was not long delayed. They were to join the 3rd Commando Brigade in the Far East, at Poona. In point of fact the precise location of the base to which the brigade had returned after the most recent mission in Burma was at Khadakvasala, some fifteen miles from the town of Poona.

Before the reinforcements departed on the long voyage to India they were granted 14 days embarkation leave.

14

PREPARED TO FACE
THE MUSIC

Though word there was of dangers ahead
The words they sang gave pleasure instead.

They went their ways with the days refrain
But knew not if they'd meet again.

Though they and the tunes have long since gone
The memr'y of both still linger on.

While it would be sheer nonsense to state Jim was glad when his two weeks leave expired, nevertheless he was spared everyone's opening question to welcome him home – "When are you due to go back?"

In another respect, it had not escaped his notice how everyone to whom he disclosed news of his approaching draft to the Far East shook their heads or wrinkled their brow, as though to emphasise that the dangers in that theatre of war were insurmountable.

Undeniably, among themselves who would make up the draft, all manner of grotesque and grossly exaggerated threats to their well-being were bandied about; but always in obvious jest. Mickey-taking impersonations of retired colonels, recalling their far-off exploits when they were big-game hunting in 'Poon...ah', comically inferred those to be posted there would be little more than fodder for the tigers and other animals partial to raw meat: but among the civilian population the attitude of mind was decidedly more sinister. Their comments were of the tenacity of Japanese soldiers. Prevalence of disease and inescapable, venomous reptiles of the jungle were all adduced. The conjecture gave the impression of a despondent punter assessing form and weighing the odds at a race meeting.

Believing his former workmates would be more light-hearted, he spent a whole day at the Ministry of Information, better known among boy messengers appointed to work there as the Ministry of Constipation on account of the length of time it took to pass anything. Within this fiefdom, throughout the entire day and from around the world reports of all imaginable occurrences flooded in, in almost every conceivable language. Some accounts were phoned in. Dozens and dozens of telephone booths stood in the vast area referred to as the pressroom. All of the national and many of the less well known newspapers had a line on which calls were received and, after ultimate clearance, relayed to editors. Handed in at the press counter, messengers conveyed the reports not requiring translation to the censors department; the others to the particular room which housed interpreters able to translate in that particular tongue, and, on completion, on to the censors.

It was incredible in how many languages most of the interpreters were proficient. Achievement in only four or five languages was thought quite unremarkable. One individual, a Finnish gentleman, seemed to have the ability to translate almost any European language. If all other interpreters in his room were busy, with an additional pile of reports awaiting their attention, messengers felt confident they could place any of the dispatches in the tray of the Finn.

Expecting to be recognised only by other messengers with whom he had worked at the ministry from time to time, Jim was very surprised at the number of interpreters and censors who paused for a few words with him. In light-hearted conversation with one of the latter and knowing disclosure of his sins were beyond rebuke, Jim humorously confessed that messengers were apt to read the reports they took to and fro in the building and how, not infrequently, they hardly recognised what remained of the article they had earlier handed in. Expressing no surprise at the revelation but taking up Jim's earlier disclosure that he was on leave prior to embarking for India, the censor mentioned he was born and bred there. Giving no indication whether he too was joking, he remarked that Poona was in an area prone to earthquakes. He added that after experiencing one Jim might similarly have some difficulty in recognising what was formerly before his eyes. On his journey back home Jim wondered what odds Seismic Eruption would enjoy among the despondent punters.

Wrexham did not delay the departure of the reinforcements for very long. On returning from leave the time was spent in queues at the quartermaster's stores awaiting issue of tropical kit, and at the sick-bay awaiting injections with what mostly felt like somewhat blunt needles.

Tailoring of tropical attire seemed better skilled than all previously issued uniforms. In places, it fitted. Without suggesting the range of items were in the made to measure category, assorted shapes and sizes of those in the overseas contingent did not appear too swallowed up within the garments nor, around the waist, exceptionally hideous squeezed into them. A far greater cause for derision was with regard to bared knees which just about protruded from or appeared substantially abandoned by the khaki shorts hoisted above them. Essential though they are to the performance of the lower limbs, even the most shapely pair of legs of the pick of the most gorgeous models are not enhanced by knee-caps. As he studied the exhibited patellae of the males surrounding him, knobbly, many of them pimpled, some scarred and the occasional pair seemingly not thoroughly washed, the motley collection gave rise to the thought knees should be banned from display in public places.

Vaccinations and numerous jabs to protect against this and that epidemic came to an end with a roll-call to ensure that each individual had survived the onslaught. On the following morning and en route to Liverpool to board the ship bound for distant shores, throbbing arms encouraged belief that odds on Pestilence in the Survival Handicap stakes would be drastically shortened.

Like most other places, Liverpool was not seen to advantage viewed from the carriage windows of the train as it picked its way through a maze of railway sidings and goods yards. Blessed with a generous sense of humour, neither were many Liverpudlians likely to object to the observation that their city was not foremost in mind of those contemplating an exotic holiday; but the fact remains it has nurtured a Scouse settlement throughout the era of Anno Domini.

Once aboard ship in Liverpool's famous dockyard and unencumbered by kit, from an upper deck of the *Scythia* Jim watched a huge waterfront building gradually disappear from view in the fading evening light as the liner sailed slowly down the River Mersey, towards Liverpool Bay and the Irish Sea. He contemplated the voyage over the next few days. Although he had not the slightest idea of the number of knots of which the *Scythia* was capable, he figured that during the night it would probably clear the Irish Sea and would be in the Celtic Sea, heading in the direction of the maligned Bay of Biscay. If the surmise was correct dawn would disclose that land was no longer in sight nor, he reckoned, would it again be visible before the ship passed Cape Finisterre at the tip of the Iberian Peninsular or, if not then, until it approached Gibraltar, which gave rise to thoughts of shore leave.

Once the evening meal had been consumed and after he had staked out a place on the mess deck where he would sleep, like practically every other passenger he went to survey his new home. Inwardly he felt a wild excitement. The expectation felt at the thought of visiting places which in his wildest dreams he could never have envisaged was immense. Even when he had entertained thoughts of life at sea before discouragement by his parents, he had not actually given thought to the specific destinations he might visit. Now he knew where he was bound. That is until he came to retrace his steps to his particular mess deck. On such a large vessel as the *Scythia* it was not difficult to get lost, which fact was realised by hordes of other service personnel as they lurched from foot to foot trying to keep in step with the tempo of the ship, itself dancing to the tune of the then, turbulent sea.

In a similar manner in which he had also befriended Jim, a member of the ship's crew came to the aid of the group who had lost their bearings, and obligingly conducted them to the position where a large plan of the vessel was displayed. Extremely ungrateful as it would have been to declare the seaman's assistance was everything short of being helpful, it was undeniably the case. The exhibited anatomy of the *Scythia* was as it had been when constructed in a more peaceful era, and when as a cruise liner it catered for the pleasure of more affluent passengers than those gathered studying the plan. Enviable thoughts of a pre-lunch aperitif or of an after-dinner liqueur in a magnificent cocktail bar, and highly fanciful vision of spacious, sumptuously appointed cabins for just two persons quickly evaporated when Jim finally found his way to the crowded mess deck. Sharing the sleeping quarters with the large contingent of Royal Marines was a considerable detachment of the Royal Scots

Regiment, both of which units were commonly referred to as The Royals. As he thoughtfully surveyed the recumbent, huddled bodies, facetiously he wondered whether there had ever been an occasional in the nation's history when so many royals had slept together.

In spite of the fact that morning light disclosed that shores were beyond the horizon, judged by the large number of the squaking seagulls circling the ship in anticipation of the swill emptied overboard, land could not be thought very far distant. However, during the day, as the distance increased while the refuse decreased as overnight squeamish stomachs became less rebellious, the gulls finally withdrew from the scene. Beyond the rail of the ship the interest of most passengers also melted away. Viewed from the forecastle, each bow wave left the same impression as had countless previous ones: stood in the stern, attention did not remain riveted for very long on either the wake or the instrument in tow which measured the ship's speed on the dial fixed on the taffrail. Inevitably attention was transferred inboard.

Energetic activities found only little favour. Though proper quoits and net were not available, with makeshift gadgets, deck quoits and deck tennis managed to cling to the participation of a few individuals for a while – a very short while. Effortless pleasures attracted extensive support and were found more sustainable by the languid majority. Those who were smitten with a gambling streak tucked themselves in an out of the way spot, knowing they risked not only the loss of the little money they possessed but detection by the onboard military police, though what that consequence would be nobody seemed to know. Nevertheless cards were shuffled and dealt, dice were thrown and coins were pitched at a mark and then tossed in the air. Those who engaged in such pursuits never seemed to tire. While some individuals quietly read, the more vociferous discussed topics which would not have been promoted by the Women's Institute, nor would some of the terms used have been pardoned by them. Some of the opinions freely aired were deliberately provocative and were loudly voiced to entice response. Though the motive was good-humoured, in those who took the bait without realising it was in the nature of badinage, tempers sometimes became a good deal more than just irritable.

What came to contribute most in the way of pleasurable entertainment throughout the long voyage, and to the greatest number of people aboard, was provided by a band which soon came into existence. Coming from different parts of the ship, from time to time ears became conscious of faint strains of melody played on an assortment of musical instruments. When investigated it was usually found that the maestro in question was playing mostly for his own benefit or was practising his talent, though in a few instances attracting the interest of one or two deck-mates who happened to be within hearing distance. Upon other musicians the renditions seemed to have the luring effect of a mating call between birds of a feather, and in the space of three or four days after sailing from Liverpool quite an appealing brood hatched. Quite obviously, the lack of space in kitbags completely ruled out the transport and thereby possession of large instruments, but regardless of such deficiencies the ensemble attracted large audiences on the upper deck on each evening. Gathered beneath the stars in the cool evening air listening, singing or whistling to the tune being rendered, the ship was a very contented speck in the vast ocean. Before 'Pipe Down' was sounded by the bosun over the ship's tannoy system at the end of each day, the evening's performance concluded with the band's adaptation of *The Song Of India*, which mystical sounding melody was most haunting, possibly the more so by virtue of the fact it was without words which tended to concentrate minds on the tune.

Since departing from Liverpool the *Scythia* had steadily sailed more or less due south, in which latitudes the temperature became progressively more unbearable. Battledress attire gave way to tropical wear in one unit after another, and knock knees together with other human imperfections lost their initial interest and were looked upon as minor freaks of nature. What was also painfully established was how parts of the torso, unaccustomed to much sunshine, quickly blistered. Sleep on the lower, inadequately ventilated and crowded decks became almost impossible and as a result countless numbers remained on the upper deck where they slept the night.

Much to Jim's disappointment it was during the hours of darkness that the ship passed through the Straits of Gibraltar. Since the first light of day there had been distant views of land

on her port side towards which she altered course slightly during
the late evening, presumably in the direction of Punto Marroqui,
the most southerly point on the European mainland. Pin points
of light gradually became visible on both the port and starboard
beam, but searching eyes were denied all sight of land. Instead,
as along one side of the ship the distant lights of Spain and on
the other side those of Morocco slipped from sight, it became
disappointingly obvious there would be no shore leave in
Gibraltar.

It only gradually but irritably began to dawn on him that from
the very commencement of the voyage from Liverpool he had
stupidly looked upon it as a pleasure cruise. Careful to dispel
belief that no major port of call would be omitted from his
imaginary itinerary, he condescended to waive thought of going
ashore at Vigo, from where the Spanish Armada had set sail and
to which Columbus had returned following his first voyage to
the New World. With even greater reluctance he relinquished
the prospect of a few hours in Lisbon, once the wealthiest city
on earth: but a day among the Barbary Apes on the Rock was a
foregone conclusion. Reluctantly he came to the disappointing
belief that in all likelihood he would not set foot on land again
until the *Scythia* ultimately reached India.

On awakening early the next morning, long before the shrill
sound of the bosuns pipe and the accompanying acerbic voice
which ordered 'Rise and shine: lash up and stow' came over the
vessel's deafening loud speakers, Jim returned to his final
thoughts of the previous day. While he no longer entertained the
slightest prospect of going ashore, he resurrected hope of seeing
a little of some of the countries in which they docked for one
purpose or another. He considered there was a chance of a stop
at Malta. Most of the crew with whom he had come into contact
on board ship were Lascars and rather difficult to understand,
but one of them had left him with the impression the liner
frequently called at the island to refuel or take stores on board
and to collect mail. If such should turn out to be the case on the
current voyage, Jim enthused, the aspect from the rails of the
ship would be far more varied than vast expanses of sea.

Warming to his rekindled hopes of satisfying his interest in
alien lands, he appreciated that though a stop at the redoubtable
fortress of Malta was only a possibility, passage through the Suez

Canal was a certainty. The longer he dwelt upon that stretch of the voyage the more enticing it became. Over a hundred miles where the ancient land of Egypt would be only a few yards away on either side of the ship and where, he presumed, along its entire length progress would be at a restricted rate of knots, allowing ample time to absorb everything. He felt it would turn out to be a journey not only measured in terms of distance but also in time; through a land with a history which stretched back to the beginning of civilization. By the time he went below for breakfast the despondency he had endured only a few hours earlier had completely vanished.

During the last few days it took to reach Port Said at the northern end of the canal, without the conjectured call at Valletta, or elsewhere, there was very little activity during the daytime other than to watch bodies become more tanned and on moonlight evenings to listen to the band, tasks which very few on board found unendurable. For much of the time on that leg of the voyage the coast of North Africa was visible but too far distant to distinguish any particular features: but there was no mistaking what met the gaze of all on board the troopship as it anchored at Port Said.

Laden with all manner of merchandise, crews aboard boats of every type frantically jostled for what they believed to be the most advantageous position alongside the assembled lines of ships at anchor, awaiting their turn to sail through the canal. In next to no time and in the process of conducting business with the *Scythia*'s passengers, the entire hull of the troopship was festooned with lengths of frayed though dependable ropes, each one hoisting crudely made raffia baskets containing goods for sale, or lowering in them sums of money for the items purchased. Each transaction, even if identical to a previous one, involved considerable bargaining. It was perfectly clear that some of those aboard the troopship had passed that way before and were well practised in the expertise required in the haggling ritual. From the experienced among their fellow passengers the novices quickly learned. As conflicting offers were bawled between vendors and prospective clients, the former striving to achieve an exorbitant margin of profit, the other intent on securing a give-away price, so the intensity and the diversity of wrangling fluctuated. The gestures and the scurrilous patter of the Egyptian salesmen would not have escaped tut-tutting by indignant clientele of Knightsbridge salons, but among the customers congregated along ship's rails in the harbour of Port Said they were a source of great hilarity.

Short of the figurative kitchen sink, between them the boatmen seemed able to supply whatever might be desired. From a most evil-looking one, but for a small fortune, was the offer to provide the services of his young sister. Among the more conventional and cheaper transactions, everything which could be made of leather was on display in the bottom of the boats, as were heaps of wares claimed to be made of brass. Wrist watches were on offer at prices which did not inspire much confidence in their time keeping. There were smallish rugs: smaller, stuffed toys and wisps of women's revealing underwear, the expanse of which was not much greater than the tabs attached to them which professed their manufacture was from silk.

A number of water-borne hawkers traded in fruit. Despite advice from medical staff to refrain from purchase, the availability of hands of bananas and of unlimited supplies of oranges could not be resisted by some.

Preceded by the engine propelled boats already alongside the *Scythia*, hordes of totally naked, young swimmers began to arrive on the scene. Although the children swam with the expert ability of adults, had they lived in England it was doubtful whether the eldest looking one would have progressed beyond infant school. Though tender in age their vocabulary was distinctly more developed. They set out their objective with loud shouts of "Hey! Johnny! You throw me effing penny". Hands of most onlookers were thrust into their pockets for loose change and the coins were tossed overboard. In hectic pursuit of the money the water-babies plunged to out of sight depths, to re-emerge a moment later with the same cry. Using their mouth in which to deposit the gathered coins, on each occasion they surfaced the ever increasing bulge in each cheek made them a hideous sight on which to dwell. But far greater significance than their distorted faces was their less apparent plight.

Jim clearly recalled to mind that while on embarkation leave and when listening to the radio it was revealed the war was currently costing Great Britain, alone, the sum of 24 million pounds each day. What the global investment in the human slaughter might be he shuddered to think; yet, in order to survive, the mites swimming in front of him in the sewage infested and oil polluted outer harbour were compelled to incur all manner of risks for the sake of a few paltry pence. Loitering on the crowded deck only sufficiently long to contribute what coins were in his pocket, with a feeling bordering on shame he flung them into the water and slunk from the scene

Below the deck his thoughts eventually emerged from a labyrinth of utter disbelief and contempt as his mind strayed from the present to the forthcoming voyage through the Suez Canal. He had been given to understand that at each end of the waterway there was always a considerable delay to shipping due to the fact it was not wide enough to safely accommodate vessels sailing in opposite directions, other than where the canal passed through the Bitter Lakes, one of which was known as Crocodile Lake. According to a now familiar but no less imprecise member of the ship's East Indian crew it would take "very much long more twelp hoors", but as Jim could not be sure whether that period of time referred to how long it would be before the voyage commenced or to how long the voyage would take, he put both uncertainties to the seaman. Given the answer of yes to both questions, and nodding his head as he backed away, Jim sheepishly intimated that he understood.

Although his imagination deliberately refrained from promising his eyes any specific sights en route, it aroused determination for vigilance throughout the duration of the lengthy passage. However, if crocodiles did continue to lurk and prey in the shallows of Lake Timshah (to give the murky water its correct name), none of the reptiles seemed intent on dining out during the passage of the *Scythia* across its uninviting depth. In point of fact, during the entire day there was little sight of man or beast but of the two categories there were unquestionably more of the latter. Aboard two or three antiquated ferries which crossed from one side of the canal to the other, each vessels' erratic course dangerously close to the bows of the *Scythia*, donkeys, herds of goats and crated chickens vastly outnumbered human passengers who tended them.

On the starboard side, along the banks of the upper reaches of the waterway there were a small number of villages, although only little evidence of the inhabitants. Those who were clearly visible encouraged the opinion the chief occupation was that of playing a table game, not dissimilar to dominoes, which demanding effort compelled resort to narcotic relief with the aid of a shared hookah. As respite from such demanding industry, in their hard earned leisure they presumably harvested the dates of the iniquitous palms which they had previously pollinated by hand during their annual holiday, taken to coincide with the only fortnight of the year during which the trees were fertile. Other than these hives of industry, and with the exception of Port Said and Port Suez, Ismalia on the western shore of Lake Timsah was the only place of significance. From what could be seen of the city, when for some inexplicable reason the *Scythia* dropped anchor close by, it made a restful and favourable impression.

By the following morning the ship was in the Gulf of Suez and was heading towards the Red Sea. Although the restriction on the vessel's rate of knots during the passage through the canal had duly been lifted, the anticipated sea breeze did not result. The atmosphere was as still, as the surface of the sea was un-ruffled, and the direct rays of the sun were exhausting. What energy bodies were able to muster was reserved exclusively for the purpose of searching for a shady spot on the upper deck where they could deposit themselves and restrict their function to that of breathing. Conversation was non-existent and eyelids firmly shut, not in pursuit of sleep but to eliminate all concentration.

Try as he did to stifle mental activity, Jim found that after a while it required more endeavour than allowing the mind to roam. It did stray, to port. To Sinai; at different times and in different areas of the peninsular, looked upon as holy ground and fought upon as battleground. To the north, where the Holy Crusades spilled over the border with the neighbouring Kingdom of Jerusalem, the soldiers of Christ under the banner of Richard Coeur de Lion had claimed God was on their side. In the jihad against the western infidels and led by Salah-ad-Din, the warriors of Mohammed swore they had the support of Allah. Seemingly, among enemies, claims of heavenly support had not much changed.

Even in the considerably wider expanse of the Red Sea which was reached later in the day there was still little more than a suspicion of gentle breeze, but the soaring temperature was unmistakable. Giving rise to the impression that the shimmering dark blue water was too warm for their comfort, a small school of porpoises and a larger shoal of flying fish rose out of the sea. Whether the former quickly discovered their blunder or were simply unable to remain airborne for long, they soon plunged back again: but with their wing like pectoral fin the flying fish were able to glide for considerably longer, and expertly skimmed the waves of the sea for quite appreciable distances, before they too eventually disappeared from sight beneath the water.

During the night there was every cause for considerable concern, though the incident which caused it was known only to a handful of people when it took place. Among those on board were a small number of women, mostly nursing auxiliaries for one branch or another of the armed forces. Allocated a few of the available cabins but finding the portholes did not provide sufficient ventilation in the tropical heat, some doors were left ajar at night. During the hours of darkness one of the nurses was awakened by an intruder fumbling among her bedding, but as soon as she raised her voice the groping ceased and the culprit fled. Each night thereafter guard was stationed outside each cabin. The effect was demoralising. The camaraderie which had blossomed since leaving Liverpool was never quite restored.

*****

On the starboard side, and in turn, the shore of Egypt gave way to Sudan, Eritrea, Djibouti and Somalia, beyond the last view of which Jim contemplated the voyage across the Gulf of Aden and the Indian Ocean – Bombay next stop. Or so he thought.

Ignorant of the fact the *Scythia* was due to make a call at the port and naval base in the Crown Colony of Aden, and not conscious of the fact the ship's course continued in an easterly direction towards the Arabian Sea instead of south easterly towards the Indian Ocean, it came as a complete, not to mention unwelcome, surprise to be awakened very early one morning by the prolonged, rumbling sound of the ship's anchor being lowered. Scarcely light enough to discern the shore when he was first disturbed by the commotion, once the sun managed to climb above the mountain peaks it revealed rather an inhospitable landscape. To the harbour-master's staff and particularly to the Royal Navy, dawn undoubtedly also disclosed a vessel dressed in such manner that they were not impressed, either.

As was not difficult to recollect from when off the coast of Normandy, salt water soap failed to produce any significant amount of lather when used with sea water. As that was all which was available for washing purposes on board the troopship, the troops were compelled to devise other methods for washing clothes. Every night, items which were to be laundered were very securely attached to lines which, before being cast into the sea, were also very carefully tied at the other end to the ship's rails. Dragged through the briny in this manner throughout the night, when hauled in on the following morning the articles were well and truly dhobied.

However, to the disdainful powers that be in the naval base, line upon line of socks, vests, pants, shirts, towels and other items were not acceptable rigging, as was made unmistakably clear.

All day long the ship rode at anchor a short distance off shore. From whichever of the vessel's two watches were off duty for the day, several seamen went ashore on the first liberty boat of the morning. If the aim of any of them was to call upon a girl-friend in that particular port, at such an ungodly hour the visit was not likely to be very welcome. On later excursions to the town a few women among the passengers, in the main members of Queen Alexandra's Royal Navy Nursing Service, were accompanied by a small number of the ship's officers. Understandably, at first there was widespread envy among the troops denied the opportunity to stretch their legs on terra firma, but as the day progressed and the temperature climbed relentlessly higher and higher, and those remaining afloat were compelled to find what shade they could, so the desire for exercise on the sun-baked streets of Aden diminished appreciably. Without leaving a shred of hope of a subsequent change of mind, so debilitating was the heat that, in order to conserve what little energy had not been drained from themselves, the musicians made it known they would not be putting in an appearance that evening.

With a degree of accuracy which could not be ascertained, Jim's mates speculated the temperature was well in excess of 100 degrees. Yet in the sweltering heat, and from small lighters tied up alongside the troopship, ragged but unflagging native labourers humped heavy-looking sacks of coal to the *Scythia*'s stokehold throughout the day. According to one of the liner's crew, a few of the labourers were from the island in the East Indies from which he came. If it was correctly understood by Jim, for their exhausting work the coal-heavers were paid a derisory pittance equal to just a few pence for each day's work.

Just to be on the move again the following morning was a great relief, although for some on the ship the pleasure was short-lived. Within 48 hours or so the sky became more threatening and the wind turned ill-tempered.

The frolicking porpoises had lost all inclination to caper in the waves and the flying fish suspended all flight on account of the inclement conditions. During the afternoon a storm began to brew, with a vengeance, and by the time the evening meal was dished up many individuals had already decided to batten down the hatch giving access to their stomach. Having been tossed about by the sea on many occasions in the English Channel but firmly convinced he had been spared attacks of sea sickness due to the fact he was positioned in the open air, Jim tried to persuade those who were lying down and looking green around the gills that they would probably be better off above deck in the fresh air, but his conviction was not shared by any who were afflicted.

As it transpired the gale did benefit some on board in one respect. On the day before it struck, the officer in charge of the contingent going to join the 3rd Commando Brigade raised the subject of a spot of physical training. It was an undeniable fact that since departure from England none of the marines had been called upon to exert themselves for anything more strenuous that the acts of breathing and blinking, but precisely why the indolence should be detrimental only to them, as appeared to be the case in their eyes, none of them could begin to fathom. However, Jim was instructed to submit a programme for the officer's perusal which, after minor additions, was authorised to commence on the day on which the storm broke. If in such manner it may be expressed, it was fortunate the storm and the ensuing swell dragged on and on. By the time the latter moderated Bombay was no more than 24 hours away and all thought of physical training was conveniently shelved.

Stomachs which had previously been in revolt relented and

permitted gullets to dispatch whatever they wished and as frequently as nourishment was available. By some individuals on the recovery list letters were composed, perhaps annulling bequests penned in disorderly haste during the height of the storm. As priorities were swiftly revised among the most morbid, who had abandoned all wish to celebrate another day on the face of the earth regardless of whether their onward journey was upward or in the opposite direction, gambling again became popular. Knowing full well there were no pockets in shrouds, each reprobate decided that if he could not take his ill-gotten gains with him on his journey into the hereafter, then he wouldn't depart.

15

STUNG INTO INACTION

Now it's not good for the Christian's health
To hustle the Aryan, brown.
For the former riles, and the latter smiles
Which wears the Christian down.

And the end of the fight is a tombstone white
With the name of the late deceased
And the epitaph drear – "A fool lies here
Who tried to hustle the East".

The Naulahka.
Rudyard Kipling, 1865-1936.

Like all good things which come to an end, after three weeks at sea the curtain was about to come down on the honeymoon.

Soon it would be back to the grindstone: to training in jungle warfare. Not that there was the slightest glimpse of jungle from the deck of the *Scythia*.

Once those aboard, who continuously searched the expanse of the horizon, established that the distant blur was in fact land, word rapidly spread and more and more bodies crowded the ship's rails.

As none among them could possible anticipate whether the side to which they had flocked would turn out to be the side which would eventually dock, every time the vessel altered course presumably to avoid sandbanks, or other charted, under-water hazards, droves of the jostling spectators attempted to find space on the newly fancied beam. The toing and froing only ceased when, still quite some distance from shore, the ship's engines were stopped and anchor was dropped. The rumour which circulated was to the effect that the procedure of docking would not take place until the following morning, whereupon the groups dispersed. With the elbows of other individuals no longer in his midriff nor their feet crushing his, it gave Jim an excellent opportunity to leisurely scan the coast. The structure which first caught his eye and the one to which his gaze constantly returned reminded him of another one, several thousand miles away.

During his earlier years as a boy messenger, delivery of telegrams to the Mount Royal and to the Cumberland Hotel in Oxford Street, as well as to Grosvenor House and the Dorchester Hotel in Park Lane, probably took him past Marble Arch many times on most days. Curious as to the meaningless position in which it was erected and the purpose it was meant to serve, he learned that it was originally intended to serve as the main entrance to Buckingham Palace, which proposition had to be scrapped following extension to the palace which left insufficient space for it. The less grandiose place subsequently decided upon for it's location and where it now stands, was where plans of other misfits came to grief – at Tyburn. Named after a tributary of the Thames, and at the junction of two old Roman roads where Stane Street (which connected Colchester and Chichester) met Watling Street (which linked St. Albans), for centuries it was the site of gallows last used for public execution in 1783.

As to the edifice on the water front at which he peered, it looked as though the centre arch of three was of far greater height than those on each side of it, but even these, he thought, well exceeded that of Marble Arch. Unlike that arch, intended for use by the monarchy, ' the Gateway to India' upon which he gazed was built as a commemorative monument to mark the spot where, as Emperor of India and accompanied by Queen Mary, King George V stepped ashore over 16 years before it was built.

Quite unknown to the troops as below deck they later ate their evening meal, a pilot came aboard to conduct the ship towards the Gateway. The sound of the anchor being weighed must have gone unnoticed among the lively hubbub, while the sea, as calm as a mill pond, gave no indication the ship was again under way. In consequence it was not until the mess decks were vacated, and steps were made in the direction of where the band would subsequently be giving their final performance, that it was realised two tugs were nudging the *Scythia* the last few yards to the dockside. Lines had already been made fast on the bollards on the quay and as the liner was edged closer to the side the slack was taken up by the bowman, and another in the stern. With a slight grinding noise against three or four very substantial wooden fenders, each about ten feet in width and floating in the water between the dockside and the ship, it came to rest. The voyage of a lifetime was at an end after three weeks.

As at Port Said, no sooner was the vessel stationary than it was besieged by bands of pedlars who appeared to be stocked with a selection of every product under the sun, but due to the fact that on the next day the passengers would be ashore and would have a wider selection from which to choose, the transactions were relatively few in number. The renewed advice not to purchase any type of fruit appeared to find more receptive minds than when at the entrance to the Suez Canal. Though expressed more in the nature of insinuation rather than established fact, the mere hint that on occasions human excrement was used to fertilise the soil was more than enough to discourage all desire for all fruit.

As was to be expected on the final night aboard, the tune with which the musicians concluded the evening was emotional Auld Lang Syne. Of the several hundred passengers aboard the ship hardly any were inclined to disperse immediately and make for their sleeping quarters. The majority were gripped with nostalgia. It seemed totally untenable that circumstances which brought together so many individuals would, at a stroke, terminate on the next day.

To give to the maid of the seas her initials despite the fact she was not at all times throughout the voyage regarded with affection, the next morning S.S. *Scythia* would cast off her devotees and silently steal away. Those jilted and abandoned on the quay would feel they had been deprived of something more than the mere source of board and lodging. They would fully understand why mariners fondly refer to the ships in which they sail as 'She'.

In enthusiastic mood at the prospect of a fresh chapter in life, Jim felt there would be no point in him going below and turning in for the night as he knew only too well sleep would be elusive. Among a group which gradually diminished as the night slipped away, he witnessed the sun slowly rise over the Gateway to India.

*****

No printed words or painted scenes nor lessons taught at school could have prepared the new arrivals for the culture into which they were thrust. Scarcely had they ventured beyond the metaphorical gateway than they were all eyes – but speechless. Of the senses, only those of taste and touch were not overwhelmed, and they solely because in the back of lorries those faculties were restricted to the confines of the transport.

The journey to Poona during the course of a sweltering day was in a convoy of bone-shaking trucks, fortunately each of them uncovered. From the very first moment minds and buttocks found the bumpy trip most absorbing, as well as a very long one which took the greater part of the day.

Beyond the environs of the docks Bombay was a frantic hotch-potch. Of humans and of animals: of traffic and an abundance of litter. Among backfiring vehicles, some conveying almost as many passengers precariously clinging to the outside as were more securely seated inside, a variety of livestock gave the firm impression they were as much at ease on the bustling roads as in the secluded countryside. Conceding that what is loosely referred to as breakfast time is vague to an extreme degree, nevertheless the hour of day was sufficiently advanced to assume it was well past. Yet on many pavements, and in several instances in the gutters, numbers of citizens still slept oblivious to innumerable flies which nestled on them.

Among the active population, beggars (some of whom were mere infants) desperately held out battered tin cans and pleaded or pestered for alms. In a water-front area through which the convoy travelled, which initially tended to give the appearance of rubbish strewn along the sidewalk, rows of laundered belongings were spread out to dry. In the same vicinity and harbouring what seemed to be the mother of refuse dumps, toil-worn mothers suckled babies perilously close to where their earlier-born valiantly contested the putrefying garbage with a pack of snarling dogs.

Toward the busy centre of Bombay the fleet of lorries cautiously picked its way through traffic-jams, and crawled past magnificent temples, most of which caused the troops to catch their breath in admiration. In a number of places and in close proximity stood squalid, corrugated-iron shacks which compelled the onlookers to hold their breath in commiseration.

In their nostrils, aromatic smells which could not be identified mingled with odours which were unmistakable and most unpleasant. To their ears, from unfamiliar-sounding instruments came discordant if not torturous sounds which vied with the incessant cries of the street vendors, each of whom tried their utmost to entice the surrender of a few rupees. Wealthy customers must have been even fewer in number.

Though the final impression was superficial, it did seem that none of the children who were on the streets were playful or mischievous, nor did there seem to be many smiling faces among the adults milling around. It was as though the continual struggle for survival had drained them of all pleasure and ruined every expectation.

In due course the drivers skilfully managed to extricate their vehicles from the infuriating congestion, in spite of rather than due to the intervention of the policemen controlling the traffic. Leaving the city behind but continuing to dwell upon the preliminary shock of making its acquaintance, it was some considerable time before Jim came to realise that the line of vehicles in which he was travelling was laboriously climbing the densely wooded slopes of the Western Ghats, which mountainous chain rose steeply from the narrow coastal plain.

Once on the summit and for mile upon mile the only traffic encountered was an occasional bullock-drawn cart. Each of the beasts brazenly persisted in ambling along in the middle of the now narrow road, with the arrogance of having right of way by virtue of the fact that, in evolutionary terms, they preceded motor transport.

Around midday and in the nick of time for brimming bladders, and not before time for empty stomachs, the drivers stopped for what one of them, in Hindi lingo, referred to as tiffin. Though there was neither sight nor sound of habitation, from out of the blue and in the buff a small group of young children appeared and stood gaping at the lorries, creating the impression that motor transport, like clothing, was a rarity in the area. Their little, emaciated bodies also indicated food was not over-abundant, either. This supposition was confirmed by the minor stampede which erupted when the surplus food was offered to the youngsters, the tussle for which morsels further added to the sorry spectacle of deprivation witnessed in Bombay.

Towards late afternoon and about a dozen miles from Poona

the convoy reached its destination. The 3rd Commando Brigade which the newcomers were urgently reinforcing comprised two army formations, number One and number Five Commando, and two Royal Marine Commandos, number 42 and number 44. Jim was posted to 42 Commando and was placed in W Troop. The back to nature accommodation was in large bell tents which slept a dozen men. Apart from the essential provision of a dozen charpoys, the canvas castles boasted nothing more extravagant than a paraffin burning, hurricane lamp. Well intended as no doubt the gesture was regarding the provision of such luxuries, the beds and the lamp exacted as much in the way of displeasure as they contributed in the form of comfort. On the very first night each of the disadvantages soon became apparent.

If blessed with the benefit of exceptionally good eyesight, the lamp just about managed to shed sufficient light to enable letters to be read or for card games to be played. Unfortunately for those assembled in the illuminated radius it also attracted swarms of various, repulsive insects, among which were clusters of blood-thirsty mosquitoes. Each of these seemed to know the exact spot between shoulder blades to which they could cling, secure in the knowledge that the arms of their host could not dislodge them as they supped blood.

But the greater cause for calamity arose in consequence of the struggle to obtain a decent night's sleep. As Jim twisted and turned in search of a modicum of comfort on the coarse rope netting which took the place of springs on his charpoy, it occurred to him that his ground sheet would solve the itchy problem. Though it did eliminate the chaffing effect on his bare back, being rubber it caused him to perspire even more profusely in the enclosure of the airless mosquito net. It was not long before he found himself slipping in pools of sweat as he desperately continued to toss from side to side in pursuit of sleep, or as he repeatedly flailed at mosquitoes which had managed to get inside the net when he leaned out to reach the groundsheet. However, if the end of the first day in India bordered upon being intolerable, the next one commenced most promisingly.

*****

In addition to the four commando units and brigade headquarters stationed at Khadakvasla, over a period of time and on the fringes of the camp a number of nondescript lodgings had sprung up, as more and more camp-followers came to the site in the hope of scraping a living on the base. Disregarding the chimney-sweep wallah who was placed on the payroll on account of scheduled visits to several camp cookhouses, all of the other wallahs were self-employed. To the troops newly arrived, the staggered arrival of the entrepreneurs was totally unexpected but unreservedly welcome, not least by Jim.

It was to such surprise that he slowly opened his heavy eyelids when gently aroused from the snatch of sleep he managed to obtain during that first night. The mug of sweet tea offered by the chai-wallah a few minutes before reveille was well worth the few annas which were entailed. No sooner was the refreshment pleasurably swallowed, and Jim once again horizontal on the charpoy, than came the shave-wallah, whose dexterity with a cut-throat razor further added to the feeling of living in the lap of luxury. Hardly had the notes of the first bugle call of the day faded away before the dhobi-wallahs turned up at each tent to distribute the previous day's immaculately washed and ironed items, and to collect other garments for laundering. At the head of each line of tents, haircut-wallahs unfolded small stools in anticipation of scalps requiring a trim.

Of a much younger generation than any of the specified wallahs, each tent collectively employed the services of a bearer, further reducing more of the daily chores. He polished whatever items of brass and footwear were required by the occupants of the tent, and generally kept it and its immediate surrounds tidy. Although the hire of bearers was not frowned upon by those in authority, it was made perfectly clear that the job of cleaning rifles or other weapons was not to be entrusted to them. Indeed they were expressly forbidden to as much as touch any firearms. Whatever the reasoning which gave rise to the order, the decision was never made known to the troops and in consequence some of their odd, theoretical motives were wildly speculative.

In addition to the difference in age between the wallahs and the bearers there was an indisputable generation-gap in attitudes towards service personnel, as well as towards the British in general. Respectful or servile, as in the estimation of the beholder, there were seldom matters of significant dispute with any of the wallahs. Such minor differences which occasionally cropped up were good natured wrangles in respect of the amount charged for laundering, or the effect upon the stitching of washed clothing as a result of its repeated thrashing against a collection of large rocks in the river, which site and facilities constituted the camp laundrette.

On the other hand, uneasy periods of neutrality punctuated by frequent outbursts of verbal hostility were more the case in dealing with the teen-aged bearers. Born in an era of rapidly increasing resentment towards British sovereignty in their country, and conversant with Britain's humiliating defeat and surrender to Japanese forces in one country after another, all insinuations of superiority or thinly disguised insults from the commandos met with instant and well chosen response. Within the space of only a few minutes of his arrival, the young Gujarati who was bearer for the occupants of Jim's tent became heatedly embroiled in an argument with one of them, and was told by the marine to "Get out of my effing tent and out of my effing sight". Not for a single moment prepared to bite his lip, the immediate and uncompromising reply was "Get out of my effing country and take your effing tent with you". As neither of the effing antagonists seemed inclined to heed the advice, Jim thought it not untoward to mutter 'Touche'.

It came as a complete surprise to the brigade newcomers to be almost entirely re-kitted very soon after their arrival, the more so considering that most of the items issued were designed for American troops. The Lee-Enfield rifles conveyed several thousand miles since departure from England were withdrawn and replaced with Yankee, semi-automatic Garrand carbines, the use of which in the impending assault on Malaya would greatly enhance fire-power – that is provided they could be properly reassembled.

The consignment of weapons had only just arrived from the United States. In preparation for the long sea voyage the mechanism and the barrel had been thickly smothered in grease. Obviously the carbines had to be completely stripped and thoroughly de-greased, which was not difficult. The snag was, without the manuals, which had not been dispatched by the manufacturers or the responsible department in the US, putting them back together, in working order, was another matter. Some individuals managed to fit together some of the parts but had bits left over. Until an unknown genius in the armoury finally solved the embarrassing problem the war looked likely to drag on and on, ad infinitum.

Though the standardised, heavy-studded, leather boots were not similarly confiscated, possibly an ominous indication that square-bashing should not be considered unfashionable and out of the question, but pending, such clodhoppers were supplemented by the distribution of American style jungle boots. With thick rubber soles and waterproof, canvas uppers, when laced across the inner gusset to just below the knee they completely stopped the incursion of leeches, which feat the British footwear miserably failed to hinder, let alone prevent.

As with one extremity, so with the other. Causing very little in the nature of gnashed teeth at their downfall, rounded steel helmets of British design were discarded in favour of the American type. Unimaginatively listed in service inventories and referred to in military circles as Helmets/bucket, the detachable, outer shell did come in handy as an economical wash-basin. The supply and conservation of fresh water in the area of the proposed invasion, especially in the initial phase and even more so by units or individuals who became isolated, did pose a serious problem. The metal, water-bottles which were a component of the rig for battle but had a capacity of only a pint or two would be pitifully inadequate. To replace them chagals were issued. Manufactured from canvas and lined with goatskin, in contrast to the metal water-bottles they held two gallons. Awkwardly dangling from webbing waist belts, their anchorage was shared by a machete for the clearance of jungle undergrowth and a kukri for the severance of over-exposed enemy heads. Khaki tropical wear was withdrawn and replaced with jungle-green clothing. While green berets were not relegated to second place, for everyday wear in camp Australian bush hats were doled out.

Equipped with American firearms, steel helmets and jungle boots, Indian chagals, Caribbean machetes, Nepalese kukris and Australian hats, about the only recognisable thing that was British was the unmistakable bad language which the incongruously dressed troops hurled at each other.

Escape cum-survival kits were supplied. A tiny compass, small enough to be securely secreted in the hollow globe in the centre of the cap badge of marines, complemented an indestructible, printed, silk map of the invasion zone. A multi-purpose jack-knife equipped each recipient with gadgets for most eventualities. In addition to two cutting blades it incorporated hacksaw blades of various gauge, a wire cutter, pincers, screwdriver and a tin-opener. Aimed at supplementing emergency rations, means in the form of fishing line and tackle were provided. In case the escape and survival aids failed in their purpose, troops stored about themselves photographs of loved ones who would be with them at the end.

The period leading up to the brigade's departure from Khadakvasla did not last long and only permitted one opportunity to visit the centre of Poona.

Even the lowest paid among Jim's companions were comfortably able to afford quite a sumptuous feast in one of the town's restaurants: but after dining and making their well satisfied exit onto the rain drenched pavements, barefoot, hungry looking youngsters pleaded for baksheesh. One or two children had a limb missing which, it was said by one old campaigner in Jim's party, was the result of deliberate mutilation in order to gain more pity and hopefully greater generosity. One young boy, barely out of infancy, mutely thrust a scribbled note into Jim's hand. Written in simple English, it explained that the lad was dumb and was the oldest of three children who had been abandoned by their parents. Of his two younger brothers, one was blind: the other a cripple. Whatever may have been the true circumstances, the message lightened the pockets of Jim's companions and himself by more than might otherwise have been the case. More than had been the effect of the deprivation witnessed from the back of the lorry as it sped through Bombay, grim though they were, the experience on the streets of Poona went deeper.

On the camp site there were other close encounters with poverty-stricken existence. At the entrance to the mess, every meal time women and children pounced upon troops who made an exit with uneaten portions of food, imploring the overfed to tip the morsels into their outstretched tins rather than into the swill bins. Until a halt was finally called to the little by little daily encroachment on the very dining tables immediately eating utensils were set down, competing hands snatched from plates every scrap which remained. Utterly deplorable as were the circumstances which gave rise to the scavenging, and sympathetic as most troops wished to be towards those banned from the area around each mess, swill bins were positioned between the inner and outer doors and orders were imposed that no food whatsoever was to be conveyed beyond them.

During the monsoonal month of August instructions were received to decamp. Preparing for the early morning scheduled departure, while shoving his folded groundsheet into an already crammed haversack Jim pricked his thumb on a sharp object – he believed. Spontaneously withdrawing his hand, a scorpion was revealed attached to his digit. A fraction quicker to realise its peril, than was Jim his mistaken belief, the scorpion relaxed its pincer-like claws, dropped to the ground and scurried out of sight in the dimly lit tent.

The short interval between the misconception he had merely pricked his thumb and the severe pain and swelling, which indicated he hadn't, lasted only a moment. The excruciating pain surged along the length of his arm and in next to no time he had the sensation of a small lump forming in the armpit, difficulty in breathing and involuntary contraction in some of his muscles. Unable to do little more than nurse his paralysed right arm with the left, a chai-wallah motioned to Jim. Enticed to seat himself on the edge of his charpoy, the entrepreneur squatted on his haunches immediately in front of Jim. He took the throbbing limb between his thighs and, in the manner of a masseur, hand over hand applied powerful pressure on the arm in a downward direction from the inflamed arm-pit.

As in a multitude of subjects, Jim's knowledge was minimal in the realm of scorpions and such that he possessed was only so-so. He knew they stung but did not know that, of the species to be found in India, only one group had venom potent enough to cause death. Adding conviction to his grim misunderstanding (and not until much later regarded as comical), as the wallah massaged he muttered away. Each time his incantations paused for want of breath he lifted his face skyward, causing Jim to fear prayers were being offered for his doomed soul. Certainly the wallah's utterances gave no relief from the pain. Nor was there anything but guffaws from those he had come to look upon as bosom pals.

When the call came for muster prior to departure Jim was unable to hoist his large pack on to his shoulders. Instead he placed it on the ground to his front. Noticing his condition, the medical officer accompanying the draft sent him to the camp sick bay for treatment. The hour of day was not much after 0500 hours. Not due to leave with the brigade, at that time of day the medical orderly was not best pleased at being roused and sent Jim on his way, back to the parade, with nothing more than a small wad of cotton wool saturated with iodine. A haunting sense of impending doom grew stronger. Luckily and for whatever purpose the MO had to make his way to the infirmary, he ran into Jim. On learning of the futile treatment dispensed and after attending to other matters, the officer administered an injection at the base of the thumb on each side of the bone.

At a break in the journey, in Bombay a visit was laid on to a nearby army hospital for further treatment which gave relief for a further span of hours: but once the effect wore off, and into the next morning, the pain continued to be difficult to bear. If, in a single word, a scorpion's sting can be described, Jim thought the only one which was anywhere near adequate was (so to speak) unmentionable.

The mission upon which the brigade was about to embark was code-named Operation Zipper, and in terms of importance and magnitude was spoken of as second only to the landing in Normandy, still vivid in the mind of those who took part. The assault was destined for Port Dickson on the western coast of Malaya, and was to be followed by an advance on Singapore, to the south. The landing force consisted of four Indian divisions, a British parachute brigade and 3rd Commando Brigade. Opposing forces known to be in the vicinity were two divisions of the 29th Japanese Army with support from an independent, mixed brigade and a tank battalion.

As it transpired, thankfully, at the eleventh hour the intended landing was aborted. The lesser of two diabolical options brought the war to a very sudden end with the capitulation of Japan on August 14th. Unprecedented and horrendous as was the effect of the atomic bombs dropped on Hiroshima in the early hours of August 6th and (in the absence of a definite offer of surrender) three days later on Nagasaki, there could not be the slightest doubt that loss of life would have been immeasurably greater but for resort to nuclear weaponry; and such consolation was not solely in respect of the Allied lives which were spared.

The samurai code of honour ingrained upon the minds of the Japanese, of glorified death in preference to cowardly surrender, exemplified time after time during the conflict in South East Asia, would have been even more fanatically upheld in defence of the land of the rising sun. Accounts of exhortations from Japanese officers were common knowledge to the allied troops who had suffered grievously in consequence of compliance with the entreaties. So called death squads were insatiable in their desire for blood, in which pursuit they boldly sacrificed their own. Snipers roped themselves to branches of trees, never to descend. They did so without reluctance. They knew that when dispatched from the land of the living, deceptive glimpses of their presence among the foliage would be enough to draw fire from enemy patrols, thereby giving away the position of the forces advancing through the jungle.

[1] On the island of Saipan the process of self-immolation was sickening to witness. In one notable instance, incredulous Americans watched helplessly as in the distance enemy troops lined up to await decapitation by their officers. The garrison of nearly 32,000 died almost to the last man. In this, Saipan was no different from all earlier campaigns, but this time there was one very real change.

On Saipan the garrison had been matched by an equal number of Japanese civilians, and over 22,000 of those chose to join their service compatriots in death rather than allow themselves to be taken prisoner by the Americans. These suicides involved whole families, children being killed by their parents before the latter killed themselves. Scenes of unparalleled horror were played out in various caves or squalid buildings, but mostly at two bluffs: the 1,000 feet Suicide Cliff over which hundreds threw themselves onto the jagged rocks below, and the 80 feet drop into the ocean at Banzai Cliff near Marpi Point. There the dead and dying were so thick that they fouled the propellers of the destroyers trying to rescue the would-be suicides. American ships and boats moved over a carpet of drowned and injured but plucked hundreds to safety.

---

[1] From *June 1944*, by H.P. Willmott.

However the two atomic bombs brought to a swift end the call for such doctrinaire stoicism and courageous defiance. The upshot was that within the course of the week following the end of hostilities the brigade stood ready to re-occupy Penang, in the Straits of Malacca.

Prepared though the force was for the task, but themselves not unmindful as to whether the Japanese troops would obey instructions to lay down arms, at much higher levels there was more widespread procrastination which delayed the mission for a further number of days. But in the first hours of August 27th the occupation force anchored off the coast of their objective. Yet almost another week passed by before the terms of surrender were agreed and the brigade, known as Force Roma, went ashore.

It was said (seldom were details authoritative) there had been a rather contentious issue. Quite apart from the military application, in another highly ticklish, sphere 'Unconditional Surrender' had a different significance. Instantly recognisable by their working outfit as they lounged on several verandas outside a number of army huts, Japanese comfort girls also came into the imbroglio. Among those conducting the delicate negotiations the senior British officer proposed that the ladies should be treated as prisoners of war and interned on the mainland of Malaya, with which the Japanese delegates strongly disagreed. They vigorously maintained their womankind should be allowed to remain on the island under the protection of Japanese guards, to which preposterous suggestion the British firmly objected. In the mood for reconciliation the latter relented and announced they would be allowed to stay; in the care of marines. As though extended an invitation to a convivial get-together with a blunt hara-kiri dagger, the Japanese feverishly chose to adopt the original proposal.

It was only a matter of days before the brigade handed over the various duties on the island to a contingent from the Royal Air Force. Nevertheless, from the moment when the Union Jack was unfurled and triumphantly hoisted and the Royal Marine bandsmen from one of the large warships rendered the national anthem in the main square, until the sight of Penang disappeared as another voyage on another mission for the brigade got under way, every moment was enthralling.

Jubilation among the population on their unexpected liberation was incredible. No less was their intoxication which was every bit as apparent. All manner of shapes and sizes of bottles and other vessels were in evidence, many more of them on the nearly empty side rather than practically untouched. The variety of alcoholic liquor was vast. Some bottles, giving the impression they had been buried for some length of time, had tattered labels of well known spirits. Names on others were not recognisable, not even by those who under the pretext of fellowship had got pxxxxd the world over, as they gracefully put it. To keep the secret to themselves, donors of unlabelled bottles only made mention of the proof of the contents. One individual, who claimed to be the local commander of the Malayan People's Anti-Japanese Army, boasted his hooch would fuel aircraft.

For those in the brigade who had never encountered the Japanese in battle, the tendency of prisoners to bow their head whenever approached was in complete contrast to the atrocities committed by them, as related by numbers of Malays and Chinese. While in some captives there were sullen indications of resentment at being searched, their disarmament was eventually completed without any actual difficulty.

However, like a festering carbuncle threatening to erupt, one blemish did surface to spoil the semblance of a clean bill of health. The concern centered on a number of 'un-opened sardine tins', the jargon for midget submarines armed with limpet mines, still believed to be hostile. A number of such vessels had ignored orders to return to base and were reputed to be at large in the sea between Sumatra and Malaya.

Whatever may have been the actual truth of the matter, after the brigade was relieved of its duties on Penang Island orders were received to embark for a destination which would considerably add to the distance from the British Isles, to where eventual return was the predominant thought. First and foremost as the hankering was, when packing each item of kit in his haversack Jim was also mindful to ensure none of his digits upset the tenancy of any resident scorpion.

16
XIANG – GANG

East is East, and West is West
And never the twain shall meet
Till earth and sky stand presently
At God's great judgement seat.

But there is neither East nor West,
Border, nor breed, nor birth
When two strongmen stand face to face,
Though they come from the ends of the earth.

The Ballard of East and West.
Rudyard Kipling, 1865-1936.

As the vessel conveying the troops progressed southward towards the equator, conjecture among the passengers regarding its ultimate destination was endless.

On the ship, as part of the strength of brigade headquarters, was a small contingent of Dayaks, members of the indigenous group of people inhabiting southern Borneo. Though famed throughout the world as expert trackers, whose expertise in dense jungle was invaluable, on the deep they had no more idea where they were bound than the other troops.

Alphabetically, speculation included every place imaginable between Aachen and Zurich, but as nobody was able to come up with a location within South East Asia Command which commenced with X, unsurprisingly the letter never came into anyone's reckoning. Then again, none spoke Chinese, not even among the three or four individuals who were from Chinatown, in the East End of London, and who were of Chinese origin.

After a few days the ship's course turned northward. Within the same week and with darkness descending the troopship eventually dropped anchor at the entrance to Causeway Bay, the narrow stretch of water separating the island of Hong-Kong and Kowloon. Disembarkation had been envisaged on arrival but a series of unexpected events had played havoc with the timetable, in consequence of which it was postponed until the following morning. All that was visible from the vessel were the onshore illuminations, a cheerful sight following so many years of black-out. Until sleep overcame him and put an end to his idle curiosity Jim was baffled by the incessant sound that came from every direction. It was like the sound from an unimaginable number of castanettes.

During the course of the next day and dependent on the distance involved, the various units which made up each of the four commandos were either transported or made their way on foot to the areas they were to garrison. In the cases of W Troop and X Troop of 42 Commando, their bases were in the New Territories, on the mainland of China opposite Hong-Kong. Like the island, the New Territories were leased to Britain towards the end of the 19th century and were looked upon as a buffer-state from which to defend Hong-Kong from attack from the north. In area it is about 400 square miles and stretches from Mirs Bay in the east to Deep Bay in the west, and from Sha-Tau-Kok on the border with China to Kowloon in the south.

En route to their respective bases, in the light of day the quandary of the previous evening was resolved on the journey through the streets of Kowloon, where small groups of people squatted as they shuffled around dozens of small tiles. For most troops it was their introduction to mah-jong.

Travelling in convoy to the eastern side of the mainland, W troop were bound for the typically English named location of Clearwater Bay, while the destination of X troop was the distinctly more oriental sounding village of Sai- Kung. Beyond the well constructed roads in Kowloon, in a number of places and especially so along the more elevated parts of coastal sections where landslides had ruined long stretches, drivers were compelled to hug the landward side while driving with the utmost caution. During the period the troop were stationed at Clearwater Bay more than one vehicle came to grief and had to be winched from where it came to rest.

Such was the lack of navigable roadway leading to the isolation of Sai-Kung, impeding delivery of rations, stores and other essentials, that the commanding officer of X troop, Captain Hiram Potts, put his men to work on the construction of a decent road. In doing so he created a little fame. Initially named by the marines in his troop as Hiram's Highway, the road was later adopted by the legislative council of Hong-Kong. To the present day it continues to appear on maps and in guide books under that name.

At Clearwater Bay W troop were cosily billeted in a modern, American, missionary school, which elegant building looked rather out of place among the surrounding dilapidated dwellings. At the cluttered entrance of a number of them were hung a variety of weird objects to ward off evil spirits, the inhabitants prayed. In close proximity though very far removed in splendour, in a temple commemorating Tin Hau, Goddess Of The Sea, sacrificial first-fruits probably took the place of good luck tokens – a sort of two-way bet, just in case the supplications to the tin-gods outside their shacks were unfruitful.

The extensive but neglected grounds of the school were over-looked by barren hills on three sides and fell away sharply toward the sea on the other. Vehicular access was through impressive wrought iron gates flanked on each side by large, grey coloured pillars, on the other side of which was a smaller entrance for pedestrians. Neither one nor the other, the mules of the captive Japanese unit took it upon themselves to decide through which to leave and enter or, on the occasion when they were exceptionally awkward, whether to bother with either. Except for where a stretch of walling stood to left and right of the smaller gates, entry was possible practically anywhere, though not without misfortune as Jim later found – if not to his cost, financially, to his detriment, fractionally.

Contrary to the instilled belief of the dishonour of captivity the prisoners came to terms with the disgrace. Though in W troop there were those who had good reason to regard the Japanese with hostility, little by little the barrier was broken down with the passage of time, during which victor and vanquished were thrown together in the daily round of duties in camp. It was probably true to say that most found it required too much effort or mental strain to keep alive past hatred. Even if forgiveness was not quite the attitude maybe there was recognition that, in the heat of battle, revenge was not entirely one-sided. Few deeds acclaimed as brave by one side were thus voiced by those upon whom they were inflicted.

Apart from the tedious nature of tasks within the base life was quite agreeable. After six wearisome years of warfare it seemed almost unreal not to be under some form of violent threat. Tomorrow, next week, next year were far more likely to be greeted; but in many parts of the world and for all and sundry life would be altogether different to what it had been in far off 1939. Horizons had shifted and attitudes had changed.

Not unmindful of the unfortunate ones who would never again see another dawn, or those who would but under some form of handicap, thoughts turned in the direction of rehabilitation in civilian life. Like many others with whom he spoke, Jim could not really contemplate resumption of his previous employment, regardless of which grade he had achieved as the result of the exams he sat prior to enlistment. He wished to provide Widge and the intended quartet with far more than that which income from even the highest grade would enable. Yet all that he possessed which to an employer was remotely estimable was a substantial geographical knowledge of the streets of inner London.

However, as had happened on a good number of occasions during his life Jim was favoured with a stroke of good luck. Not long after W troop occupied the school a lieutenant/schoolmaster in the service of the Royal Navy was posted to Clearwater Bay. Just a couple of weeks after his arrival Jim was appointed his assistant and was placed in charge of and actually housed in the very considerable library situated in the grounds of the school. Surrounded by so much literature there was acute awareness and embarrassment at the thought of his limited vocabulary. The opportunity to improve it was eagerly seized, fully conscious of the fact he was blessed with a retentive memory; at least for such matters earnestly committed to it.

Without aiming to swallow the entire dictionary yet keen to satisfy an appetite for greater literacy, he managed to digest a generous portion of it. At the start of each day and commencing at the page previously reached, he swotted up on the meaning of a new list of words. During every evening the expanding number of definitions were reviewed, but the knowledge so laboriously acquired served only a limited purpose when engaged in conversation. Though usually sure of the existence of the word which he required, invariably there was an inability to call it to mind. Annoying as it was that command of the required word was lacking, he persevered with the daily exercise convinced that it would more adequately enable understanding of those persons who possessed better diction. However, encouraged by the naval schoolmaster to think more objectively of prospective employment, hunger for a larger slice of vocabulary gradually diminished.

The ritualistic daily dozen from the dictionary was replaced with tuition in a variety of subjects at a naval establishment on Hong-Kong island, together with participation in a fee-paying correspondence course conducted from further afield and covering subjects not available under the official scheme. Frequent and long conversations with the schoolmaster, who had been a head teacher in civilian life immediately prior to enlistment, began to stimulate Jim's interest. Memories were rekindled of pre-war occasions when former pupils made return journeys to schools to visit teachers, obvious testimony to the benefit they had derived and, for their teachers, immense satisfaction at the development of juveniles whose characters they had helped to mould and whose progress in life they had assisted.

When it became known that an official body was visiting units in each theatre of war in order to promote teaching as a career, Jim took the plunge and applied.

The twice postponed notification to appear before the selection board strained his fragile patience, but the lengthy interview was less daunting than had been anticipated: the successful outcome was more than he had dared to expect. The only cause for a degree of consternation arose from the projected date of his demobilisation. From the intersection of length of service and date of birth, on a chart which was produced, it would be March 1946, on which precise date, it was explained, the first interns would still be in residence at the appointed teacher training colleges. The recommendation was to think in terms of entry into college in spring of the following year. And was it, he vexatiously asked of himself, by fair means or foul that he was expected to survive for the intervening 12 months or so.

Though far removed from an ideal solution, the recommendation put to him was to sign on for a further period of service. Lacking a better option he agreed. As soon as the return to Clearwater Bay was accomplished an explanatory letter was written to Widge. He felt quite sure she would acknowledge that the improved standard of living they would enjoy, and the better start in life they would be able to provide for their children, would more than compensate for the sacrifice of just one further year of separation. Striving to convince himself more fully that the extra year would soon pass, he consoled his troubled mind with the thought that if Widge's discharge was at a later date than March 1946 the delay in setting up home would be less than one year. A comparable period in terms of days or even months was deliberately avoided.

In the exalted role of custodian, each weekday evening Jim operated a lending library: three mornings each week he found himself acting as a glorified errand boy. What, at meal times, was loosely referred to as food was several levels below the standard of putrid. The only substance that was determinable, not by taste, smell or appearance but on account of the vast quantity dished up in one form or another at every sitting, was apple – not completely reconstituted from its dehydrated state. So many were the boxes containing the wizened flakes of fruit, from floor to ceiling they occupied the very large dormitory previously devoted to band practice. The unambiguous notice previously etched on the door denoting the room's earlier function had been painstakingly obliterated and neatly replaced by unknown hands with 'The Bountiful Orchard'.

To keep pangs of hunger at bay personnel contributed to what was called the famine fund, armed with which proceeds Jim was driven to Kowloon to shop around in the market place for all sorts of produce – except apples. By sight he became fairly well known to the stall-holders. By word of mouth, in his capacity of buyer he was probably also well known as an easy touch, but if among mongers of Mong-Kok the view was all marines could be fleeced their vision was short-sighted.

In the sly manner of a wolf lurking in sheep's clothing, Jim's driver was engaged in a different transaction with other entre-preneurs. Beyond the border, in China, there was substantial demand for British manufactured cigarettes which were only obtainable via the black-market, the source of which was in Kowloon. There the quantity of cigarettes allocated to British troops was over-generous and supplied in cylindrical, hermetically sealed tins containing 50 – but not when they came to be sold.

Given a less dignified title by his mates than the one of a feather plucker chosen by his peacetime boss on a poultry farm, in camp and manipulated by his ingenious mind, the plucker's nimble fingers successfully removed labels gummed around the tins. With a fine file, tins were parted around the middle, cigarettes were removed and replaced with a tightly rolled strip of cardboard which, when it unwound inside the tins, wedged the two halves together again. He then refixed the labels. After sale in the market-place the counterfeit contents were resold, smuggled across the border and finally unloaded on distant Peking and Shanghai streets.

It took ages and ages for news of the fraud to filter back to Kowloon, but when it did the wary customers in the market tightly gripped and twisted the top and bottom of each tin before proceeding to hand over money to itching palms. To prevent the neck of the lorry driver being likewise twisted, he was replaced by another marine.

Subsequently seated next to the replacement driver in the cab of the lorry on a combined shopping and sales undertaking, some distance ahead a couple of coolies were noticed. As the vehicle drew closer the two Chinese veered to one side of the road and lowered the long bamboo pole to which there burden was attached. As they did so, Jim and the driver were astonished to see the object was a huge fish: in fact, a shark. Secure in the knowledge it was well and truly dead, motions signalled the offer of a lift. Smiles and gestures indicated its acceptance. While, balanced on the pole resting on a shoulder at each end, the weight of the shark had been manageable, from the struggle to shift it deadweight it was evident they needed assistance to hoist it on to their shoulders in the first place. Together, the four managed to heave it into the back of the lorry.

No person claiming to know Jim would describe him as discerning. The closest he came to appreciating the value of perception was when surveying the sexes. Should an object be remarked upon, or if something was pointed out to him he would take note of the disclosure, but he had precious little ability to judge things in terms of quantity, age or size. Of the shark, in Jim's mode of expression it was closer to quite a few feet in length rather than just a few. Equally vague, it was too large to be accommodated within the width of the lorry and was placed length wise. Fascinated in a gruesome sort of way, Jim remained in the back of the vehicle for the remainder of the journey, captivated time and again by sight of the monsters wicked looking teeth as its jaws were repeatedly prised apart by its captors, rather like a couple of dental students peering at molars in the gaping mouth of an anaesthetised patient.

As the year drew towards its close with the approach of Xmas, the first one since 1938 in which peace reigned, the initial group of repatriates departed for Blighty. Those who remained plotted and schemed to make the festival merry; with a decidedly capital M. Though it was not to be in the guise of Santa Claus, a brief visit to the base by the Allied Supreme Commander in South East Asia was announced. In preparation for the occasion everything, in and out of immediate sight was polished, painted, whitewashed, washed, neatly folded, or renovated. In neither breath-taking nor in eye-catching magnificence could Paradise, itself, have surpassed the camp – until the day of the visit by Lord Louis Mountbatten arrived.

Following one of the brigade's bloody but highly successful missions in Burma, in his capacity of supremo it was alleged that Lord Louis had implied the troops could expect to live off the fat of the land once the war was over. When dawn came on the day of his visit, on a wall directly opposite to where W troop would be lined up for his inspection an image of Mr Chad had been scrawled. He was a cartoon character popular with civilians and service personnel on account of his grumbling at shortages of every description, each of which complaints commenced with the caption 'Wot! No (followed by the commodity)

The figure of Chad's unsmiling face appearing above a sand-bagged parapet protested 'Wot! No Fat Of The Land!' Pools of sweat testified to the effort required in the race against time to erase the light-hearted sarcasm, but when vehicle after vehicle in the cavalcade bringing Lord Louis and his retenue drove through the gates the resemblance to Shangri-La had been restored.

Like those of previous years in the corps, Christmas morning was not ushered in by the bugler's blast of reveille accompanied by the duty sergeant's suggestion as to how hands might be better employed. Instead all the senior NCO's served tea to other ranks still in bed. Each of the bearers of tea and tidings clutched a sprig of mistletoe, but as none of the battledress Magi were loaded, neither with frankincense nor myrrh, let alone gold, their bedside manner and flirtatious chat was unavailing.

Breakfast left the feeling that those who had remained in bed had made the better choice. It also enticed suspicion that the cooks, too had made the very same decision. The difficulty experienced in scraping from enamelled plates the burnt offering congealed on them left no doubt the substance had been prepared on the previous evening and placed in the cookhouse ovens overnight.

Whether or not individuals had bothered to tumble out of bed to partake of breakfast, at the sitting the duty officer announced the gladdest of tidings for one and all. He disclosed that following lunch and without any formalities a number of lovely bits of crackling would be introduced. Slices of bread faltered between plates and mouths as wanton thoughts envisaged intimate moments with nymphs in nylons, who were regarded as more than just stocking-fillers. Anticipation of the midday feast and fraternisation whetted the appetite of every individual.

Hardly had lunch finished than the moment of truth arrived. Never can any child have felt so much disappointment as the items in its Xmas stocking were unwrapped as did the diners on surveying the contents of the small packages they received. Under the corny pretence that it came with the compliments of Lord Louis, inside was a crisp though fatty portion of skin of roast pork. Although unseasonable remarks were all but drowned out by the shindig which erupted, the more restrained points of view were to the effect that the day's tastiest morsel had been the Mepacrine (anti-malarial) tablet, which treat had not been enjoyed by the whole of W troop.

Prior to Christmas a small number of them had been detailed to act as escort for a party of Japanese prisoners of war who were being repatriated. It was debatable whether the envy among some of those not selected to accompany the captives was rational. On the slender supposition by the malcontents that among those returning to their homeland there might be a number of comfort girls, the voyage represented a romantic cruise to the land of the rising sun. Those in the troop with different desires of the flesh preferred not to expose theirs to the possible danger of residual radiation.

While there was not a shred of evidence as to the reliability of the assertion, the return of the escort party had been spoken of as "in good time for Christmas". That had arrived, but not them. As they were not back speculation on their whereabouts and upon valid reasons for their predicament were many, highly imaginative and helped to pass away an hour or two of an otherwise dull evening. The send-up which best suited the one established fact revolved around the name of the commissioned officer in charge of the escort party. In both rank and name befitting the satire, Lieutenant Pinkerton was adjudged to have jumped ship, in Honshu, in pursuit of 'Madam Flutter-By', leaving those in his charge up a creek in Kyoto, without a paddle.

Spoiled for choice with the silence of the grave, or the wail of bagpipes lamenting the absence of Bonny Prince Charlie with the dirge of 'Will ye no come back again' (on the face of it a shade doubtful in the 20th century), weird plans to celebrate a less funereal new year concentrated minds. Although some of the suggestions were novel, only one was realistic.

Together with nearby X troop, approaches were made to an adjacent naval establishment with the suggestion of a get together for hogmanay. Inexplicably named HMS *Nabcatcher*, to most service personnel it was known as HMS Crab-catcher, suggestive of shirt free arms stretched aloft and trouser free loins exposed for examination by a medical officer at periodical delousing inspections. In the spirit of camaraderie the marines pledged to drink a toast to HMS *Nabcatcher* and to all who itched aboard her, provided the host supplied the rum.

Uneventful was not the most appropriate word to describe the manner in which the evening unfolded; nor the consequences. Though issue of rotgut rum commenced in modest tots, due to never-ending queues for replenishment the quantities progressively increased and culminated in mugsful, as nothing larger was to hand. When, just short of dawn and those still conscious few in number, time for departure loomed, they who were horizontal were loaded into the back of the lorry head first. Stowed in this convenient position, with each pair of boots over-hanging the tailgate, soles were chalked with the destination of either Sai-Kung or Clearwater Bay to ensure correct delivery. Once those carcasses intended for the latter base were off loaded and dumped on bunks, Jim and two others able to keep themselves upright decided to give three Japanese trained mules the benefit of a breath of fresh air and a little, gentle exercise. As a result of previous instruction by the former muleteers but overconfident in their own personal ability due to the consumption of liquor, they saddled the beasts and off went the trio.

In the estimation of some people mules are stubborn: in the estimation of some Jim was stubborn. In the latter instance, he alone remonstrated, purely an example of misinterpretation. Whereas he displayed unflagging determination, he kidded himself, others saw it as obstinacy; but in the case of mules their stubborn streak was more in the nature of a chasm, the inscrutable, waterlogged surface and impenetrable depth of which ruled out all pretence.

On the outward, reluctant journey each step of the way was contested. Every time Jim's mount stopped and was urged forward with the slightest nudge of the heel it simply edged sideways, menacingly always towards the side of the road skirting the cliff-top. There it defiantly pawed the ground and tossed its head back and forth, cannily imprinting on Jim's mind it would toss him over the edge if there was so much as just one more prod with the heel.

However, once its head was turned in the homeward direction it gave the impression of winged flight upon reaching the padlocked gates of a knacker's yard. There was no stopping it. So he thought. On reaching the perimeter of the camp and without bothering to continue in the direction of the proper entrance, it galloped its headstrong way towards the stables. Most unfortunately this once defensive zone was scarred with trenches now overgrown and hardly visible from a distance, but over which, and in a fashion, the mule leapt – with Jim, also in a fashion, still in the saddle. Very shortly afterwards was the moment when life's little pleasures almost came to a premature end.

Until arrival in Hong-Kong Jim had not had much association with beasts of burden. Such dealings as there had been with horses were not in pursuit of recreational enjoyment seated on their back, arrayed in breeches and spurs, but in commercial employment in their path, armed with bucket and spade. He had never been to Aintree, either, but was firmly convinced none of the Grand

National obstacles were as formidable as the towering one which suddenly came into view and toward which his far from trusty steed was heading, full tilt. Dreading the mule might steamroller him if they fell, at next to the last moment he withdrew his feet from the stirrups. As though it had run into buffers, one moment later the mule suddenly stopped. Jim didn't. As he sailed through the air he contemplated the impact his descent might make and what impression it might make on him.

Of all the space to be found in China on which to alight, the spot which he picked was a poor choice. If, as he had heard, there was a place in the Crown Colony named Happy Valley, the gully in which had been cemented a rusty, but nevertheless sturdy-looking, girder did not encourage belief that was where he was heading, nor did it provide a happy landing. He knew his head would be all right. It had come up against far more solid surfaces than soil without causing him to bite the dust, on many occasions; but it was not dust and his skull which became unexpectedly acquainted.

The consequences of the irresistible force of gravity and the immovable iron post had an undesirable effect upon his torso. Winded was totally inadequate to describe the result of the amount of oxygen of which Jim's lungs were deprived; but the thorax was not the precise area introduced to the girder.

His two companions who dismounted and came to his aid said he looked bloody awful, which, perhaps, might better have been described as pale. He felt cold yet his skin was sweaty to the touch, and his throat was parched. Surprisingly there was no sign of blood anywhere. At first he declined their offer to get him on his feet again as he felt too giddy to get up, but hurriedly changed his mind upon the remark that if there was nothing more they could do they might as well go back to the billet. Once back there he flopped onto his bunk, from which he did not budge until the following morning; and then, only at Nature's insistence. For the first time he noticed a small amount of blood on his underpants. When passing water he found it in his urine, the upshot of which was his removal to 28th Indian General Hospital, on the outskirts of Kowloon. The card standing on the bedside locker which greeted him and which had presumably been left behind by the previous patient mockingly proclaimed 'Happy New Year'.

Although 28IGH was staffed almost exclusively by Indian doctors and nurses and the beds were mostly occupied by troops from the sub-continent, two wards were set aside for European, service personnel. If there were no more inmates in the second such ward than in the one to which Jim was admitted, business would appear to be rather on the slack side. In fact so short in number were the British invalids, it was jokingly said their discharge was invariably thwarted by the staff on almost any pretext. These injured and ailing seemed to be regarded as trophies; though it had to be conceded the amputated limbs and removed organs were not exhibited on plaques above each bed, bearing the date of severance.

Jim underwent X-rays, probes of a nature and duration he would sooner have been spared, and intimate examinations which warranted arrest, but nothing was discovered. Or next to nothing. Gazed upon by turbaned medical students, at arm's length the consultant handled Jim's John Thomas as one tends a withering bloom. After fumbling less gently than Jim would have preferred, the consultant spoke in subdued terms to the juniors who subserviently nodded their agreement. Possibly Muslim brethren who all devoutly observed the rites of their religion, recollection of the assenting audience prompted Jim to seriously consider the principal's strong recommendation during the following 24 hours. As for the wicked, cursed with no rest during the night he repeatedly delved into whether the unanimous advice was anything more than an ingenious attempt to delay release from hospital, but for the sake of Virginia Margaret and her siblings he decided to agree to circumcision.

The pre-surgical preparations and post-surgical exclamations of acute discomfort were along similar lines to those that damned memories of Newton Abbot, although on that occasion there was the prospect of 14 days sick leave which acted like balm on stretched stitches, and anticipation of arms stretched around Eileen, but when he finally managed to escape the clutches of the warders he knew there would be no prospect of arms encircling Widge.

Nor, he well realised, would there be the slightest compassion when he eventually got back to Clearwater Bay. The encounter with the scalpel would raise nothing more than smirks. Admittedly trivial and distinctly different as was his operation compared to the much later 'take off' of the first man to land on the moon, and despite the fact that Jim's surgical ordeal was not likewise televised, comparably it was one small snip for the surgeon but a giant leap for manhood.

In grim reality, his minor surgery served only to emphasize the hardly imaginable misfortune which befell another member of W troop. Swimming in the bay, a sergeant was attacked by a voracious fish. Taking him first by one ankle then the other, the outcome was both of his feet had to be amputated. Explaining the horrific ordeal while recovering in hospital, he felt that what attacked him was probably a barracuda rather than a shark. He maintained he would not have been able to wrench the grasp from his first attacked ankle, as he did manage, had it been a shark: but before other swimmers were able to come to his assistance his second one was lacerated.

Another tragic event occurred some time after Jim was discharged from hospital and happened while he was in the library, situated next to the room from which came a loud bang. There was no mistaking the sound of a weapon which had been fired. The scene at which he arrived as fast as his legs would carry him was ghastly. Three or four room mates of the casualty surrounded the body and, perceiving that life was not extinct, took means to stem the profuse bleeding to prevent him choking. Another individual had dashed to get transport to rush the lad to hospital. Lying motionless except for the slight sign he was still breathing, he had shot himself in the head using the pistol of an officer in the troop for whom he acted as batman.

When something approaching normality was resumed and his personal belongings were gathered together for safekeeping in the stores, a letter found under his pillow revealed that the correspondent had terminated their relationship. It was concluded by room mates this was probably the letter he had been seen reading on several occasions during the day. One of those gathered at the scene in the room was fully aware of the effect such letters can have on individuals so far removed from the consolation of home and who, perhaps were still highly-strung as the result of what they endured during the war.

Though the bullet had entered his right temple a little above the height of the right ear and made its exit just above his left jaw, miraculously he too managed to survive, although as those who visited him while he was in hospital discovered, his speech was incoherent. In what manner he and the sergeant would manage to cope with their life, which had been spared in war and tragically spoiled in peace, was difficult to imagine.

In sombre mood the unit continued with the daily routine, fancying it to be more mundane than ever before. Now regarded more as a chore than a pleasant diversion, visits to the market place in Kowloon proceeded as before, but on one occasion the bountiful stalls were fewer in number than was usual. Gesturing his puzzlement with outstretched and up-turned palms of each hand while shifting his glance from left to right, from each and every street trader the only response he obtained was 'Tai Fung'. Jim's Cantonese being even less than the scrap of Hindi which he had mastered, he hadn't the slightest clue as to their explanation. He was left in no doubt as the day wore on.

From late afternoon and increasing in intensity during the evening a strong wind blew. Throughout the night which permitted precious little sleep it raged more and more, falling objects interrupting whatever snatches of light slumber did overcome him from time to time. Though during the hours of darkness the fury of the elements was disconcerting, at day-break and until evening when the strength of the wind abated he found the forces of nature absolutely spellbinding. With stern implications of being blown off their feet, the recommendation was not to venture out. The inclination was otherwise and the reality was that nobody was uprooted, but in varying degrees a few individuals did finish up the worse for wear as a result of falling debris. Far more entitled to sympathy were those units under canvas who, during the night and in torrential rain, were deprived of their tents by the typhoon.

No mean feat in itself, if with tongue in cheek it is possible to smile to oneself, Jim did so at the thought of how simple it was to convert Cantonese into English, or vice versa. Tai-Fung: typhoon. He repeated the Chinese expression over and over again. Practising very careful attention to his own tuition, perfect pronunciation was gradually achieved by lengthening the letter U to OO, and by softening the letter G. Watched inquisitively while verbally struggling to translate English obscenities which might come in handy in a Chinese slanging-match, the expression of concern on the face of a perplexed oriental bystander was for Jim's softening brain.

Symptoms of another kind were perceptible on the border with China. The fragile truce between the Kuomintang Government forces led by General Chiang Kai-Shek, and the troops of the Chinese Communist Party under the chairmanship of Mao Zedong, came to an end with the defeat of Japan. The resumption of open hostilities between the two factions was not long delayed, and the stronger forces of Chairman Mao were soon driving hell for leather southward towards the New Territories, through which the British were fully prepared to allow the nationalist armies to withdraw and, in Hong-Kong, embark for the Kuomintang stronghold of Formosa. The question which everyone weighed was whether the communist troops would attempt to cross the border in pursuit.

Not surprisingly, when 42 Commando were moved up to the border and surrounding zone, with the prospect of it becoming a battle area, there was little scope for the presence of the lieutenant/schoolmaster. Instead, he was posted to brigade headquarters. By that time looked upon as the officer's number one (by virtue of the fact there was no number two), Jim went with him.

As had consistently been the sarcastic jeer by troops in each of the four commando units, life was cushy at HQ. For one thing the food was edible and more than adequate in quantity; and for another, though at a cost, there was choice at lunch time and at dinner. In addition to the food served in the mess which by and large was placed in the ambiguous category of not too bad, a Chinese couple had been authorised to open a restaurant within the premises occupied by the brigade. The agreement stipulated the tenancy would be entirely free but on the understanding the price of all meals on the menu would be subject to the consent of a small committee within HQ, and that the restaurant was out of bounds to all except headquarters personnel. With no overhead expenses at all, the meals were provided at very attractive prices which in turn generated a large turnover for the proprietors. For a while the venture ran smoothly and was greatly appreciated by all concerned.

Though the concession was good-hearted, unwisely, troops were allowed to obtain meals on tick. Chits for the sum involved were signed on the express understanding they would be honoured following the next pay parade. Mostly they were, but as always seems to be the situation when privileges are granted, a small number of individuals were prepared to take advantage of the arrangement and unpaid bills mounted. Harshly, if understandably, the powers that be refrained from direct intervention and passed the buck to a substandard type of intelligence section, consisting of one junior NCO.

Examining the signatures on the long overdue chits, Jim knew that Mickey Mouse and Donald Duck were not on the staff of HQ and he had grave doubts about Peter Pan, too. There were also many others which would never be traced. In bold letters he made out several notices to the effect that meals would only be provided on credit on production of service pay books, which notification was placed underneath the sheet of glass covering each table. With gestures and in conjunction with the use of his own pay book he indicated to the proprietors they should satisfy themselves that the person presenting the pay book identified with the photograph on the inside cover and, alongside the signature on the chit, they should copy the service number shown beneath the photo. Through motions he also made it clear the chits with the false signatures should be torn up as they were never likely to be redeemed. Though anger must have been felt, the smiles of the owners of the business signified their gratitude for the advice given, while the disposal of the chits indicated their acknowledgement of the bad debts.

The relatively small help which they had received gave no reason for them to dwell upon thoughts of an appropriate manner in which to return the favour, but just around the corner, both in terms of time and in distance, an entirely chance encounter by Jim led them to do so without the slightest hesitation.

There were of course no longer any shopping sprees in the street markets of Kowloon in the hapless quest for inexpensive vegetables. Instead, and in the capacity of assistant to the naval schoolmaster, journeys of another nature were just as frequent both in the New Territories and on the Island of Hong-Kong. The purpose was to establish a small library in each location where troops of marines were stationed. On the whole the buildings were stocked with reference books and pamphlets

containing information and designed to assist personnel returning to civilian occupations. Quite apart from the considerable
number who had very little enthusiasm for a return to their
previous employment, it was more than probable many would
discover their services were no longer required due to the fact
many businesses had simply folded in consequence of the war or
had been drastically affected as a result of a crop of innovations.

It was when en route to the docks to collect a consignment of
books, and on the very day when Jim first encountered Chang,
that the naval schoolmaster happened to mention a novelty
which, he predicted, would give rise to the end of another
hitherto thriving enterprise – that of the manufacture of
blotting-paper. No longer an essential on every school desk
throughout the British Isles nor by pen-pushers in every office,
a Hungarian had very recently patented a ball-point pen. Named
after him, the mass production of biro pens did completely
dispense with the need to blot wet ink.

The journey to the wharfage was on an uncomfortably hot
day, with the blazing sun turning the cab of the lorry into a
heated oven. To provide respite the officer parked the vehicle in
a cavernous area beneath a disused building. It turned out they
were not the sole occupants of the dilapidated and unsanitary
premises. Except for one, the remainder of the squatters fled,
leaving behind what it would have been shameful to
acknowledge as personal belongings. Still bedded on its sorry
heap of tatters and unkempt in its pitiful clothing, a child whose
gender was indeterminable, and whose age was debatable, glared
its resentment at the blasted intrusion. Its privacy was not disturbed for an unendurable length of time. Enquiry ascertained
that the ship conveying the awaited literature had been delayed
at Singapore and would not arrive until the following morning.

At many cracks after dawn Jim again stood on the quayside.
Surveying the activity with the driver who had brought him,
from opened holds of berthed ships towering cranes hoisted
nets crammed with cargo. At far more than sufficient height to
ensure safe clearance, jibs were swung landward and, in
accordance with weird gesticulations from watchful stevedores,
loads were carefully lowered and by different means dispersed in
various directions. Off watch crews came down gangways, at the
foot of which tipsy-looking seamen paid for the hire of

rickshaws in which they had returned to commence theirs. In a different direction and in the company of another, Jim was sure one of the pair was the youngster who had seen off the schoolmaster and himself on the previous day. Halting every now and again, among the litter something edible was pounced upon and contested, which morsel of grub seemed to be sufficiently palatable to line a hungry stomach. As they drew closer the NAAFI van with the elevenses happened to arrive, from which was obtained tea and a couple of packets of biscuits. As neither the driver nor Jim fancied the contents, each of the children were given a packet.

The sturdy wooden boxes containing the books were off-loaded and given clearance. Far too heavy to be lifted on to the truck, they were opened and the contents safely stowed on the vehicle. One of the two juveniles was still at Jim's side and presently began to hand books up to the driver who was stacking them. Not nearly as quick to realise the faux pas he was committing, as was the lad who jumped at the chance of a ride in the lorry, he was still loitering outside HQ on the following morning. When Jim set out for breakfast he had not noticed him. But, seated at the foot of the steps leading to the mess, when Jim came out there was no possibility of overlooking him.

It did not require either a high degree of intellect nor a vivid sense of imagination to grasp the situation, literally on the doorstep: but the wisdom of Solomon would have been an asset in deciding how to handle it. As is always the desperate habit of sterile minds, Jim resorted to the hope the problem would simply go away. Yet he was aware that if, when he again ventured outside, the waif had disappeared it would be some time before his conscience was clear. In fact at lunch time he was still at the entrance to the mess. The pleading look which the youngster gave could not be ignored. Backing away from the entrance, with a jerk of his head Jim gave notice to follow. The lad was not slow to do so.

Though he knew full well it was in conflict with the agreement with the restaurateur, with his young companion Jim boldly entered the premises. If an explanation was required he would give one, though he thought it more expedient just to order some food and then provide motives once the concession had been achieved. Quite deliberately he chose to order for his young guest first, employing the assistance of the proprietor in helping with the choice. There was no hesitation in making his recommendation but, Jim thought, far more discussion than the contents of the menu could possibly warrant. During the course of the ravenous consumption of what was chosen, the owner took the opportunity to relate as best he could details of the boy's background, obviously obtained in the course of the dialogue.

The sketchy disclosure which most struck Jim concerned the age of the lad – he did not catch the name the restaurateur mentioned. The probable reason why it was so difficult to appreciate he had seen his twelfth birthday was due to the fact he was so small in stature. Though he was Chinese his place of birth and early upbringing was Macau, a tiny Portuguese dependency less than 40 miles distant. Together with both of his parents he had returned to Canton following the Japanese seizure of Manchuria and Peking. Whether his father was killed while resisting the occupation of Canton was not revealed, nor how he came to be abandoned by his mother: but orphaned he was. Under whichever of the international auspices he entered Hong-Kong could not be remembered, but of his terrible daily struggle for survival and the hardship he suffered on the cruel streets there was full account.

Ignoring the adage directed towards those once bitten, and indifferent to whatever philosophical remarks Confucius may have had for such folly, Jim abruptly swept to one side the obstacles to be overcome. Through the owner of the business he enquired whether the youth would be interested in a little job in the junior NCOs mess, with a little pay attached. Another drawn out conversation took place between the oriental countrymen, firmly impressing on Jim's declining patience the notion their language lacked the convenience of yes and no. During the tête-à-tête the wife of the proprietor appeared on the scene and joined in. Temporarily stranded with his own thoughts, boomerang fashion the earlier problem of the lad's entire welfare returned to play havoc with Jim's mind, most particularly in respect of some form of accommodation. His presence while just assisting in the mess would be met with little more than raised eyebrows by senior NCOs or officers, should they encounter him, but none of them would turn a blind eye if he was found in the lodgings. Fortunately it was never put to the test. The restaurateurs offered to provide a place in their quarters. Furthermore, in order to eke out his income from the junior NCO's mess they promised to put him to use in the restaurant, helping to wash up and to sweep up after each meal time.

From the very outset more readily accepted while working in the busy restaurant, in the corporal's mess Jim made a firm point of explaining the boy's presence behind the bar and at tables, emptying ash trays and collecting glasses. Still without knowledge of the boy's actual name, he was given the one of Chang to which he quickly became accustomed. Obviously unaware of what was said of him, in the early days of his adoption his features expressed doubt bordering on unease but, in the course of time, across his broad face the smile which lit it and replaced his frown was clear indication that he felt at home.

When Jim ultimately departed on the long voyage to England more than 12 months later, Chang was still at home.

17

HOMEWARD BOUND

I read within a poet's book
A verse that stole the page –
"Stone walls do not a prison make,
Nor iron bars a cage".

That may be true. But something more;
You'll find where'er you roam,
That marble floors and gilded walls
Can never make a home.

But every home where love abides
And friendship is a guest,
Is surely home, and home, sweet home,
For there the heart can rest.

Home Song. Henry Van Dyke

Although at Brigade Headquarters new friendships had developed with other marines and pongos in number one and number five army commandos, sketchy contact was still maintained with other, longstanding comrades in 42. What with one thing and another on the border their hands were pretty full.

In addition to the military aspect on the frontier, smuggling (in both directions) and the flow of refugees (only in one direction – southward into the New Territories) made constant demand upon those stationed there. Quite obviously not the only unit who, before their transfer to the border, flogged tins of cigarettes on the black market in the back streets of Kowloon, where successful their tasks included confiscation of the tins – full or otherwise.

Although it was not actually whispered behind raised hands that the feather plucker in W troop, who had devised the means of extracting cigarettes from sealed tins, also 'liberated' some of the impounded tins – thereby ensuring for himself a perpetual source of income – few in the troop were so rash as to dismiss the speculation completely.

Tending to exonerate suspicious minds, in Kowloon relays of

refugees streaming south from the border were arrested and found to be in possession of contraband fags.

From the increasingly troublesome border with China, the main highway through the New Territories and towards the south led to Nathan Road, the principle thoroughfare in Kowloon.

Situated as brigade headquarters was in Mody Road, a comparatively serene byway off Nathan Road, the clamour of humanity threading its way along the latter turning was inescapable.

Those in the form of Chinese nationalist troops who were often to be seen passing through Kowloon, en route to their future but highly unpredictable existence on the island of Formosa, looked pathetically dejected and miserably armed to continue their struggle against the communist forces, let alone to overcome them.

The weapons in their possession were limited to light calibre, antiquated rifles and pistols which, brandished in the faces of travellers on the public highway, would not have caused a great deal of alarm nor resulted in the meek surrender of personal property. If it could be remotely viewed as such, transport consisted of little more than small, rickety hand carts, much like those knocked together in next to no time in Jim's boyhood. In those days, and drawn along in the small, wooden apple box mounted on an axle with a wheel at each end, (which combination had been retrieved from a discarded pram), fire wood or horse dung was conveyed from door to door. Along the main thoroughfare of Kowloon those who dragged behind them no better version of Jim's mode of transport, conveyed in theirs no greater treasures.

If ludicrous means of conveyance, sundry equipment and weapons were well past their prime, the ages of vast numbers in the crestfallen procession were incompatible with the concept of veterans. Though Jim was fully aware he had badly underestimated Chang's years when he first encountered him, there was no mistaking the fact that, among the passing faces, the dejected jowls of quite a considerable proportion were still covered in bumfluff. He wondered whether, like young Chang, some had been orphaned and had sought basic necessities in the form of food, shelter and clothing within the ranks of the

Kuomintang forces streaming southward from the frontier. Reports which regularly filtered through from the border spoke of their continual harassment once in the British sector. There was good reason to suspect the intimidation was by communist supporters from within Kowloon walled city. Violence from that quarter was not unknown to brigade headquarters.

Due either to an appalling oversight or to misunderstanding when the New Territories were ceded to Britain, a small enclave in Kowloon remained under Chinese jurisdiction. At one time the location had been a Chinese garrison, around which had been erected a defensive wall. Though the troops had been withdrawn, the civil population who later came to occupy the area within the abandoned fortification considered their overriding loyalty was to China and their morality not answerable to colonial rule. Over succeeding years it became a notorious den of thieves and a hot bed of insurrection. A veritable no-go area.

Times without number all available ranks at HQ were called out when riotous crowds got beyond the control of the constabulary. Although in the course of their every day duties small revolvers were carried by the police, when troops were called upon they were forbidden to arm themselves with anything other than the short handle of an entrenching tool. By those in authority it was thought a display of weapons would be likely to incite the situation and provoke shooting by known armed gangs within the walled city.

On occasions when rushed to the scene of uncontrollable rioting, with truck drivers giving little, if any, regard for speed restrictions, on arrival troops were unfailingly met with a barrage of missiles, against which the only protection was a steel helmet. From a distance, some in the reception committee hurled bottles. Others pitched in with stones, bricks or chunks of concrete, according to strength of arm. Facing the unruly mob, the devised routine saw ranks drawn up in open order with military precision, though an unsanctioned step to one side to dodge the flight of a missile was not frowned upon as un-disciplined. When, frequently in error, it appeared stocks of missiles were running out, the order was given to advance, on which command all semblance of control was lost. The rioters fled in all directions with the troops in pursuit. All that continued to be hurled was abuse. Any of either side who stumbled or fell were savagely beaten up by equally angry antagonists, rather diminishing the likelihood of gentlemanly handshakes at the conclusion of the squabble.

There was good reason to suspect that the flight of the protesters was a lure; to entice those in hot pursuit towards the enclave, the outcome of which was only too predictable in the clutches of groups of Triads who were known to rule the roost in the walled city. Their triangular symbol, outwardly indicating the serene coexistence of heaven, earth and mankind was a familiar sight on many old buildings. Details of their origin, and insight into the brotherhood's none too subtle, criminal threats were brought to Jim's attention in a most bizarre fashion.

Sitting in the room in which the library was established, early one evening a young lieutenant entered. While motioning to Jim to remain seated, from his own head the officer removed his green beret. He was noticeably agitated and spoke with emotion. Talking of two small holes in the centre of two slightly singed patches, he said he had been fired at and the holes were where a bullet had gone through and out of his beret, miraculously without causing any injury. It had happened in Mong Kok, adjacent to the quarter in which Triad gangs existed. He never went so far as to declare he was fired upon by a member of such gangs, but before leaving the library he went into considerable detail about their formation. According to whatever or whoever was his source of information, the origin of the organisation was in the interior of China and came into existence 300 years ago. Its objective was to restore to power the Ming Dynasty following its overthrow by Mongols in 1644. For what purpose the history of the cult was thrust upon the lieutenant, and for what reason he was shot at, Jim found so odd he could think of nothing to say except for how lucky the officer had been.

What, if any, connection it may have had with the lieutenant's strange encounter was entirely speculative, as precisely what was laid bare was never divulged to all and sundry, but a short time afterwards the officer was discharged on medical grounds and returned to England.

Apart from the involvement in periodical, riotous dust-ups, existence at HQ was agreeably placid or downright boring according to one's temperament. However there were a couple of typhoons which happily broke the monotony suffered by the more venturesome. Due to the intensity of one of the storms and because of what was left in its wake, several parties of marines were detailed for an unusual mission in conjunction with the Royal Navy. Manned by the senior service, on board a number of motor torpedo boats the troops went to the rescue of a number of Chinese boats which had been unable to reach the safety of typhoon shelters at Yau Ma Tei, or at Tung lo Wan, and which had been washed up on stretches of the mainland and a number of remote islands.

As the bows of the MTBs plunged into deep troughs, only to be rocked from side to side on the crest of the next huge wave, the feeling was either one of exhilaration or of excruciation depending on what each individual had hurriedly swallowed at breakfast a short time beforehand, and upon its even more rapid rejection by churned up stomachs. For considerable lengths of time completely hidden from sight by mountainous swell, menacing rocks suddenly and frequently appeared, the skilful and split-second, evasive action taken by the person at the helm further deranging the flow of bile.

Once vessels that had been forsaken were located, from as close to the wreckage as it was safe for the torpedo boats to venture, troops clambered over the ships rails and waded ashore. The unappetising rations which had been issued were nibbled with little enjoyment during what remained of the ill-tempered day, mostly spent surrounding the wrecks: throughout the hours of darkness armed guard was mounted over them. Within hearing distance of any cry for assistance, those not keeping guard spent an interrupted night beneath tentage, which filtered the downpour rather than prevented its entry. Thankfully morning dawned more promisingly.

On an oscillating receiving and transmitting set the signaller in the salvage party picked up a message that at 1000 hours aircraft would approach the island on which Jim's party were marooned. From a safe altitude they would release containers in which were food and drink as well as other essentials. With make shift devices for beacons, a dropping zone was marked out and they waited. Until the canisters came floating down, not by any means entirely within the designated area, none in Jim's party had the slightest idea the rocky island was inhabited: but, as they found out when they gave chase after the multitude who made off with what had providentially descended from heaven, a sheltered bay provided quite a substantial harbourage. Tied up along side their water-borne neighbours, and thus existing cheek by jowl as undoubtedly had been the custom among countless generations, hundreds lived aboard tiny sampans and slightly larger junks.

As with the Greeks, with the reputation of a word for everything, the Chinese may have had a term for the ease with which the marauders leapt from boat to boat with what they had plundered. Jim certainly had a word for it: suicidal, in consequence of which he believed further pursuit would have been unproductive, except, perhaps, for any peckish sharks lurking beneath the waves.

Relieved by other sentinels on the following day, for a considerable while existence at HQ was unruffled by typhoon or riot. The period of the year for the former disturbance was coming to an end. Unconstrained by season, the latter lacked spontaneity due to preparations for the much celebrated Mid-Autumn festival, but like all good things the tranquillity came to an end, and in a totally unexpected manner for Jim.

A handsome profit, which materialised due to the unquenchable thirst of practically the entire membership of the junior NCO's mess, was used to purchase a small number of musical instruments, which items became available on the disbandment of a touring entertainment group prior to their return to England. In due course the small band which came into existence made the mess well known among several other units, from whose patronage the accumulated profit funded a further increase in the number of instruments. Unfortunately, it was the dubious disappearance of a couple of them that were instrumental in bringing about Jim's disappearance.

He was formally approached by an officer's batman in one of the army commando units, which was awaiting repatriation, following its replacement with the arrival in Hong-Kong of 45 Royal Marine Commando. The batman's inquiry was as to whether on the approaching weekend the band would provide musical entertainment at the planned farewell party. After checking the service of various members of the band would be available and willing, their agreement was passed on to the batman.

Evidently the performance went on until well into the early hours of the particular Sunday morning, when the ability of any musician to drive back to HQ was quite out of the question, on account of which the instruments were left on the premises hired for the occasion. It was not until an advanced hour on Monday morning that a truck was laid on and called to collect them, when it was found two of the instruments were missing.

While from the outset of the disclosure Jim suspected he would have a struggle on his hands in obtaining compensation for the corporal's mess, he was furious to find that no matter by whom his grievance was heard the response was always along the same lines – to the effect that the arrangement had been an unofficial matter between the committee of the junior NCO's mess and the since departed officer. No claim, whatsoever, could be said to rest with the officer's mess.

Ultimately permitted the opportunity to appear before the Brigade-Major (the final arbiter) but not for one single moment expecting the outcome to be any different, prior to the anticipated confrontation Jim made a decision regarding the level of resentment he was inclined to think he could display, without landing himself in yet further trouble. Each of his assumptions proved to be accurate. The judgement on the matter of recompense was final. Careful to avoid giving the impression it was the opinion held by himself, the major propounded the view that the disposal of the instruments by one of the musicians during the weekend in question could not be altogether ruled out.

On the other subject the major seemed indifferent to Jim's resolution to relinquish two chevrons and revert to the rank of marine, signifying belief Jim's demotion would not vastly impair the entire structure and competence of South East Asia Command.

In spite of the brigade-major's attitude, perhaps perfectly aware the final throw of the dice was his, in Jim's estimation the officer did seem to relent, well somewhat: to the extent that Jim would be sacrificing not solely his daily rate of pay as a substantive corporal, but also the sum due as gratuity pay on eventual demobilisation … but then the major could not possibly be expected to know the deficit would be compensated by a corresponding increase in the balance of pay made to Jim by the General Post Office, on whose payroll he continued to exist and would remain until his discharge from the Royal Marines.

It was while thus meditating and inwardly congratulating himself upon the degree of compassion his ostensibly selfless cause had managed to restore in the aching heart of the officer, and when contemplating if it would result in a most generous whip-round among the more senior officers, that the proceedings were brought to an abrupt end in accordance with Jim's perceived self-sacrifice.

Almost on his feet before the ink was dry, the brigade-major's order was as brief as it was devastating. In conformity with service regulations regarding demotion, when reprisal by other ranks for past acts committed by the demoted was the foremost consideration (and, Jim thought, an excuse for riddance), he was to be transferred with immediate effect to 'Four Five', as the recently arrived commando was designated.

Though not actually nursing a grudge against the BM, the posting was contrary to what had been expected. Yet again esteemed friendships would be severed and as a result of a loss for which Jim did not consider himself primarily responsible.

With the exception of the words spoken by Chang, on the last evening Jim closed the bar in the corporal's mess it was most difficult to estimate whether strong drink may have contributed to the sincerity of some of the parting remarks. In the case of Chang's farewell its brevity was its sincerity, as well as being a mystery to most who overheard it.

Though Chang understood most of the English spoken to him, little of the English he had learned to speak was recognisable by most individuals. The main drawback to grasping what he said was due to his faulty pronunciation of the letter R, which always sounded like the letter L. Jim had discovered this defect in the youngster's speech quite by chance, when he came across him seated in the mess one morning during a break while re-stocking empty shelves. Chop-sticks in hand, he was tucking into a bowl of 'Flied Lice', a most generous offering of which Jim swiftly declined.

To Chang's "Cheelio colpolal", in his no better and far more limited Cantonese, Jim departed with "Ch'ing-Ch'ing". No longer an NCO, Jim handed over the keys of the mess.

*****

Though never previously stationed in Hong-Kong, he had made the short trip to the island on the Star Ferry from Kowloon a large number of times, when attending the makeshift school in the building appointed by the Royal Navy, but while making the crossing to join Four Five, it struck him as never before that with countless sampans, junks, ocean-going liners, troopships and warships discharging every imaginable category of waste into the stretch of water, the Chinese appellation of 'Fragrant Harbour' was a Confucian masterpiece of 'triumph of mind over matter'.

He did not proceed to his new quarters full of the joys of spring. Feeling more than a trifle peeved at the outcome of the loss of the instruments for which he was not to blame, when, a few days after his arrival at Stanley Barracks harsh quarantine was imposed, he began to wonder if he would be held responsible for the loss of liberty which that entailed.

Within a matter of days some in the room in which he was quartered were affected by bouts of vomiting. Several suffered severe attacks of diarrhoea: a couple were subject to both ailments. Described as rice water runs by a sick bay attendant who first treated the patients who was renowned for a glossary of medical terms of his own, the medical officer was more precise and diagnosed cholera which brought down the curtain for shore leave for everyone in the block. Not even allowed out of the dormitories for meals, food was conveyed to the inmates by a couple of Chinese commis chiefs who were employed at the barracks. With vigorous taps on the row of window panes of the building to ensure the delivery was noticed and the containers were gathered, those who had nervously deposited the meal on the sills scampered away like greased lighting before any of the stricken occupants could get to the windows.

Reading, letter writing and various forms of gambling occupied most dull hours of most individuals, but not sufficiently. Every day seemed to exceed 24 hours duration. The tireless padre, adding to his task of saving depraved souls, also came to the rescue of sanity with several board games, but that which he produced and which contributed most in the way of relieving tedium was a small, though largely wheezy, portable gramophone and a huge pile of records.

Although before leaving England for the Far East everyone in Four Five had been inoculated against cholera, they were given a 'lucky' booster to increase immunity, but for a further few weeks all precautions remained in place. During that interval, which produced no other suspect cases, the period of incubation passed. Like jailbirds whose release was pending, talk was of getting out.

Situated as the barracks were, close to the lower terminus of a funicular railway, the spectacle of carriages ascending and descending Victoria Peak had revived a long held urge to visit a site which attracted Jim's attention whenever waiting to board the Star Ferry in Kowloon. The towering object of his curiosity stood towards the top of the peak.

Curiously named by the Japanese 'The Temple Of The Divine Wind' and neatly emblazoned with fifteen feet high Chinese ideograms meaning 'Heroic Memorial', when it was built Shinto priests presided over the ceremony, at which a sacred sword was embedded in the masonry once the foundations were laid. When finally erected it was supported on a dozen concrete legs and stood eighty feet high. Following their conquest, during the occupation the Japanese treated the prisoners of war brutally and, with few exceptions, the civil population only a little better. Unsurprisingly, neither the rescued inhabitants of Hong-Kong nor the troops who came to their rescue saw the slightest connection between the monument and anything even remotely divine with regard to the 'Japs'.

On the day quarantine was ultimately lifted the weather was beautiful, with clear blue sky; though regardless of its mood Jim would have pursued his intention. Awaiting the cable drawn carriage which would take him to within walking distance of the memorial, Jim was surprised to learn the height of the peak was only a little above 1,800 feet. From across the harbour, in Kowloon he had formed the impression it was far higher. He was even more surprised to hear the distant rumble of thunder. Continuing to read the typed notes about the railway which hung in the little booth, he was impressed by the fact that since its opening well before the end of the previous century there had not been a single accident.

Sincerely hoping his first ever conveyance by funicular railway would not spoil the record as he stepped aboard, he was more than a little amazed at the gradient of the track, especially when, on the upward journey, he turned to look behind. It gave the uncanny sensation of being suspended in mid-air. The thunder also increased its threat, he seemed to think. A short walk from the terminus at the summit he was confronted by a military policeman. What Jim had taken to be claps of thunder were, in fact, a series of detonations. In retribution for many past atrocities in Hong-Kong, work was in progress to demolish the detested Japanese shrine.

Back in barracks that evening, when the topic of conversation was mainly of how various individuals or groups had spent their reinstated liberty, a copy of the morning edition of the South China Post was thrust into Jim's hand. A short paragraph on an inside page revealed what was due to take place, and what the provost-sergeant stated was happening on the hillside. On the following day but now on the front page of the same publication the headline was even more brief. Comparable with the bizarre newspaper heading disclosed when on the NCO's course at Deal, giving the impression that in the First World war 50,000 stranded Germans had enabled the French to 'recycle' 50,000 bottles, news of the event on the peak on the previous morning could also have been better composed. On the somewhat blunt side of forthright, to the embarrassment of the devout it confessed DIVINE WIND BROKEN!!!

The period of time spent in barracks on the island was short-lived. Amid ever-increasing tension on the border with China, Four Five were despatched to the frontier.

At Lo Wu facilities were not over-elaborate. For the troops there were flimsy tents, in which to pray they would withstand the weather and enable sleep at night, and in which to eat the food dished up at the field kitchen by day. For the isolated Chinese community existence also appeared a touch unsophisticated. In snake infested paddy-fields where darting eyes kept careful watch for ineradicable and highly venomous, banded kraits as they wriggled through the ooze, rice was still laboriously planted by hand. In closer proximity to the tireless, stooped backs, threadbare clothing gave indication the reward for their labour left little for its renewal. Whether in or out of the rice-beds, feet were unshod. Toil in the fields was interrupted only to answer the calls of nature.

The pitiable shacks to which they retired when darkness compelled a halt suggested the dwellings had not actually been erected, but had occurred as boulders and boughs of trees came to rest following an avalanche. The spectacle of the rather young and the elderly clutching heaps of brushwood or carrying cans of water, of which they had gone in search hours earlier, gave an atmosphere of timelessness to the woe-begone settlement. In typical service fashion, between the troops the place acquired the name of 'Lo, woe'.

During the time Jim spent in the locality there was little to write home about. Other than a solitary shot now and again, as foot patrols along the border angered trigger-happy troops on the other side of it, the threat of open hostilities never materialised. In camp, boredom was the chief enemy. The daily routine entailed nothing more exciting than spud-bashing which task Jim was no longer spared, now a common or garden marine. More and more the thoughts of many troops revolved around eventual repatriation. While there were some regulars enlisted in Four Five with varying lengths of service to complete, the majority were in the category referred to as Hostiles Only – a constant cause of complaint by several of them who argued they should no longer be in uniform. In countless personal diaries and on calendars attached to tent poles, agonising days of delay were impatiently crossed off.

As for a few others, for Jim the date of departure for England finally came through. It was stipulated as March 15th. He dwelt upon whether the date was that of the ides of March and, if so, upon what state of affairs the ill-omened day might have in store.

Standing on the dockside waiting for the order to board the homeward-bound troopship, Jim scanned each of the lorries which arrived with other marines due for repatriation. He knew that his oldest friend, one with whom he had trained long before the formation of 606 flotilla, was also due to sail on the same vessel. But he was not on the truck which turned up with the home-going marines from 42 Commando. Together with a number of others, his pal had been injured when the vehicle in which they were returning to base, after a farewell celebration on the previous night, overturned. He was in hospital in Hong-Kong, in a critical condition.

At first the officer in charge of embarkation was hesitant to grant Jim's request, but relented on Jim's promise of all the tea in China if he failed to return before the ship sailed. At the hospital he found his oppo on a trolley, sedated and waiting to be wheeled into the operating theatre. His pelvis was broken. Until he was admitted Jim just laid a hand on his friend's shoulder and assured him he would be OK. It was the last occasion on which they met.

He managed to get back from the hospital with plenty of time to spare. After staking out a space in which to sleep on a lower deck he went aloft to take leave of the Orient. As the thrust of the ship's propellers infinitesimally reduced the distance from home, his mind slipped back to the journey on which he had set out on the very morning on which war was declared, unbelievably more than seven and a half years previously.

*****

Without even the foggiest notion as to where in the adjacent county of Hertfordshire the village and sanctuary of Chipperfield was situated, or any idea as to how long the journey would take, it was to there his former school chums had been evacuated and they who he wished to locate. From the sombre news bulletin heard on the radio before setting out, Jim was aware that if, by 1100 hours, Germany had not agreed to withdraw its troops from Poland, then a state of war would exist.

On his bicycle he was travelling through Enfield when the air raid sirens sounded. Police constables and air raid wardens quickly appeared, wearing steel helmets, bearing gas masks slung across the shoulder, blowing whistles, or ordering everyone to take cover. Householders threw open their doors to all who were on the streets. Motorists abandoned their vehicles and gratefully accepted the offered refuge, as did Jim. In the basement of the house to which they had rapidly retreated someone remarked it was 1115 hours.

Though from within the cellar neither aeroplanes nor explosion of bombs could be heard, when after about 30 minutes the all-clear was sounded and he emerged, Jim fully expected to find the entire landscape flattened. In the vicinity there was no visible damage. He turned and looked in the direction of London. As far as the eye could see the capital had escaped destruction.

*****

Now he was heading for London, in a land at peace. Whereas, on arrival in the village of Chipperfield, the fourteen year old cyclist had found the exiled youths, sailing from the other side of the world the returning man had lost the exuberance of youth.

Yet … acknowledging that spent years can never be reclaimed, Jim knew full well that he had been extremely fortunate compared with millions of others. At the one nearest to his home, Widge was at the bus stop to greet him. Reunited, thus they remained for the following 57 years.